— COMPLETELY REVISED AND UPDATED EDITION —

TOWARD SUSTAINABLE COMMUNITIES

• • • • • • • • • • • • • • • • • •

RESOURCES FOR CITIZENS

AND THEIR GOVERNMENTS *157138*

Mark Roseland

with Maureen Cureton and Heather Wornell

Foreword by Hazel Henderson

NEW SOCIETY PUBLISHERS

Cataloguing in Publication Data:
A catalog record for this publication is available from the National Library of Canada and the Library of Congress.

First published by Canada's National Round Table on the Environment and the Economy as *Toward Sustainable Communities: A Resource Book for Municipal and Local Governments*, by Mark Roseland, 1992. This is a completely revised and updated edition.

Cover design by Miriam MacPhail.

Graphics credits: Grahame Arnould, pp. 31, 46, 101, 109, 111, 113, 213; City of Vancouver, pp. 118, 119; Greater Vancouver Regional District, p. 131; *RAIN Magazine*, p. 137; Recycling Council of British Columbia, p. 71; Eva Riccius, pp. 49, 58, 72; Mark Roseland, p. 61; David Rousseau, pp. 132-134; Christopher Small, p. 114; Ray Straatsma, p.171; Denise Taschereau, pp. 42, 43, 45, 47, 48, 115, 150, 173; Heather Wornell, pp. 55, 60, 90.

Printed in Canada on acid-free, partially recycled (20 percent post-consumer) paper using soy-based inks by Best Book Manufacturers.

Inquiries regarding requests to reprint all or part of *Toward Sustainable Communities* should be addressed to New Society Publishers at the address below.

Paperback ISBN: 0-86571-374-X

To order directly from the publishers, please add $3.50 to the price of the first copy, and $1.00 for each additional copy (plus GST in Canada). Send check or money order to:

New Society Publishers,
P.O. Box 189, Gabriola Island, BC V0R 1X0, Canada.

New Society Publishers aims to publish books for fundamental social change through nonviolent action. We focus especially on sustainable living, progressive leadership, and educational and parenting resources. Our full list of books can be browsed on the world wide web at: http://www.newsociety.com

NEW SOCIETY PUBLISHERS
Gabriola Island BC, Canada and Stony Creek CT, U.S.A.

H
10/05/04
9:06

Toward Sustainable Communities

TABLE OF CONTENTS

PREFACE TO THE SECOND EDITION

Many of our most critical global environmental issues are rooted in local, day-to-day problems. Atmospheric and potential climate change, for example, can be altered by local citizens and government officials making enlightened decisions about local traffic congestion and inefficient land-use patterns. Local decisions about such issues benefit all of us globally.

While global environmental change is accelerating, there is a wealth of important and exciting information that can help us set the planet on a sustainable course. Unfortunately, most of this information is not available through the mainstream media. I have endeavored to make these ideas, tools and resources accessible. Those concerned citizens, elected officials, and municipal staff who prompted me to write this book are the people for whom it is written.

Toward Sustainable Communities: A Resource Book for Municipal and Local Governments was originally published in 1992 and distributed by the government of Canada's National Round Table on the Environment and the Economy. Over 12,000 copies were distributed internationally, and the book was also used as a textbook in several university courses.

The book received much critical and popular acclaim. Jeb Brugmann, Secretary General of the International Council for Local Environmental Initiatives, called it "a rare compendium of tested, practical suggestions, helpful contacts, and essential references to use in setting community planning and development on a sustainable course." Doreen Quirk, President of the Federation of Canadian Municipalities, said it "will assist your municipality in developing an integrated approach to sustainable development for the 21st century."

This edition is similar to the original, but differs in several important ways. First, the orientation has changed slightly, as reflected in the new subtitle: *Resources for Citizens and Their Governments*. Second, the conceptual framework has been revised and is more explicit. Third, this edition is *completely* revised and updated, and now includes numerous internet and e-mail resources. Fourth, the chapters are written in a more narrative style, although tools, initiatives, and useful resources are emphasized as before. Fifth, the sequence and organization of the chapters differs significantly from the original edition. Sixth, some chapters have been added and some dropped or incorporated into other chapters. Seventh, an appendix of organizations and publications has been added to provide general resources on sustainability. Eighth, this edition is fully indexed. Finally, this edition is longer than the original and has a much more appealing design. To summarize, *this edition is substantially different from — and better than — the first.*

The book is designed to be both stimulating and useful. Part 1 explores the meaning of sustainable development and its implications for communities, and develops a framework for sustainable community development. It concludes with a chapter on thinking strategically, which examines policy instruments for sustainable community development.

Part 2 is a set of sustainable community "building blocks." Each chapter provides an overview explaining the topic and its relevance to sustainable communities, followed by a set of "Tools and Initiatives" and "Resources." These building blocks are a set of planning tools, practical initiatives, and associated resources that have helped citizens and their governments move toward sustainable communities. While not every tool will fit every community, many of them will fit quite well. The resource sections for each chapter are accompanied by bibliographic references and other resources.

Part 3 focuses on mobilizing citizens and their governments toward sustainable communities. It concentrates on governing sustainable communities and tools for managing community sustainability, and concludes with some lessons for designing effective sustainable community development policies and thoughts for the challenge ahead. It is followed by an appendix of additional sustainable community resources.

The book is not intended to be comprehensive; rather, it attempts to identify and document the current range of initiatives toward sustainable communities. Dozens of tools, initiatives and resources are presented in these pages, accompanied by hundreds of references to aid interested readers in their own research. Certain tools and initiatives may be missing because we didn't know about them, but many others were omitted because of space and budget limitations. We have presented those that seemed most readily transferable to other communities.

The term "North America" in this book refers primarily to communities in the developed countries of North America, in other words, those in the U.S. and Canada. The term "community" refers to a group of people bound by geography and with a shared destiny, such as a municipality or a town.

The mixed use of Canadian and U.S. spellings throughout the book (e.g., centre versus center, neighbour versus neighbor) is due to keeping the original spellings intact in all excerpts from the literature of Canada, the U.S., and other countries. As well, measurement units are original in these excerpts, while the equivalents of SI and Imperial units are provided throughout the text (with the exception of an equivalent for "ton," as the unit is nearly equal in both forms of measurement).

This volume is part of a larger, ongoing research project. If you are aware of sustainable community initiatives and resources other than those described here, or are involved in developing your own sustainable community initiatives, please send your information and/or documentation to me at the Community Economic Development Centre, Simon Fraser University, Burnaby, B.C., Canada V5A 1S6.

This book is dedicated to the citizen activists and local government officials around the world who have developed the wide array of initiatives that make it possible. Your efforts to create a sustainable future have sustained me as well.

Mark Roseland
Vancouver, British Columbia

FOREWORD

by Hazel Henderson

It is my privilege to introduce this completely revised and updated edition of *Toward Sustainable Communities*. The promise of its subtitle — *Resources for Citizens and Their Governments* — is filled to overflowing! My hat is off to Mark Roseland, Maureen Cureton and Heather Wornell for the wealth of inspiring examples, useful pilot projects, fabulous tools and resources in this book. Many were news to me — and I cover these fields extensively. I shared this manuscript enthusiastically with my friend Carol Spalding, a member of that City's Transportation Board and Executive Vice President of Florida Community College at Jacksonville. On perusing Chapter 9: Transportation Planning and Traffic Management, Carol asked for her own copy by courier!

I am also delighted to find included so much of the wisdom from *RAIN*, the magazine I frequently wrote for in the 1970s and early 1980s, and where I met Mark Roseland. All the concepts of sustainable communities and local initiatives which keep our planet in mind were seeded back then. After their temporary absence during the recent reactionary "Politics of Instant Gratification," it is thrilling to see all this common sense making a big comeback. I went on to become involved with many of the visionary young entrepreneurs and renewable-resource technologists I met and wrote about in my book, *Creating Alternative Futures* (1978), now happily back in print from Kumarian Press (1996). I joined the Advisory Council of the Calvert Social Investment Fund in 1982 when most Wall Streeters told us we were crazy to try to screen mutual fund portfolios to exclude weapons makers, heavy polluters, and those companies unfair to workers and minorities. We proved them wrong by proactively including emerging young enterprises of the solar age in services, information, software, solar and renewable energy, demand-side management, recycling, remanufacturing, clean foods, organic agriculture, preventive healthcare and fitness, as well as hosts of new environmental and socio-economic consultants offering life-cycle costing and product analyses, "green" and social audits.

Today there is a global green boom. *The International Environmental Monitor's Global Opinion Survey* released at the United Nations Earth Summit II, June, 1997, in New York, showed that in 24 countries in both North and South, covering 60 percent of the earth's population, environmental concerns have grown considerably since the first Rio Summit in 1992. Conducted with partner polling firms, including MORI International between January and April of 1997, the survey showed majorities of respondents citing personal concern for the environment: 94 percent in India; 90 percent in Chile; 89 percent in the U.S. and Poland; 88 percent in Canada and Korea; 87 percent in Nigeria; 86 percent in Mexico; 85 percent in Hungary; with Japan and Britain at 83 percent and 82 percent respectively; and Germany, Russia, and Finland in the 70 percent range.

Green investors have been banking on these trends for the past 15 years. Since the early 1980s when the first U.S.-based, socially responsible mutual funds were founded, assets managed in such screened portfolios have grown to $650 billion in the U.S. alone. Today, this social screening of portfolios itself is becoming a new financial services sector. The green and "ethical" asset group has its own stock market index, which regularly outperforms the Standard and Poors: The Domini Social 400 Index.

The survey shows that "citizens around the world are even more likely today to say that economic growth should be sacrificed if necessary to insure that the environment is protected." Yet this *false choice is imposed by obsolete economics* challenged today by environmentalists and dynamic chaos models. These show that consumers are changing as people learn and cope with changing conditions. Yet economists still assume a "rational economic man," constantly calculating and maximizing his self-interest in competition with others. I and other critics have pointed out for decades that this unrealistic economics leaves societies backing into the future looking through the rear-view mirror.

This narrow "economism" still driving national statistics, and gross national product (GNP) and gross domestic product (GDP) has steered societies off course toward pollution and depletion of natural resources. One of the Earth Summit agreements calls for the 170 signatory countries to overhaul their GNPs/GDPs to take account of social and environmental costs and benefits. GNP/GDP still over-counts material goods and under-counts services, as well as ignoring the 50 percent of all unpaid productive work (volunteering, parenting, do-it-yourself, etc.); for example, some 89 million Americans volunteer at least five hours per week.

GNP/GDP has no asset budget but expenses in a single year: vital, long-payback investments in infrastructure, the new info-structure, education, training, and human capital, as well as maintaining national assets such as dams, bridges, parks, forests, and public lands. GNP/GDP still values bombs, tanks, and aircraft as useful production, while setting the value of the environment at zero. The Calvert-Henderson Quality-of-Life Indicators, based on my Country Futures Indicators (CFI), coming soon from the Calvert Group, Inc., will offer a broader view of wealth and progress in the U.S.

National tax codes are similarly biased against the environment, human capital investments, and full employment, while encouraging waste and pollution. We should shift taxes from incomes and payrolls to waste and pollution. A 1997 report from the Earth Council, Costa Rica, "Subsidizing Unsustainable Development," documents the ways nations annually waste $700 billion on accelerating resource depletion and pollution. All these errors in policies and statistics lead to prices that exclude full costs. This is why consumers still are given the false choice: that they must sacrifice a prosperous economy for a clean environment — even as the emerging sustainable economies of the 21st century are now visible and booming.

As we eliminate the $700 billion in subsidies from propping up the obsolescent, resource-intensive corporations of the Industrial Era (coal, oil, gas, nuclear, mining, transport, chemicals, construction, and fossil-fueled agriculture), societies can reap a huge "sustainability dividend." Today, Ralph Nader, Congressman John Kasich, the Cato Institute, and most environmentalists agree that we must end "corporate welfare." This would allow the emerging sustainable industries of the 21st century to compete on a level playing field, including: the companies in renewable energy and resources; companies in solar, wind, fuel cells, flywheels, hydrogen propulsion, new materials, "smart glass," energy-efficiency, recycling, re-manufacturing, preventive and alternative health care, fitness, clean, pesticide-free food and agriculture, education, training, human development, entertainment, and eco-tourism.

This still statistically invisible new economy is changing the true composition of GNP/GDP, confounding policy makers and investors alike. As we reclassify and recalculate GNP/GDP and move from its material goods focus (autos, housing, etc.) toward services and information, we will see the direction of growth for this new "attention economy" where the crucial resources are individuals' attention, time, and knowledge itself. Many surveys show people in post-industrial societies are turning their attention from consumerism to more emotionally satisfying concerns and values of family and community, quality-of-life, and environment.

While globalization is accelerating, and $1.4 trillion sloshes around our planet in a daily global casino, local communities must create "permeable membranes" to screen such global speculative flows of "hot money" and preserve local options and cultures. It is even more important to overhaul old economic statistics underlying trade policy and the World Trade Organization. If not, today's short-term market evaluations in the unregulated global casino will continue to reinforce competitive global economic warfare and further loss of national sovereignty. International agreements are now being forged in the private, public, and civic sectors, including those on eco-labels and the ISO 9000 and ISO 14000 standards for products. Codes of conduct such as the CAUX, CERES, and McBride Principles are also helping to place an ethical floor under the global playing field so that the most ethical companies and countries with the highest standards for democracy, human rights, accounting, disclosure, treaty compliance, and environmental protection can be the winners in the future. Many of these international agreements have been fostered by the United Nations, the world's indispensable organization for the 21st century.

The most crucial factor is the new "third force" in the world today. This is the booming civic society of newly-aware global citizens, voters, consumers, employees, and investors who care for the planet and future generations and are determined to hold corporations and countries fully accountable. Bet on the green global boom and the good common sense of local communities!

Hazel Henderson
Florida, August, 1997

ACKNOWLEDGMENTS

In the five years since the first edition of this book appeared, interest in sustainable communities has exploded (due at least in part to the impact of the book). What was a difficult but possible task for one person to accomplish in 1992 is no longer possible today. Fortunately, many people helped directly or indirectly in making it possible to complete this edition.

First and foremost, this book came together with the assistance of Maureen Cureton and Heather Wornell. I could not have been more fortunate than to have these two talented and capable people working with me, and both were instrumental in producing part 2 of this edition. Maureen joined the project after a three-year stint with the Rocky Mountain Institute in Colorado. She is an experienced researcher and writer with considerable expertise in many of the topics in the book. Maureen revised the chapters on water and sewage, energy efficiency and renewables, and community economic development, co-revised the chapter on housing and community development, and contributed substantially to the entire project. Heather will soon be completing her graduate work with me, and has been invaluable as a researcher and editorial assistant both on this book and on *Eco-City Dimensions: Healthy Communities, Healthy Planet* (New Society Publishers 1997). Among her many contributions to this project, she revised the chapter on greening the city.

Thanks also to my colleagues in the Department of Geography at Simon Fraser University for allowing and encouraging me to teach courses on sustainable communities. My students used the first edition as a text and provided valuable feedback as well as new material for this edition. My students in the Community Economic Development Program at Simon Fraser also provided valuable research assistance, much of which made its way into the chapter, "Community Economic Development."

In conjunction with my sustainable communities courses, I have run two graduate research seminars which resulted in much of the revised material in part 2 of this edition. Karen Asp, Maureen Cureton, Gavin Davidson, Zane Parker, Angela Smailes, Denise Taschereau, Kelly Vodden, and Heather Wornell provided a great sounding board for proposals and ideas as well as proving to be excellent researchers. Denise Taschereau and Karen Asp revised the chapter on waste reduction and recycling. It is extremely heartening to work with a bright new generation of thinkers and future leaders who will be making important contributions to sustainable communities for many years to come.

Several other individuals also deserve specific mention for their contributions. I am delighted and honored that Hazel Henderson wrote the foreword, and my thanks go to Chris and Judith Plant at New Society Publishers for encouraging this revised edition, and to Sharon McCann for wonderful copy-editing. Graham Arnould provided cartoons which grace these pages, Heather Wornell, David Rousseau, and Christopher Small provided drawings, and Denise Taschereau, Eva Riccius, and Ray Straatsma provided photos which appear throughout the book.

I am obliged to Joan Fletcher for background research on social capital; to Gavin Davidson for contributions to the transportation and water chapters; to Ryan Hill for research assistance on policy instruments; to Dorli Duffy for research on shared decision-making; to Zane Parker for research on sustainability indicators; to Jay Lambert for researching internet sites, updating addresses, and general "gophering"; and to Penny Simpson, SFU Community Economic Development Centre, for all kinds of administrative assistance. We also thank Scott Chaplin of Rocky Mountain Institute's Water Associates for his technical review of the chapter "Water and Sewage," and for generously sharing his published works.

I gratefully acknowledge financial support for this project from the President's Research Fund at Simon Fraser University, and from the Science Council of British Columbia for research on policy instruments. Support for the original edition came from The Forum for Planning Action, The University of British Columbia Centre for Human Settlements, The University of British Columbia Task Force on Healthy and Sustainable Communities, Friends of the Earth, and from the National Round Table on the Environment and the Economy, which published and distributed the first edition.

I am obliged to Professors William Rees and Brahm Wiesman of the University of British Columbia's School of Community and Regional Planning; former Councilmember Nancy Skinner of the Berkeley, California, City Council; Jeb Brugmann of the International Council for Local Environmental Initiatives; and secveral anonymous reviewers for reviewing all or parts of the original manuscript prior to publication.

An earlier version of chapter 3 first appeared in *Local Environment* 1(2) 1996, and a chapter based on material in chapter 1 is appearing in *Community Perspectives on Sustainability* (edited by John Pierce and Ann Dale, and to be published by UBC Press).

Last but by no means least, I am beholden to Susan Day, my friend, confidant, advisor, and partner, for carrying much of my load during this long and demanding process, and for sustaining our dreams; and to Sean Rigby, who represents the future we are trying to make sustainable.

PART I

SUSTAINABLE COMMUNITIES, SUSTAINABLE PLANET

CHAPTER 1

THE CONTEXT FOR SUSTAINABLE COMMUNITIES

A quiet transformation is taking place in communities all over North America and around the world. Thousands of citizens and their governments are embracing a new way of thinking and acting about their future.

Motivations for involvement vary, but they include a desire to improve the quality of community life, protect the environment, and participate in decisions that affect us; concern about poverty and other social conditions, whether in far away countries or in our own towns; longing for a sense of satisfaction that money can't buy; and pride in the legacy left for our children.

These motivations are all coming together now in a movement toward sustainable communities. As the following chapters demonstrate, this synergistic approach will enable our communities to be cleaner, healthier, and less expensive; to have greater accessibility and cohesion; and to be more self-reliant in energy, food, and economic security than they are now. Sustainable communities are not merely about "sustaining" the quality of our lives — they are about *improving* it.

This chapter explores the context for sustainable communities. Acting locally is more significant when we think globally, so that is where we begin our discussion of "sustainable development." We then examine the concepts of "natural capital" and "social capital" as ideas that can help us to "do development differently," as well as to begin building a framework for sustainable community development.

THINKING GLOBALLY

Many people around the world are starting to consider that the population problem in the South is less significant a problem than over-consumption and wasted resources in the North. For example, in the U.S., the total agglomeration of oil and hydrocarbon pollution caused by pleasure boating, some 1.6 billion liters (420 million gallons) per year, is the equivalent of up to 40 Exxon Valdez disasters every year (Mele 1993). Another example is the 8-million hectares (20-million acres) of U.S. lawns that claim 30 percent to 60 percent of urban water use while causing pesticide pollution, adding significantly to solid waste (Borman, Balmore, and Geballe 1993).

During 1986-90, the average person in a developed country used nine times as much fossil fuel and 20 times as much aluminum as his or her counterpart in developing countries. In terms of waste, the average person produced four times as much household refuse, 11 times more carbon dioxide, 26 times more chloroflourocarbons, and 75 times more hazardous wastes. Average Americans use 43 times as much gasoline as average Indians, 45 times as much copper, and 34 times as much aluminum (ICPQL 1996).

In 1991, the U.S. consumed almost three times as much energy as Japan in order to produce $1 of GNP. With only 4.6 percent of the world's population, the U.S. produced 22 percent of the global carbon-dioxide emissions in 1991 — more than the combined totals of China, India, South America, and Africa (ICPQL 1996).

Many in both northern and southern countries now argue that gross population figures must be corrected by adding figures reflecting per-capita resource consumption. By these calculations, the U.S. population is in the tens of billions, and is viewed as the biggest contributor to the global population problem (Henderson 1996).

Bringing the Third World up to North American living standards would require a five- to 10-fold increase in world industrial output (WCED 1987), yet the contingent combination of depleted resource stocks (e.g., fossil fuels, fisheries, forests) with degraded life-support systems (e.g., ozone depletion, global warming, acid rain) demonstrates the impossibility of the entire world consuming and polluting at the rate of North Americans.

SUSTAINABLE DEVELOPMENT

In December 1983, in response to a United Nations General Assembly resolution, the U.N. Secretary-General appointed physician Gro Harlem Brundtland of Norway as Chairman of an independent World Commission on Environment and Development. In April 1987, the Commission released its report, *Our Common Future*. The report showed that the poorest fifth of the world's population has less than 2 percent of the world's economic product while the richest fifth has 75 percent; the 26 percent of the world's population living in developed countries consumes 80 percent to 86 percent of nonrenewable resources and 34 percent to 53 percent of food products (WCED 1987). At the core of the report is the principle of sustainable development. Embracing sustainable development as an underlying principle gave political credibility to a concept many others had worked on over the previous decade. The Commission defined sustainable development as meeting "the needs of the present without compromising the ability of future generations to meet their own needs."

The term sustainable development has been criticized as ambiguous and open to a wide range of interpretations, many of which are contradictory. Confusion has resulted from using the terms sustainable development, "sustainable growth," and "sustainable use" interchangeably, as if their meanings were the same. They are not. Sustainable growth is a contradiction in terms: nothing physical can grow indefinitely. Sustainable use is applicable only to renewable resources: it means using them at rates within their capacity for renewal (IUCN 1991).

Many people use the term sustainable development to simply mean either "envi-

"To attempt to deal with international disparities by trickling aid from growth-stimulated rich countries to poor countries will at best be insufficient to reduce those countries' poverty; at worst, such an approach increases their dependency on technology and oil, deepens their debt, and leads to more ecological destruction. If we in the rich countries are to help those in the poor, we must reduce our own consumption. . . . Whether or not such a path is sufficient to move toward global equality, it is necessary" (Boothroyd 1991).

ronmental protection" or else sustained economic growth (presumably to pay for, among other things, environmental protection). Even the Brundtland Commission accepted the need for a five- to 10-fold increase in world industrial output as essential for sustainable development.

The very concept of environmental protection is based on the separation of humanity from nature. As a society, we point to a few things we think of as nature — some trees here, a pond there — draw a box around them, then try to "protect" what's within the box. Meanwhile, we ignore the fact that human activity *outside* that box — housing, economic development, transportation, and so on — has a far greater impact on the environment than do our "environmental" policies.

Environmental protection is like foam padding — it offers some protection from a fall. We congratulate ourselves if we double our spending to double the thickness of the foam, because we assume thicker foam means more protection. However, *we only get more protection if we fall the same distance.* Meanwhile, *unsustainable* development constantly increases the distance we're likely to fall. Sustainable development must therefore be more than merely "protecting" the environment: it requires economic and social change to *improve human well-being while reducing the need for environmental protection.*

Social equity demands that we balance the needs of the biosphere with the needs of the vast majority of the human population, the world's poor. Within the developed nations, this in turn means that we must balance the needs of the biosphere with the needs of our own poor. But in doing so we can no longer rely on our 200-year tradition of material growth as the primary instrument of social policy.

Like other political objectives of its kind (e.g., justice, democracy), we all agree with the ideal of sustainable development and disagree over what it entails. Nevertheless, sustainable development has a core meaning which remains, however it is interpreted. According to Jacobs (1993), the three core elements of sustainable development are:

• *Environmental considerations must be entrenched in economic policy-making.* Environmental and economic objectives must be placed within a common framework in which a variety of parallel objectives can be recognized.

• *Sustainable development incorporates an inescapable commitment to social equity.* This requires not simply the creation of wealth and the conservation of resources, but their fair distribution both between and within countries, including at least some measure of redistribution between North and South. Sustainability also requires the fair distribution of environmental benefits and costs between generations.

• "Development" *does not simply mean "growth,"* as represented by faulty measures of economic performance such as increases in gross national product (GNP). Development implies qualitative as well as quantitative improvement.

In sum, sustainable development must be a *different kind of development*. It must be *a pro-active strategy to develop sustainability.*

"Sustainable development is a program to change the process of economic development so that it ensures a basic quality of life for all people, and protects the ecosystems and community systems that make life possible and worthwhile" (ICLEI et al. 1996).

NATURAL CAPITAL

Global resource depletion and pollution are forcing recognition that existing patterns of development and resource use are not sustainable. Even conservative neoclassical economists are recognizing that the sustainable component of development requires that human activities today do not deplete what can be termed "natural capital" or "environmental capital." Although the idea of natural capital originated nearly a century ago, only recently has the term gained prominence (primarily among ecological economists, themselves a relatively new breed) to further our understanding of sustainable development (e.g., Jansson et al. 1994; Wackernagel and Rees 1996). Natural capital refers to any stock of natural assets that yields a flow of valuable goods and services into the future. For example, a forest, a fish stock, or an aquifer can provide a harvest or flow that is potentially sustainable year after year. The forest or fish stock is natural capital and the sustainable harvest is "natural income."

The total stock of environmental assets which comprise this natural capital may be divided usefully into three categories:
- non-renewable resources, such as minerals and fossil fuels;
- the finite capacity of natural systems to produce "renewable resources" such as food crops, forestry products, and water supplies — which are renewable only if the natural systems from which they are drawn are not overexploited; and
- the capacity of natural systems to absorb our emissions and pollutants without side effects, which imply heavy costs passed onto future generations (such as chemicals that deplete the atmosphere's ozone layer, and greenhouse gases which may cause serious climatic imbalances).

Natural capital also provides such critical ecological services as waste assimilation, erosion and flood control, and protection from ultraviolet radiation (the ozone layer is a form of natural capital). These life support systems are counted as natural income. Since the flow of services from ecosystems often requires that they function as intact systems, the structure and diversity of the system may be an important component of natural capital (Wackernagel and Rees 1996).

Although natural capital is a relatively new way of framing choices for social policy and action, it has helped considerably to refine the sustainability debate. For example, there is no doubt that the stock of non-renewable resources is finite, nor is there any doubt that eco-systems (individually and collectively within the biosphere) have limits in their capacity to absorb pollutants. There is also agreement that some environmental assets, such as areas of outstanding natural beauty, are irreplaceable. According to Mitlin and Satterthwaite (1991):

> The debate centers on which environmental assets are irreplaceable and the extent to which current (and projected) future levels of resource use degrade the capital stock of environmental assets for future generations, the extent to which one resource can be substituted for another (for instance, a synthetic substance replacing a natural one) and the extent to which pollutants derived from human activities are damaging the biosphere.

"The opposite of wealth is not poverty but sufficiency. This is critical. Sufficiency is not a matter of sacrifice and deprivation. It is a means of working out different ways of achieving satisfaction in our own lives" (Porritt 1989).

Strong or Weak Sustainability?

Some analysts (e.g., Pearce et al. 1989) argue that "future generations should be compensated for reductions in the endowments of resources brought about by the actions of present generations"; they suggest that each generation should leave the next a stock of assets at least as great as that which they inherited themselves. There are two possible ways to interpret this: "weak sustainability," which aggregates all types of assets, and "strong sustainability," which differentiates between assets that are "natural" and those that are not. Strong sustainability argues that whatever the level of human-made assets, an adequate stock of environmental (or natural) assets alone is critical in securing sustainability (Daly 1989; Rees 1992).

Weak sustainability reflects the neoclassical economic assumption that non-natural assets can substitute for natural assets; therefore it is acceptable to use up natural assets so long as the profits they generate provide an equivalent endowment to the next generation. Yet in some cases, natural and non-natural assets are clearly not substitutable. For example, a sawmill cannot be substituted for a forest since the sawmill (non-natural capital) needs the forest (natural capital) in order to function (Daly 1989). Weak sustainability also assumes that other forms of capital (e.g., manufactured, financial, or human capital) can be converted back into natural capital. This interpretation does not take into account irreversible processes such as the extinction of species or the destruction of ecosystems.

All this suggests that weak sustainability is grossly insufficient; natural capital stock should only be destroyed if the benefits of doing so are very large or if the social costs of conservation are unacceptably large (Pearce et al. 1990). Yet this begs the key question: *are we capable of knowing the full costs and benefits of destroying or conserving natural capital stock?*

Ecological economists can put a price on resources such as timber and fisheries; but the value of ecological process resources such as carbon absorption or photosynthesis cannot easily be quantified and monetized (Rees 1991). The very concept of economic "trade-offs" depends upon being able to put a *price* on the items traded (see Pricing the Planet). Resources that cannot be quantified or monetized also cannot be priced. It may be theoretically possible to trade-off some value of a fishery for some value of a timber harvest, but it may not be possible to realistically price the value of the ozone shield.

The economic benefits of destroying natural capital stock or the social costs of conservation may *seem* large, but only as a function of our inability to adequately assess such costs and benefits. If the potential benefits of conservation approach infinity, the costs are irrelevant (Rees 1991). This suggests that it is time for a different kind of framework for planning and decision-making, guided by the understanding that *natural capital stock should not be destroyed.*

In terms of the life-support functions of natural capital, destruction of any single significant natural asset can be likened to destruction of any single bodily organ or system. The destruction of the ozone layer may have the same consequences, in planetary

"Each generation is entitled to the interest on the natural capital, but the principal should be handed on unimpaired" (Canadian Conservation Commission 1915).

terms, as destruction of the immune system has for the human body; global warming may be analogous to a high fever.

We do not ask those who suffer from heart disease to trade normal brain functioning for a healthier heart. Such choices are the stuff of literature's great tragedies; they only become more tragic if we insist upon this approach to deciding complex societal choices.

Like a thermometer registering a fever, the accumulating trends of ecological decline (e.g., decrease in stratospheric ozone, increase in greenhouse gases, extinction of species, loss of biodiversity, etc.) are the indicators of our condition.

The "ecological bottom line" is that we must learn to live on the "interest" generated by our remaining stocks of living natural capital, and not deplete those stocks. In short, we must *minimize our consumption of essential natural capital.*

This applies particularly in developed countries, where one-quarter of the world's people consume three-quarters of the world's resources (ICPQL 1996; WCED 1987). For North Americans to contribute to global sustainability will require major shifts in lifestyles of the affluent. A wide variety of approaches are called for, including reducing atmospheric emissions and water pollution, waste reduction and recycling, and greening our cities. The most important adaptation for minimizing consumption of natural capital is a reduction of our present levels of materials and energy consumption. This will require a more globally conscious kind of local development than we are accustomed to.

Minimizing consumption of natural capital has profound implications for urban form, for the material basis of urban life, and for community social relationships in the 21st century. *If the basic science is correct, we have no choice but to shift to more sustainable patterns of resource use and development.* The longer we wait, the greater the risk of having to impose rigid regulations in times of crisis. The sooner we make these shifts, the more options we will have to create mechanisms of adjustment that are socially acceptable and economically feasible.

SOCIAL CAPITAL

Despite the interest in "natural capitalism" (Hawken 1997), putting a price tag on everything in nature will not solve all of our planetary woes. Economic growth and industrialization as presently practiced are accompanied almost invariably with increasing energy demand and growing ecological waste, even when the intensity of

---

Pricing the Planet

A team of 13 ecologists, economists and geographers, in a report in the journal *Nature,* estimated the present global value of 17 ecosystem "services" at US$16 trillion to $54 trillion a year, with a likely figure of at least $33 trillion. That figure is based on the cash value of such things as water, air, forests, animals, dirt, coral reefs, grasslands, and other aspects of the natural world. Most of this lies outside formal markets and is therefore not reflected in market prices, the customary gauge of economic value. Ecosystem services are services essential to the human economy, including climate regulation, water supply, soil formation, pollination, food production, raw materials, genetic resources, recreation and culture.

To come up with the $33 trillion figure, the team, headed by University of Maryland ecological economist Robert Costanza, found published estimates of the economic value of natural ecosystems. After finding credible estimates of how much each of 17 ecosystems is worth, they multiplied that value by the total areas of each type of feature on earth.

The purpose of the study was to put a price tag on what people would have to pay to replace — if that were possible — the ecosystem services of the natural environment. In comparison, the gross national product of the world, which is all the goods and services produced by people each year, is about $18 trillion (Stevens 1997).

"The chain, economic growth-employment-political success in the form of democracy-increased resource consumption-waste and environmental damage, must be broken if we are to achieve sustainable improvement in the quality of life" (ICPQL 1996).

energy use is falling. This means that technological improvements can be expected to slow down the rate of ecological damage only marginally, so long as the scale of production is increasing rapidly. Ultimately, social issues — including the nature and purpose of economic development — must be addressed (Foster 1997).

All forms of capital are created by spending time and effort in transformation and transaction activities. Physical capital is the stock of material resources that can be used to produce a flow of future income. The origin of physical capital is the process of spending time and other resources constructing tools, plants, facilities, and other material resources that can, in turn, be used in producing other products. Human capital is the acquired knowledge and skills individuals bring to productive activity. Human capital is formed consciously through training and education and unconsciously through experience (Ostrom 1993).

Social capital is a term used by progressive economists and other social scientists to further our understanding of society and community (e.g., Coleman 1988; Ostrom 1993; Putnam 1995). It describes a norm of social responsibility, a corresponding atmosphere of social trust and interconnecting networks of communication (Jacobs 1961).

Social capital is the shared knowledge, understandings, and patterns of interactions that a group of people bring to any productive activity (Coleman 1988; Putnam 1993). The term refers to the organizations, structures, and social relations that people build themselves, independently of the state or large corporations. It contributes to stronger community fabric, and, often as a by-product of other activities, builds bonds of information, trust, and inter-personal solidarity (Coleman 1990).

The term social capital refers to features of social organization such as networks, norms, and trust that increase a society's productive potential (Putnam 1993). Though largely neglected in discussions of public policy, social capital substantially enhances returns to investments in physical and human capital. However, unlike conventional capital, social capital is a public good, i.e., it is not the private property of those who benefit from it. Thus, like other public goods, from clean air to safe streets, social capital tends to be under-provided by private agents. The ties, norms, and trust that constitute social capital are most often created as a by-product of other social activities and then transferred from one social setting to another.

Social capital is created when individuals learn to trust one another so that they are able to make credible commitments and rely on generalized forms of reciprocity rather than on narrow sequences of specific quid pro quo relationships. The shared cognitive aspects of social capital help account for two unusual characteristics that differ from physical capital. First, social capital does not wear out upon being used more and more; and second, if unused, social capital deteriorates at a relatively rapid rate (Ostrom 1993).

Social capital differs from other forms of capital in several significant ways. It is not limited by material scarcity, meaning that its creative capacity is limited only by imagination. Consequently, it suggests a route toward sustainability, by replacing the fundamentally illogical model of unlimited growth within a finite world with one of

"The main intellectual problem with the 'ecological economics' approach is that all the fancy math hides the neoclassical assumptions, which ignore disparities in wealth, income, power, and information between people and countries, as well as issues of who wins and who loses, job loss, the unpaid informal economy, and so on. The price system should be subordinated to more democratic decision making, i.e., voting"
(Henderson 1996).

unlimited complexity, not bound by the availability of material resources.

However, social capital also has limitations which other forms of capital do not. It cannot be created instantly, and the very fact of trying to consciously create it or direct it can create resistance. People resist being instrumentalized for even the best of reasons. Social capital takes time to develop, and is inherently non-transferable (Flora and Flora 1993). It is also fragile and subject to erosion not only by direct assault but more importantly, by neglect, if there are many or strong competitors for investment of emotional significance or time.

The modern concept of social capital is described as the *relations between* individuals and groups. It can take several forms, some of which are mutually recognized bonds, channels of information, and norms and sanctions.

In this sense, social capital is related to the concept of social ecology, as developed in the works of Murray Bookchin. Social ecology is the study of both human and natural ecosystems, and in particular, of the social relations that affect the relation of society as a whole with nature. Social ecology goes beyond environmentalism, insisting that the issue at hand for humanity is not simply protecting nature but rather creating an ecological society in harmony with nature. The primary social unit of an ecological society is the sustainable community, a human-scale settlement based on ecological balance, community self-reliance, and participatory democracy (Bookchin 1987).

Multiplying Social Capital

Beyond understanding the basic nature of social capital, we need to know where to locate and how to *multiply social capital* for sustainable community development.

Social networks can be divided into those with and without closure (Coleman 1988). A network with closure is one where most of the individuals within it know each other, and the relationship of each to the others. In contrast, a network without closure is one where each individual's circle of acquaintances overlaps only partially or not at all with those of the others, and the degree of overlap is generally unknown.

Formally organized groups are the necessary recourse of societies without closure. Organized groups have established procedures for adherence and keep membership lists, follow recognized procedures to conduct their affairs, and often administer budgets and own property. Examples are churches, ethnic associations, unions, trade associations, sports associations, theater societies, or environmental groups. However, a formal organization may also be a public representation of a more primary closure society. Churches, especially ethnically-rooted ones, tend to fall into this category. Organizations which have survived an intense struggle in a hostile social environment, such as some unions and environmental groups, can also take on something of this character of closure.

Informal groups can be regular customers of a shop, users of a park, sports fans, music fans, mothers of children who play together, or groups of street youth who mutually protect each other. Members of such groups may not necessarily know each other, or even that they constitute a group, yet they can be a useful resource for each other, and an immense reservoir of energy and imagination if it can be accessed and

"Social capital is constituted by cohesion, cultural identity and discipline; these are essential for our peaceful collective survival. Social capital can be depleted by inequality, unemployment, insecurity. Situations of this kind are socially unsustainable over the long term since they reduce everyone's quality of life and lead inevitably to social collapse" (ICPQL 1996).

9

Champagne on a Beer Budget

Kerala, a state of 29 million people in southern India, has a per capita income estimated by various surveys to be between U.S.$298 and $350 per year, about one-seventieth the U.S. average. Yet data for life expectancy, literacy, and birth rates for Kerala are comparable to those for the U.S. "One-seventieth the income means one-seventieth the damage to the planet. So, on balance, if Kerala and the United States manage to achieve the same physical quality of life, Kerala is the vastly more successful society" (McKibben 1996).

organized.

Multiplying and using social capital is not without its problems. By its very nature, social capital can tend to mirror existing power structures. Marginalized people are sometimes marginalized exactly because they are unable to access social capital, as is often the case with the mentally ill or other people with poor social skills.

Even in a society with closure, social capital may be divided among different factions who regard each other as rivals or threats. While there are possible tools to deal with this, their success is uncertain, and the difficulties are worse in situations like larger North American cities, where there are many groups competing with others without closure, who may not even be able to communicate because of language or cultural barriers or both. This is not to claim that we should give up on prospects for sustainable community development in urban centers, but rather that we should not deceive ourselves about the challenge involved.

Community "civicness" is key to maximizing the potential of communities as agents of sustainable development (Selman and Parker 1997). Civicness in a community will lubricate social life, enhance productivity and facilitate action; in practice, it will then become a proxy for successful policy implementation (Putnam 1993). It is also an important component of sense of place, which is critical for community sustainability.

Along with ecological carrying capacity, we also need an increase in the "social caring capacity" of our communities (UBC Task Force on Healthy and Sustainable Communities 1994). Social caring capacity, reflected by networks of social capital, is a prerequisite for sustainable development. Evidence from the Indian state of Kerela (see Champagne on a Beer Budget) suggests that quality of life can increase while industrial production decreases; i.e., social capital can substitute for manufactured capital. Furthermore, whereas natural capital diminishes with exploitation, social capital accumulates with regular use (Selman and Parker 1997).

DOING DEVELOPMENT DIFFERENTLY

"Sustainability . . . is not only an effort to be incorporated in government policy. It is a basic ingredient of the individual's duties towards society" (ICPQL 1996).

Several key arguments inform this book. First, the term sustainable development acquires tangible meaning when understood in terms of natural capital and natural income. The bottom line for sustainability is that we must learn to live on our natural income rather than deplete our natural capital. Economic growth with an ecological deficit is anti-economic and makes us poorer rather than richer in the long-term (Daly and Cobb 1989). Sustainability therefore requires that we minimize our consumption of essential natural capital.

Second, natural capital and social equity demand that North Americans, who are among the world's most inefficient and wasteful consumers of materials and energy (ICPQL 1996; WCED 1987), find ways of living more lightly on the planet. At a minimum, we will have to increase the efficiency of our resource and energy use. More likely, we will also have to reduce our present (not to speak of projected) levels of materials and energy consumption.

Third, reducing our materials and energy consumption need not diminish and, in fact, would likely enhance our quality of life and the public domain — in other words, it could multiply our social capital. It is important to distinguish here between "quality of life" and "standard of living" (Jacobs 1993). Standard of living generally refers to disposable income for things we purchase individually, whereas quality of life can be considered as the sum of all things which people purchase collectively (e.g., the health care system, public education, policing), or those things which are not purchased at all (e.g., air quality). "Standard of living" refers solely to the private domain, whereas "quality of life" refers to the public domain, the realm of social capital.

Fourth, the critical resource for multiplying social capital is not money — rather, the critical resources are trust, imagination, courage, commitment, the relations between individuals and groups, and time, the literal currency of life. Many of the social issues that people relate to most intimately — family, neighborhood, community, decompression from work, recreation, culture, etc. — depend on these resources at least as much as money. This is not to say that economic security isn't important — it is — but focusing solely on money to provide security is using 19th century thinking to address 21st century challenges.

Taken together, the direction to which these arguments point is clear. We must explicitly aim to nurture and multiply social capital in order not only to preserve our stock of natural capital but also to improve our economic and social well-being. Government and corporate decisions should be reviewed for their effects on both natural and social capital. Programs and policies need to be effected at every level to insure that natural and social capital are properly considered.

In a nutshell, we need to *do development differently.*

REFERENCES

Bookchin, M. 1987. *The Rise of Urbanization and the Decline of Citizenship.* San Francisco: Sierra Club.

Boothroyd, P. 1991. "Distribution Principles for Compassionate Sustainable Development." In *Perspectives on Sustainable Development in Water Management: Towards Agreement in the Fraser Basin,* ed. A.H.J. Dorcey. Vancouver: Westwater Research Centre.

Borman, F.H., D. Balmore, and G.T. Geballe. 1993. *Redesigning the American Lawn* New Haven: Yale University Press.

Canadian Conservation Commission. 1915. In *Towards a Liveable Metropolis.* Toronto: Metropolitan Plan Review Report. No. 13, May 1991.

Coleman, J.S. 1988. "Social Capital in the Creation of Human Capital." *American Journal of Sociology* 94 (supplement) S95-S120.

Coleman, J.S. 1990. *Foundations of Social Theory.* Cambridge, Mass.: Harvard University Press.

Daly, H.E. 1989. "Sustainable Development: From Concept and Theory Towards Operational Principles." In *Population and Development Review.* Hoover Institution Conference.

Daly, H.E., and J.B. Cobb, Jr. 1989. *For the Common Good: Redirecting the Economy Toward Community, the Environment, and a Sustainable Future.* Boston: Beacon Press..

Flora, C.B., and J.L. Flora. 1993. "Entrepreneurial Social Infrastructure: A Necessary Ingredient." *In Annals of the American Academy of Political and Social Science* 529 (September): 48-58.

Foster, J.B. 1997. "Natural Capitalism?" *Dollars and Sense* 211 (May/June): 9.

Hawken, P. 1997. "Natural Capitalism." *Mother Jone*s (MarchApril): 40-62.

Henderson, H. 1996. *Building a Win-Win World: Life Beyond Global Economic Warfare.* San Francisco: Berrett-Koehler Publishers.

Independent Commission on Population and Quality of Life (ICPQL). 1996. *Caring for the Future.* New York: Oxford University Press.

International Council for Local Environmental Initiatives (ICLEI), International Development Research Centre (IRDC), and United Nations Environment Program. 1996. *The Local Agenda 21 Planning Guide.* Toronto: ICLEI and Ottawa: IDRC.

Jacobs, J. 1961. *The Death and Life of Great American Cities.* New York: Random House.

Jacobs, M. 1993. *The Green Economy: Environment, Sustainable Development, and the Politics of the Future.* Vancouver: University of British Columbia Press.

Jansson, A-M., M. Hammer, C. Folke, and R. Costanza, eds. 1994. *Investing in Natural Capital: The Ecological Economics Approach to Sustainability.* Washington, D.C.: Island Press.

McKibben, B. 1996. "The Enigma of Kerala: One State in India is Proving Development Experts Wrong." *Utne Reader* 74 (March/April): 102-12.

Mele, A. 1993. *Polluting for Pleasure.* New York: W.W. Norton.

Mitlin, D., and D. Satterthwaite. 1991. Sustainable Development and Cities. Prepared for How Common Is Our Future? A Global NGO Forum, Habitat International Coalition, Mexico City, 4-7 March.

Ostrom, E. 1993. Social Capital and Development Projects. Prepared for Social Capital and Economic Development, American Academy of Arts and Sciences, Cambridge, Mass, 30-31 July.

Pearce, D.W., E. Barbier, and A. Markandya. 1989. *Blueprint for a Green Economy.* London: Earthscan Publications.

Pearce, D.W., E. Barbier, and A. Markandya. 1990. *Sustainable Development: Economics and Environment in the Third World.* Brookfield, Vt.: Gower Publishing.

Porrit, J. 1989. "Seeing Green: How We Can Create A More Satisfying Society." *Utne Reader* 36 (November/December): 70-77.

President's Council on Sustainable Development. 1996. *Sustainable America: A New Consensus for Prosperity, Opportunity, and a Healthy Environment for the Future.* Washington, D.C.: U.S. Government Printing.

Putnam, R., R. Leonardi, and R. Nanetti. 1993. *Making Democracy Work: Civic Traditions in Modern Italy.* Princeton, N.J.: Princeton University Press.

Putnam, R.D., 1995. "Bowling Alone: America's Declining Social Capital." *Journal of Democracy* 6:1 (January): 65-78.

Rees, W.E. 1991. "Economics, Ecology, and the Limits of Conventional Analysis." *Journal of the Air and Waste Management Association* 41 (October):1323-27.

Rees, W.E. 1992. "Understanding Sustainable Development: Natural Capital and the New World Order." Vancouver: UBC School of Community and Regional Planning.

Selman, P., and J. Parker, 1997. "Citizenship, Civicness and Social Capital in Local Agenda 21." *Local Environment* 2 (2): 171-84.

Stevens, W.K. 1997. "The Value of Nature." *New York Times.* Reprinted in *Vancouver Sun*, 24 May 1997, p. G9.

University of British Columbia (UBC) Task Force on Healthy and Sustainable Communities. 1994. "Tools for Sustainability: Iteration and Implementation." In *The Ecological Public Health: From Vision to Practice*, eds. C. Chu and R. Simpson. Toronto: University of Toronto Centre for Health Promotion; Australia: Institute for Applied Environmental Research at Griffith University.

Wackernagel, M., and W. Rees. 1996. *Our Ecological Footprint: Reducing Human Impact on the Earth.* Gabriola Island, B.C.: New Society Publishers.

World Commission on Environment and Development (WCED). 1987. *Our Common Future.* New York: Oxford University Press.

World Conservation Union (IUCN), United Nations Environment Program (UNEP), and World Wide Fund for Nature (WWF). 1991. *Caring for the Earth: A Strategy for Sustainable Living.* Gland, Switzerland: IUCN, UNEP, WWF.

TOWARD SUSTAINABLE COMMUNITIES

What is a sustainable community? The concept does not describe just one type of neighborhood, town, city or region. Activities that the environment can sustain and that citizens want and can afford may be quite different from community to community. Rather than being a fixed thing, a sustainable community is continually adjusting to meet the social and economic needs of its residents while preserving the environment's ability to support it. Here's how some Minnesota citizens defined sustainable community:

> [A sustainable community is] a community that uses its resources to meet current needs while ensuring that adequate resources are available for future generations. A sustainable community seeks a better quality of life for all its residents while maintaining nature's ability to function over time by minimizing waste, preventing pollution, promoting efficiency and developing local resources to revitalize the local economy. Decision-making in a sustainable community stems from a rich civic life and shared information among community members. A sustainable community resembles a living system in which human, natural and economic elements are interdependent and draw strength from each other (Minnesota SEDEPTF 1995).

This chapter examines sustainability at the community level. It begins with a look at communities in developed and developing parts of the world, proceeds to investigate some of the reasons why our North American communities are presently unsustainable, explores some characteristics and images of more sustainable communities, and concludes with the role of citizens and their governments in moving us toward sustainable communities.

SUSTAINABLE COMMUNITIES NORTH AND SOUTH

For the first time in history, nearly half of the world's people now live in urban areas — areas characterized by human structures and activities. The way our communities develop will largely determine our success or failure in overcoming environmental challenges and achieving sustainable development. Cities and towns provide enormous, untapped opportunities to solve environmental challenges; they must and can pioneer new approaches to sustainable development and community management.

Local governments must also assume the responsibility and marshal the resources to address the sustainability problems facing their communities (Toronto Declaration 1991).

The communities of the developing (southern) world face distinctly different challenges than those faced by the communities of the developed (northern) world. From the perspective of sustainable development, the basic problem with northern cities is that they are unsustainable, whereas the basic problem with southern cities is that they are underdeveloped. Most northern city dwellers are adequately housed and fed, but they meet their needs by consuming at rates the planet cannot afford and polluting at rates the planet cannot tolerate. Many southern city dwellers cannot meet their basic needs for food, clean water, clean air, fuel, transport and an environment free of disease-causing agents. While this dichotomy is not absolute — i.e., there is poverty in most northern cities, and many southern cities live beyond their means in terms of consumption of natural resources such as firewood and water — it helps illuminate the essential challenge of urban sustainability both North and South: meeting basic needs without depleting or degrading natural capital (Holmberg, Bass, and Timberlake 1991).

The cities of the industrial world, with their inadequate urban policies and technology, set the standard to which city managers in low-income countries aspire — low density single family dwellings, cars, expressways, waste creation, air conditioning and profligate water use (White and Whitney 1990). The role of the cities of the industrial world deserves much more scrutiny in the context of human settlements and the environmental crisis, precisely because their impact on the world's changing ecosystems is so enormous.

Approaches to accounting for the environment in urban economic development illustrate the differences between traditional environmental economics and a more ecological approach. Traditional environmental economics perceives environmental problems in terms of a deteriorating local environment, e.g., land-fills approaching capacity from the growing waste stream. Solutions are cast in terms of finding efficient trade-offs between economic growth and environmental quality and finding policy instruments that will internalize the costs of pollution to those firms causing the problems. In contrast, the ecological ("strong sustainability") approach reveals new facets of the problem that are invisible to conventional economic policy models. Here attention is on the total relationship between the human population of the urban region, prevailing levels of ecologically significant consumption, and the sustainability of the resource base (Rees 1992).

THE UNSUSTAINABLE COMMUNITY

Most North American cities were built using technologies that assumed abundant and cheap energy and land would be available forever. Communities therefore grew inefficiently, and became dependent on lengthy distribution systems. Cheap energy influenced the construction of our spacious homes and buildings, fostered our addiction to the automobile, and increased the separation of our workplaces from our homes. As described by Calthorpe (1989):

"No one fully understands how, or even if, sustainable development can be achieved; however, there is a growing consensus that it must be accomplished at the local level if it is ever to be achieved on a global basis" (ICLEI et al. 1996).

"It is becoming apparent that almost every issue of sustainable development which emerges at the local level will be replicated, in one form or another, at the provincial, national and international levels" (Connell 1991).

"*During the period that environmentalism became a force in North American public life, our cities and communities have sprawled without consideration for resource efficiency. Infrastructure has been constructed — housing, roadways and sewage systems, for instance — which encourages disregardful resource consumption. Water sources have been taxed or polluted. Built environments have been designed which alter microclimates and promote photochemical smog formation. Environmental services, such as public transit systems, have been left without public support. Our settlements have not only become less and less habitable for humans and most other species. They now stand as the geographic point sources of most regional and global environmental problems, and threaten even the most distant wild areas saved by environmental advocates*" (Brugmann 1992).

The current round of suburban growth is generating a crisis of many dimensions: mounting traffic congestion, increasingly unaffordable housing, receding open space, and stressful social patterns. The truth is, we are using planning strategies that are forty years old and no longer relevant to today's culture. Our household makeup has changed dramatically, the work place and work force have been transformed, real wealth has shrunk, and serious environmental concerns have surfaced. But we are still building World War II suburbs as if families were large and had only one breadwinner, as if jobs were all downtown, as if land and energy were endless, and as if another lane on the freeway would end congestion.

Urban sprawl is one legacy of abundant fossil fuel and our perceived right to unrestricted use of the private car whatever the social costs and externalities. Other local and regional consequences of sprawl, such as congestion, air pollution, jobs-housing location "imbalance," and longer commuting times are now commonly recognized. Yet until recently, few researchers acknowledged that the land use pattern of North American cities also has serious *global* ecological ramifications.

For example, residents of most Canadian cities annually produce about 20 tons of carbon dioxide per capita, placing Canada among the top three or four nations in terms of per capita contribution to potential climate change. In contrast, citizens of Amsterdam produce only 10 tons of carbon dioxide per capita per year. Sprawl, exclusionary zoning, and low density account for much of this difference. According to research at the International Institute for Applied Systems Analysis, if North American cities modeled future development on cities like Amsterdam, future carbon dioxide emissions here would only be half as much as current gloomy projections now indicate (Alcamo 1990).

One way to consider the impact of a community on natural resources and eco-systems is to consider its "ecological footprint": the land area and the natural capital on which it draws to sustain its population and production structure (Wackernagel and Rees 1996). Cities and towns demand a high input of resources — water, fossil fuels, land, and all the goods and materials that their populations and enterprises require. The more populous the city and the richer its inhabitants, the larger its ecological footprint is likely to be in terms of its demand on resources and, in general, the larger the area from which these are drawn.

Although some of our cities may appear to be sustainable, analysis of the ecological footprint of industrial cities shows that they appropriate carrying capacity not only from their own rural and resource regions, but also from distant elsewhere — in other words, they "import" sustainability. The flip side of importing sustainability is exporting ecological degradation, or unsustainability, since the production or extraction of natural resources in distant places often causes serious problems of environmental degradation there. Most North American cities (as well as those in Europe, Japan, Australia, and other developed parts of the world) can only have forests, parks, and nature reserves nearby because such land is not being used to meet the demand for food and other natural resources which are instead imported.

The average North American's footprint has grown to measure 4-5 hectares (about 10-12 acres), somewhat more than three city blocks, while the amount of ecologically productive land available has decreased this century from over 5 hectares to less than 1.5 hectares per person in 1994. Ecological footprint analysis shows that the residents of the Lower Fraser Valley (which includes the City of Vancouver, B.C.), with 1.8 million inhabitants and a population density of 4.5 people per hectare, depend on an area 19 times larger than that contained within its boundaries for food, forestry products, carbon dioxide assimilation, and energy. The country of Holland, with 15 million people, or 4.4 per hectare, requires about 15 times the available land within their own country for food, forest products, and energy use, even though Dutch people consume less on average than North Americans (Wackernagel and Rees 1996).

Ecological footprint analysis confirms our need to minimize consumption of essential natural capital. If everyone lived like today's North Americans, it would take at least two additional planet Earths to produce the resources, absorb the wastes, and otherwise maintain life-support.

THE SUSTAINABLE COMMUNITY

The postwar pattern of Western urban development is not only ecologically unconscionable but economically inefficient and socially inequitable. In contrast, sustainable development implies that the use of energy and materials be consistent with production by such natural capital processes as photosynthesis and waste assimilation (Rees 1990a,b). To some authors this implies increasing community and regional self-reliance to reduce dependency on imports (California Office of Appropriate Technology 1981; Morris 1982; RAIN 1981). The benefits would be reduced energy budgets, reduced material consumption, and a smaller, more compact urban pattern interspersed with productive areas to collect energy, grow crops, and recycle wastes (Van der Ryn and Calthorpe 1986).

Movement toward sustainable communities requires a new kind of ecosystem thinking about human settlements. As described by Brugmann and Hersh (1991):

> In this century, the city has been imagined by sociologists, planners, and engineers as a bazaar, a seat of political chaos, an infernal machine, a circuit, and, more hopefully, as a community, the human creation "par excellence." These different ways of thinking about cities, their social forces, their market behaviours, their reliance on materials and processes from the natural world, both shape and constrain the programmes and policies that local governments put forward to serve the needs of urban people.
>
> The city can also be imagined as an ecosystem. Such a concept provides a tool to understand the complex relations between human activities and the environment, and how communities can organise their activities to both meet human needs and benefit the environment. . . .
>
> Like a natural system such as a pond or forest, an urban ecosystem transforms energy (human labour, capital, fossil fuels) and materials (timber, iron, sand and gravel, information, etc.) into products that are consumed or exported, and into by-products. In natural systems by-products are recycled. We have designed and managed our cities so that these by-products often go unused as wastes. The impact of

human activity on the environment can be highlighted by charting the dynamics of the system — the movement of materials and people, the flows of energy and capital, the locations where energy is stored or expended, the rates at which wastes are generated and recycled. By looking at the city as a whole, by analyzing the pathways along which energy and pollution move, we can begin to see how human activities create and direct pollution into local, regional, and global ecosystems. We can also see how these activities can be reorganised and reintegrated with natural processes to increase the efficiency of resource use, the recycling of "wastes" as valuable materials, and the conservation of energy.

Australian researcher Peter Newman (1990) notes that "the most unsustainable form of settlement yet developed — the low density suburb — has been a relatively recent phenomenon, motivated by a strong anti-urban Anglo-Saxon sentiment and facilitated by the automobile. Social organisation for ecological sustainability will need to reverse this settlement pattern." His analysis of settlement patterns and sustainability suggests that sustainable settlements require making cities more urban and making the countryside more rural.

Making cities more urban can be accomplished by "re-urbanizing" city centers and sub-centers; re-orienting transport infrastructure away from the automobile; removing subsidies on the automobile; and providing a more public-oriented urban culture, assisted by attractive urban design (townscapes, streetscapes, malls and squares) and by "traffic calming" measures to facilitate bicycle and pedestrian use of residential areas and major roads. Making the countryside more rural can be accomplished by means such as protecting and encouraging sustainable agriculture and forestry in rural areas and moving towards bioregionalism (e.g., air- and watershed management) as the basis of local government boundaries and responsibilities.

The ideal urban form for a particular locale will depend to some extent on the nature of the energy supply options: for example, higher densities make most efficient use of district heating and public transport networks, while lower densities may make solar energy more viable. The location, gross density and form of new development should therefore be determined in conjunction with programs for energy supply and conservation technologies (Owens 1990). This principle is illustrated by a San Jose, California study that compared development pressures with or without a "greenbelt" to constrain development. Without it, 13,000 exurban homes would be developed which, compared to an equivalent number of units downtown and along the transit corridor, would require at least an additional 320,000 kilometers (200,000 miles) of auto commuting plus an additional 11 million liters (three million gallons) of water *every day,* as well as 40 percent more energy for heating and cooling (Yesney 1990).

Another study, by Montgomery County, Maryland, found that continued growth in an automobile-dependent pattern would produce traffic congestion levels high enough to choke off economic development. However, an anticipated doubling of population and employment could be accommodated without excessive traffic problems if most new growth were clustered in pedestrian- and bicycle-friendly centers focused on an expanded rail transit and busway system. Through such strategies, the share of county work trips made by non-auto alternatives could double to 50 percent,

"Sustainable urban development is ultimately a cultural statement about ourselves, how we want to live, and our ability to manage our needs, desires, and dreams in ways that are effective and caring. . . . Ultimately the city is the expression of the only ecosystem that we have helped to create; it is the unique contribution of our species, and the creation against which we are most likely to be judged" (Jacobs 1992).

resulting in only half the level of energy use and air pollution compared to the sprawled, automobile strategy (Replogle 1990).

As these examples demonstrate, *the pattern of growth is more important than the amount of growth* in determining the level and efficiency of resource use and traffic congestion. They also show that a critical sustainability objective for our communities is more *efficient use of urban space.* This objective, as we will see throughout this book, is very compatible with the objectives discussed in chapter 1, *minimizing consumption of natural capital,* and *multiplying social capital.*

Images of Sustainable Communities

Yaro et al. (1988) developed practical planning standards which rural New England towns can adopt to protect their distinctive character, while at the same time accommodate economic growth. Illustrating actual sites in western Massachusetts, their drawings show each site before development, after conventional development, and after what the authors call "creative development" (figure 1). In both development schemes, the same number of units have been added. While many aspects differ between the two development approaches, the most critical is that the conventional approach dramatically alters the land-use pattern (e.g., agricultural lands are lost to suburban sprawl), while the creative approach absorbs growth without destroying future options (e.g., agricultural "capital" remains intact).

Norwood (1990) illustrates a similar concept, but within the setting of a typical suburban block (see figure 2). Variations on this theme are increasingly popular in new private-market developments. In this case, an existing single-family neighborhood, characterized by under-utilized backyards, garages, attics, basements, and bedrooms,

Reprinted with permission from the Center for Rural Massachusetts/ University of Massachusetts at Amherst, *Dealing With Change in the Connecticut River Valley: A Design Manual for Conservation and Development* by Yaro et al.

Figure 1a: Before Development   **Figure 1b: After Conventional Development**   **Figure 1c: After Creative Development**

Before development, after conventional development, and after "creative development."
In both development schemes, the same number of units have been added

Figure 2: An Urban Cooperative Block
An existing single family neighborhood (above) has been transformed into an urban cooperative block (below) — an urban "village cluster" which could include a community house, common back yards, common parking, and common resources

Reprinted with permission from the Shared Living Resource Center, a non-profit organization dedicated to creating supportive shared living communities that integrate housing with cooperative living, ecological design and affordability. Shared Living Resource Center, 2375 Shattuck Avenue, Berkeley, California, USA 94704; tel: 510/548-6608

Figure 3: A Sustainable City Vision
This sustainable city vision emphasizes mixed-use zoning, pedestrian-, bicycle- and transit-friendly streets, renewable energy sources, and urban greenery

From a drawing by Diane Schatz, reprinted with permission from *RAIN* Magazine, P.O. Box 30097, Eugene, Oregon, USA 97403; tel: 503/683-1504 has been transformed into what the author calls an "urban cooperative block." The urban cooperative block concept could be organized around one or more small or home businesses; it could be designed to "recycle" obsolete corporate/industrial parks, shopping centers, and office complexes; or, as shown here, it could be the center of a "village cluster" typical of the popular Danish cohousing communities, with a community house, common backyards, common parking, and common resources. Many forms of ownership are possible, ranging from a condominium corporation to a non-profit corporation with resident control, a limited equity cooperative, a community land trust, or a mutual housing association. Potential economic advantages include lowering housing costs through creating additional units and/or bedrooms, renting rooms and units, and allowing cottage industries or home businesses. By improving affordability, this model has the potential of serving a diversified and intergenerational cross-section of the population.

Figure 3 illustrates a similar concept, but this time the setting is in a downtown core. Many ideas for urban sustainability are illustrated in this drawing, such as mixed-use zoning; streets devoted to walking, cycling, and public transport; heavy reliance on renewable energy sources; rooftop gardens and greenery; and separate "waste" containers for compost and trash. Note the integration of work and home, which reduces the need for travel. As described earlier, a San Jose, California study compared the impacts of 13,000 units of this kind of development downtown and along the transit corridor to an equivalent number of exurban homes. It found that the kind of development pictured here saved at least 320,000 kilometers (200,000 miles) of auto commuting plus an additional 11 million plus liters (three million gallons) of water every day, and required 40 percent less energy for heating and cooling (Yesney 1990).

Figure 4 brings the discussion to the level of the urban region, using the City of Berkeley, California as an example. Although these maps may at first appear to show the *history* of Berkeley, they actually demonstrate a sustainable *future* development pattern for this urban region. The first map in this set shows Berkeley and its town and neighborhood "centers." These centers were selected as a compromise between the "ideal" centers — according to the natural features of the landscape such as ridge lines and steep slopes — and the existing centers. Over time, urban development is concentrated near these centers while surrounded by non-urban lands. Once again, the key feature is the *pattern* of urban growth.

These drawings demonstrate a "nodal" rather than a "centralized" vision — a network of smaller, compact communities surrounded by *non-urban land*. As the city grows, and its centers become increasingly compact, the surrounding land can be reclaimed — as open space, forests, agricultural land, and wildlife habitat — to simultaneously benefit people and the environment.

On Natural and Built Environments

"We must recognize that the distinction between environment as commonly understood and the built environment is artificial and that the urban [arena] and everything that goes into it is as much part of the solution as it is a contributing factor to ecological difficulties. The tangible recognition that the mass of humanity will be located in living environments designated as urban says that environmental politics must pay as much if not more attention to the qualities of those built environments as it now typically does to a fictitiously separated and imagined 'natural' environment. . . . A crucial preliminary is to find an adequate language in which to discuss possible futures in a rapidly urbanizing world, a language that actively recognizes that urbanization is both a constituent of, as well as constituted by, the ways such possibilities might potentially be grasped" (Harvey 1996).

Berkeley and its Centers

Berkeley, 15 to 50 years hence

Figure 4: A Nodal Vision of Urban Development

"The underlying concept behind drawing these circles [in Berkeley and its Centers] is simply that distance requires energy and time to traverse. The greater the distance people have to travel, the higher the use of resources and the greater the pro-duction of pollution and waste of time. Therefore, we should build relatively compact centers. These areas will then work well with any public transit connecting them to other relatively high-use areas. Within and between the spots of higher activity, people can find it easy and pleasant to walk and bicycle.

MOBILIZING CITIZENS AND THEIR GOVERNMENTS

There is no (and perhaps should not be any) single accepted definition of sustain-able communities. Communities must be involved in defining sustainability from a local perspective. The dilemma is how to encourage democracy (e.g., participatory local processes) within a framework of sustainability. As we have seen, elements of this framework include minimizing consumption of essential natural capital, multiplying social capital, and more efficient use of urban space. However, a fourth element is required to coordinate and balance the other three.

There are legitimate causes for concern about the dislocations, economic costs, and potential inconveniences associated with sustainability measures and their distri-bution across society. Both the gain and the pain of adjustment should be shared fair-ly by community members. Participation in the decision process by affected groups "can help make the attendant redistribution of costs and benefits fairer and more

Berkeley, 25 to 90 years hence

Berkeley, 40 to 125 years hence

This pattern of 'spots' of development is based on the size of the human body and the speed of walking. It contrasts sharply with 'strip' (one-dimensional or linear development) and 'sprawl' (two-dimensional or flat development) created by and for things that weigh 10-40 times as much and travel up to 50 times as fast: automobiles" (Register 1987).

Reprinted with permission from Register, *Ecocity Berkeley: Building Cities for a Healthy Future.*

widely understood. Democratic mobilization is essential to the achievement of such policies in the face of the opposition [by vested interests they] inevitably engender" (Paehlke and Torgerson 1990).

Environmental organizations and activists, especially in the United States and Canada, have tended to focus narrowly on specific campaigns of one kind or another, and may find it difficult to see how their work fits into the larger social, political and economic context. Yet the current popularity of the term sustainable development requires those concerned with environmental protection to cooperate with others in meshing environmental critiques, goals and strategies with those of peace, social justice, equality and economy, etc. (Gibson 1991; PCSD 1996).

In general, sustainable development strategies should favor bottom-up over top-down approaches; redistribution over "trickle-down;" self-reliance over dependency; a local rather than a regional, national, or international focus; and small-scale projects rather than grand-scale or megaprojects. As well, they should be designed with exten-

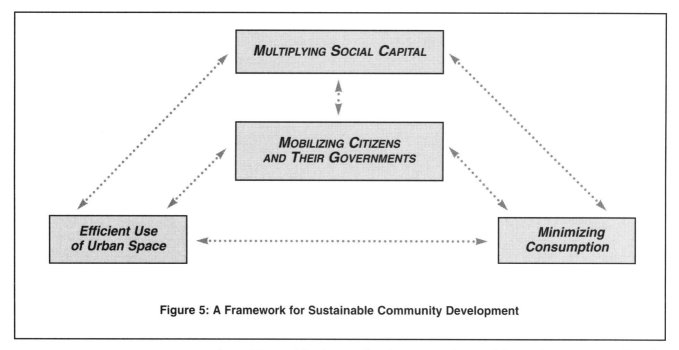

Figure 5: A Framework for Sustainable Community Development

sive public participation; seek to improve society and the environment as well as the economy; and result in increased equity, equality and empowerment (Brohman 1996).

Democracy is an inherent part of the sustainable development process. Sustainable development must be participatory development. For people to prosper anywhere they must participate as competent citizens in the decisions and processes that affect their lives (Gran 1987). Sustainable development is thus about the quantity and quality of empowerment and participation of people. Sustainable development therefore requires *mobilizing citizens and their governments* toward sustainable communities.

In summary, applying the concept of sustainable development to North American communities begins with unprecedented and simultaneous emphasis on the *efficient use of urban space*, on *minimizing the consumption of essential natural capital*, on *multiplying social capital*, and on *mobilizing citizens and their governments* toward these ends. This last element is crucial to coordinating and balancing the other three (figure 5). The significance of these criteria for the future of our communities and our society is elaborated in the following chapters.

REFERENCES

Alcamo, J.M. 1990. Compact City Design as a Strategy to Cut Dangerous Air Pollution. Presented to First International Ecocity Conference, Berkeley, California, March 29-April 1.

Brohman, J. 1996. *Popular Development: Rethinking the Theory and Practice of Development.* Oxford: Blackwell Publishers.

Brugmann, J. 1992. "Preface." In M. Roseland, *Toward Sustainable Communities: A Resource Book for Municipal and Local Governments*. Ottawa: National Round Table on the Environment and the Economy.

Brugmann, J. and R. Hersh. 1991. Cities as Ecosystems: Opportunities for Local Government. Draft. Toronto: ICLEI.

California Office of Appropriate Technology (CalOAT). 1981. *Working Together: Community Self-Reliance in California*. Sacramento: California Office of Appropriate Technology.

Calthorpe, P. 1989. "Introduction: A Reverse Definition." In *The Pedestrian Pocket Book: A New Suburban Design Strategy*, ed. D. Kelbaugh. New York: Princeton Architectural Press.

Connell, G.E. 1991. Letter to the Prime Minister. In *A Report to Canadians*. Ottawa: National Round Table on the Environment and the Economy(NRTEE).

Gibson, R. 1991. "Should Environmentalists Pursue 'Sustainable Development'?" *Probe Post* 13(4) Winter: 22-25.

Gran, G. 1987. *An Annotated Guide to Global Development: Capacity Building for Effective Social Change*. Pittsburgh: University of Pittsburgh Economic and Social Development Program.

Harvey, D. 1996. "Cities or Urbanization." *City Magazine* (London, UK) 1:2.

Holmberg, J., S. Bass, and L. Timberlake. 1991. *Defending the Future: A Guide to Sustainable Development*. London: International Institute for Environment and Development/Earthscan.

International Council for Local Environmental Initiatives (ICLEI), International Development Research Centre (IDRC), and United Nations Environment Program. 1996. *The Local Agenda 21 Planning Guide*. Toronto: ICLEI and Ottawa: IDRC.

Jacobs, P. 1992. "Sustainable Urban Development." In *Architecture in the Year 2000: Conference Proceedings*. Royal Architectural Institute of Canada.

Minnesota Sustainable Economic Development and Environmental Protection Task Force (SEDEPTF). 1995. *Common Ground: Achieving Sustainable Communities in Minnesota*. St. Paul: Minnesota Planning.

Morris, D. 1982. *Self-Reliant Cities: Energy and the Transformation of Urban America*. San Francisco: Sierra Club Books.

Morris, D. 1990. "The Ecological City as a Self-Reliant City." In *Green Cities: Ecologically Sound Approaches to Urban Space*, ed. D. Gordon. Montreal: Black Rose Books. Pp. 21-35.

Newman, P. 1990. "Social Organization for Ecological Sustainability: Toward a More Sustainable Settlement Pattern." In *Social Structures for Sustainability*, ed. P. Cook. Fundamental Questions Paper No. 11. Canberra: Centre for Resource and Environmental Studies, Australian National University.

Norwood, K. 1990. "The Urban Cooperative Block." *Permaculture Activist* VI(4) November.

Owens, S.E. 1990. "Land Use Planning for Energy Efficiency." In *Energy, Land, and Public Policy*, ed. J.B. Cullingworth. New Brunswick, NJ: Transaction Publishers. Pp. 53-98.

Paehlke, R. and D. Torgerson, eds. 1990. *Managing Leviathan: Environmental Politics and the Administrative State*. Peterborough: Broad View Press.

President's Council on Sustainable Development (PCSD). 1996. *Sustainable America: A New Consensus for Prosperity, Opportunity, and a Healthy Environment for the Future*. Washington, D.C.: U.S. Government Printing.

RAIN editors. 1981. *Knowing Home: Studies for a Possible Portland*. Portland: *RAIN*.

Rees, W.E. 1990a. "Sustainable Development and the Biosphere: Concepts and Principles." In *Teilhard Studies*. No. 22 (Chambersburg, PA: Anima Books for the American Teilhard Association.

Rees, W.E. 1990b. "The Ecology of Sustainable Development." *The Ecologist* 20(1):18-23.

Rees, W.E. 1992. Ecological Footprints and Appropriated Carrying Capacity: What Urban Economics Leaves Out. Presented to Globe '92, Vancouver, B.C., 18 March.

Register, R. 1987. *Ecocity Berkeley: Building Cities for a Healthy Future*. Berkeley, Calif.: North Atlantic Books.

Replogle, M. 1990. Sustainable Transportation Strategies for World Development. Presented to World Congress of Local Governments for a Sustainable Future, United Nations, New York, 7 September.

Toronto Declaration on World Cities and Their Environment. 1991. Presented to World Cities and Their Environment Congress of Municipal Leaders, Toronto, Ontario, 28 August.

Van der Ryn, S., and P. Calthorpe. 1986. *Sustainable Communities: A New Design Synthesis for Cities, Suburbs, and Towns*. San Francisco: Sierra Club Books.

Wackernagel, M., and W.Rees. 1996. *Our Ecological Footprint: Reducing Human Impact on the Earth*. Gabriola Island, B.C.: New Society Publishers.

White, R. and J. Whitney. 1990. Human Settlements and Sustainable Development: An Overview. Prepared for Colloquium on Human Settlements and Sustainable Development, University of Toronto Centre for Urban And Community Studies, Toronto, 21-23 June.

Yaro, R.D. et al. 1988. *Dealing With Change in the Connecticut River Valley: A Design Manual for Conservation and Development*. Amherst, Mass.: Center for Rural Massachusetts, University of Massachusetts at Amherst.

Yesney, M. 1990. "The Sustainable City: A Revolution in Urban Evolution." *Western City* LXVI:3 (March): 4-44.

Making Community Policy

There are many ways to mobilize citizens and their governments toward sustainable communities, but there are also many barriers and obstacles that hamper our progress in this direction. We cannot realistically expect most people to choose sustainable options if they appear to be more difficult or expensive than unsustainable choices. The question arises, then, how can we change the systems around us, "level the playing field," and provide ample opportunities for individuals to make behavioral choices that improve their communities?

In recent years there has been increasing interest in the use of "economic instruments" in environmental policy. These tools influence the behavior of economic agents by providing financial incentives to environmentally improved behavior, or disincentives to damaging behavior. Such instruments — taxes, charges, subsidies, tradable permits, deposit-refund schemes, performance bonds and so on — have been particularly favored within the discipline of environmental economics, where they originated. As the influence of environmental economics has grown, so the calls to introduce economic instruments in fields such as pollution control and energy consumption have grown louder (Roseland and Jacobs 1995).

Economic instruments should not be seen in isolation. When introduced they are inevitably part of a structure and process of community management which in turn reflect wider objectives — environmental, economic, social and ethical — in society.

For communities to move effectively toward sustainability, citizens and their governments should understand the range of policy instruments available to them and the wider context of how community policy is made. This chapter explores the use of policy instruments in sustainable community planning and development, and reviews the different types of instruments that are available to community decision-makers.

POLICY ISSUES FOR LOCAL GOVERNMENTS

Although the precise characteristics of sustainable communities may be debated, characteristic objectives of local activity toward sustainable development can be applied virtually anywhere. Several sustainability issues can be identified as important for local governments, as will be evident in the following chapters. (Unless otherwise noted, most examples referred to in this chapter are detailed elsewhere in this book.) These include infrastructure that results in environmentally respectful use of

Table 1: Policy Instruments

Categories	Instruments
Regulations	1. Laws 2. Licenses, Permits, and Standards 3. Tradable Permits 4. Quid Pro Quos
Voluntary Instruments	1. Information 2. Volunteers, Volunteer Associations, and NGOs 3. Technical Assistance
Expenditure	1. Expenditure and Contracting 2. Monitoring 3. Investment and Procurement 4. Enterprise 5. Public/Private Partnerships
Financial Incentives	1. Pricing 2. Taxes and Charges 3. Subsidies and Tax Incentives 4. Grants and Loans 5. Rebates, Rewards, and surety Bonds 6. Vouchers

resources; minimization of waste and proper management of residues; energy-efficient transportation; compact land-use patterns; integrated transportation and land-use planning; local environmental assessments and audits; cooperation with non-governmental organizations in the implementation of environmental programs; reducing economic and social polarization; and integration of marginalized people into efforts towards sustainable development (Gilbert et al. 1996).

Given these general concerns for local governments, some broad policy goals might include the following: reducing per capita car use; reducing per capita water consumption; increasing the percentage of local land contained in parks; and improving cycling and pedestrian infrastructure, etc. Policy instruments can be employed to achieve these specific policy objectives.

POLICY INSTRUMENTS

Two target populations for policy instruments can be identified: the general public and individual firms or industries. The use of instruments to influence the behavior of the public can be called *demand management* (see chapters on energy, water, transportation, and community economic development). One of the most important requirements for sustainability is a reduction in the per capita consumption of resources as communities grow (Wackernagel and Rees 1996). Since supply of resources can only be augmented to a certain point, this inherently requires that *demand* for resources be managed. Instruments that try to influence the behavior of firms and industries are not usually considered to be demand management, but they serve the same purpose — to reduce the consumption of natural resources. In considering particular instruments, it is important to note their target populations.

In table 1, the instruments are divided into broad categories according to Jacobs (1993), although many instruments could actually fall into more than one category. The various policy instruments can be slotted into four categories. The first is traditional regulations such as permits and licenses that have a legal basis. A second category is voluntary mechanisms or actions taken that generally do not require expenditure. The third is direct government expenditure such as money spent on improved infrastructure. Lastly, there are financial incentives such as taxes, subsidies, tradable permits, and rewards. Financial incentives do not require people to change their behavior or values, and do not usually require as much enforcement as regulations.

Regulations

Regulations are the most pervasive policy instruments. They include laws; licenses, permits, and standards; tradable permits; and quid pro quos. Requirements for catalytic converters in cars or insulation in homes are both typical regulations. Detailed regulations such as a prohibition on the use of barbecue lighter fuels make up Southern California's Air Quality Management Plan; it has an astounding 5,500 pages of regulations designed to reduce smog levels.

Laws

The traditional way that governments discourage certain behavior is by making specific activities illegal. Enforcement of laws can be a problem, but they are still useful. For example, government can manage the demand for a certain product by restricting the amount that any individual can consume. Desirable behavior can also be achieved by getting rid of outdated or inefficient regulations (deregulation), although deregulation *for the sake of deregulation* is hard to justify. Governments can use building code laws, rent control laws, and zoning laws to encourage particular kinds of community development.

A simple law can have significant effects. Cheap parking rates in urban areas are known to encourage automobile use. A simple law setting a minimum price for parking may be a substantial incentive for employees to use transit.

Washington State has gone so far as to pass a statute, named the Commute Trip Reduction Act. This piece of legislation, passed in 1991, forces large companies (more than 100 employees) to initiate trip reduction programs consisting of such measures as parking fee increases and transit subsidies (Plous 1994).

Licenses, Permits, and Standards

These are also regulatory instruments. Standards such as municipal effluent discharge standards may be based on a desirable ambient water quality level (performance standards) or industries may simply be required to use certain technologies (technology standards). Best-available-technology standards can be used for industrial effluent and emissions. Conservation plumbing standards have been adopted in New York and elsewhere (PMC 1990). For example, all new developments in the Highland Water District of New York must have 6 liters (1.6 gallons) per flush toilets.

There must of course be a penalty associated with non-compliance if legal standards are to be effective. For example, a Ride Share Ordinance in Montgomery County, Maryland, penalizes employers that do not achieve a particular increase in transit use among employees. The result was a 31.7 percent increase in carpools and a 59.6 percent increase in transit use in just one year.

Santa Monica is one of many cities that has set recycling space standards for new buildings. Residential buildings with 10 units must allocate 9 square meters (100 square feet) to recycling, and additional area for additional units. The standard is similar for commercial buildings.

A 1986 ordinance in Florida allocates housing permits to developers based on a point system. Preferences are for energy efficiency, recreational amenities, low infrastructure requirements, and landscape quality. The ordinance also requires that at least 40 percent of residential housing units be constructed as affordable housing.

Tradable Permits

Although monitoring is still required when tradable permits are used, the total allowable resource use or output level can be easily set as the sum of all permits. A community may agree on a limit for the amount of industrial waste that may be discharged into a local lake. A tradable permit system conveniently ensures that the limit will be met, as long as the system is enforced. Furthermore, the permits should end up efficiently allocated if firms have reasonable information. Depending on traditional use of a resource, permits can either be awarded to firms directly, or auctioned (Jacobs 1993). Tradable permits are a useful instrument only if they can be easily enforced and if initial allocation is not too difficult.

Quid Pro Quos

Governments may require firms to do something in exchange for the right to build or produce a product. Some U.S. cities require developers to invest in low-income housing at the same time as constructing more profitable downtown business buildings (Osborne and Gaebler 1993). The use of property is also convenient — governments may actually give land to developers in exchange for a particular type of construction.

Voluntary Instruments

Voluntary mechanisms can be defined as actions taken by firms, individuals or governments that generally do not require regulations or financial incentives. Volunteer associations and non-governmental organizations (NGOs) can be organized by firms or individuals. Some organizations use volunteers to clean up residential neighborhood garbage or carry out other activities that benefit communities. Government agencies can provide information and technical assistance to firms and individuals to promote certain behavior. Though classified as voluntary instruments, these may involve some expenditure as well. Government pleas to conserve water in times of drought are a useful alternative to shutting down water supply.

Information

Expenditure on educating the public is a valuable tool — if people know that their behavior is socially or environmentally harmful, they may change it. The Power Smart program in British Columbia has resulted in voluntary reductions in energy use in the province. This type of education is a valuable form of demand management. Community policy development should involve a great deal of public participation in general, in order to identify important objectives, to discern what policy instruments are most acceptable, and to increase the acceptability of policy initiatives (Newman 1993a). Education can be achieved indirectly as well by financial support for NGOs.

Without expenditure, individual politicians can educate people with public statements that can influence public behavior. By publicly condemning certain behaviors, people may feel obligated to stop or change them. Choice programs can also be an integral part of education. For example, if a community wishes to sustain its organic produce industry, it may initiate a program that clearly labels all produce as either organic or not. Accompanied by a public education program on the community benefits of buying organic, consumers will be well informed about the choices they are making.

Volunteers, Volunteer Associations, and NGOs

The use of volunteers is an efficient way to work towards community objectives. Not only can government choose the activities that it wants to organize, it can also help foster a healthy sense of community. Government need not get directly involved. It may instead promote volunteer associations or fund NGOs or private firms that can then organize activities. Small-scale voluntary recycling organizations are a common example.

Technical Assistance

Governments can not only provide financial resources, but also expertise for NGOs and firms. The City of Santa Monica sends brochures to small businesses which describe specific waste reduction measures in detail. Eco-counsellors are common in Europe, and provide detailed information and advice to individuals or businesses on a range of environmental issues.

Expenditure

Expenditure consists of any use of public money such as contracting, monitoring, investment, procurement, enterprise, and public-private partnerships. The Danish city of Copenhagen successfully used some regulatory and expenditure measures to reduce automobile use. In the 1960s, people wanted isolated homes and their own cars, desiring to imitate the American way of life. The city planners decided to reduce automobile use by reducing urban sprawl. Copenhagen set out to make the downtown core more attractive. It reduced parking by 3 percent each year, rebuilt city housing, and made the streets pedestrian-friendly and more hospitable by providing outdoor seating, etc. The result has been decreased traffic, a tripling of recreational and social activity in the major streets, and a decline in the market for isolated homes far from the downtown core (Newman 1993b).

Expenditure and Contracting

Government can directly work towards specific community objectives by spending money on specific activities, or by offering contracts that serve those purposes. Of course expenditure requires money (see Leithe and Joseph 1991 for a review of financing alternatives for local governments). Furthermore, traditional engineering approaches often encourage expansion of infrastructure and supply augmentation, rather than alternatives such as demand management.

Still, investment in improved technologies, such as better garbage or sewage treatment systems, can be a valuable form of expenditure. A good example of innovative use of public funds was Portland's 1991 construction of a municipal garbage composting facility, with a capacity of 185,000 tons of garbage each year. Small-scale energy-efficient sewage treatment plants such as those built in Providence, Rhode Island, and in Harwich, Massachusetts are also innovative. The technology is available for small-scale, self-contained sewage treatment plants that use sunlight, bacteria, plants, and fish to change sewage into clean water. Any technology that encourages the recycling of resources should be seriously considered by communities that attempt to plan for sustainability.

Although expenditure has been traditionally used as a solution to many policy problems, it is not necessarily effective on its own. While some increases in transit use have been observed in the U.S., the $2.5-billion a year spent by the federal government since 1979 has not been as effective as hoped; although the systems are in place, people have not been given any real incentive to try transit (Plous 1994). As long as public subsidies for roads and parking keep driving costs low, it is simply too easy to continue driving. It is apparent that federal expenditure on transit would be much more effective if it were accompanied by increased costs on automobile use.

Monitoring

A valuable form of expenditure is on the monitoring of infrastructure to ensure efficient operation. Leaks in U.S. municipal water systems range from 12 percent to 40 percent (Roseland and Jacobs 1995). Leaks cannot be detected easily anywhere in which water is not metered, simply because it is not possible to measure the volume of water arriving at a site.

Investment and Procurement

Governments can invest money in firms whose behavior is desirable in order to ensure their survival. They can also buy products from the firms that they choose, and thereby favor particular firms or industries. In an attempt to reduce waste generation by 50 percent by 2000, representatives of federal, provincial and municipal governments in Ontario have formed a committee called Governments Incorporating Procurement Policies to Eliminate Refuse. Its function is to educate its members on environmental considerations to be used during purchasing.

Enterprise

When the market fails to provide desirable outcomes, governments can create their own businesses. These may be, but are not limited to, situations in which natural monopolies exist. Governments may also create private businesses that are non-profit. Community Development Corporations are private corporations with a responsibility to meet the needs of all members of the community. Residents join for a fee and can then vote on activities to be undertaken. Community Development Credit Unions can help a community by serving low- and moderate-income individuals that may not get financial services from banks. Their goal is to empower all citizens in the community. Public enterprises may also be set up that support community agriculture or utilize forestry as a source of revenue.

Creating Markets for Recycled Materials

Many U.S. local government procurement policies give a 5-percent to 10-percent cost preference to products made with post-consumer recycled materials, even though they may initially be more expensive. In the long run, it is in the interest of local governments to build up markets — and demand — for recycled materials (Local Government Commission 1989).

Public/Private Partnerships

Governments can enter partnerships with particular firms that either have resources that are valuable to the government or have enough employees to do useful community labor. For example, Adopt-a-Park programs have evolved in Seattle and other U.S. cities, in which private companies take responsibility for the maintenance of public parks (Osborne and Gaebler 1993).

Joint developments between private firms and transit authorities in Toronto have resulted in efficient use of land around transit stations (Kenworthy 1990). High density development around stations has encouraged reduced automobile use and commuting times.

Financial Incentives

Financial incentives are an attractive alternative to traditional regulatory instruments. They do not generally require expenditure on enforcement because they create a constrained market environment in which firms behave as they normally would. Examples include pricing, taxes, charges, subsidies, tax incentives, grants, loans, rebates, rewards, surety bonds and vouchers. A water conservation program in Santa Monica, California offered rebates to cover installation of low-flow toilets and shower heads. At the same time, a conservation incentive fee (a tax) was collected from households that did not participate in the program (as part of their water bills), and this money was used to partly finance the conservation program. Per capita consumption of water for indoor use has dropped from 303 to189 liters (80 to 50 gallons) per day.

Pricing

Goods that have traditionally been provided for free can be priced as a method of demand management. For example, water metering can significantly reduce consumption. Calgary consumes twice as much water as its nearby, similarly-sized neighbor Edmonton, largely because it is only partially metered (Brooks and Peters 1988). The federal government in Canada reduced the number of employees driving to work by 23 percent after increasing parking rates. Although some equity problems emerge when pricing is used, there is a growing realization that natural-resource constraints are leaving few alternatives (Newman 1993a).

In 1985, the City of Freiburg, West Germany (with a population of 172,000), lowered the cost of season-pass fares for transit by more than a third to give people an incentive to switch from cars to transit. The result was a 23 percent increase in the use

Corporate Environmental Responsibility

The Coalition for Environmentally Responsible Economies (CERES) is a broad coalition of environmental organizations and socially responsible investment groups formed to promote environmental responsibility among businesses and local governments. In September 1989, CERES set forth the Valdez Principles as broad standards for evaluating corporate activities that directly or indirectly affect the biosphere. The principles were adopted in the hope of working with companies to create a voluntary mechanism of self-governance, and to help investors make informed decisions. The Valdez Principles call for elimination or minimization of pollution, sustainable use of natural resources, reduction and safe disposal of waste, energy conservation, environmental risk reduction, marketing of safe products and services, damage compensation, hazard disclosure, selection of environmental directors and managers, and annual environmental audits.

Several governments and corporations have signed the Valdez Principles or use environmental investment guidelines based on them. For example, Canadian corporate signatories include McDonald's Restaurants of Canada, Delta Hotels, Air Canada, VanCity Savings, and BC TEL.

CERES provides information and assistance in relation to the Valdez Principles, corporate shareholder campaigns, and community efforts to encourage local governments to adopt environmental investment policies (see Appendix).

of transit in the first year. More than 30 other German communities have adopted the same program based on the success in Freiburg.

The Greater Vancouver Regional District currently charges residents a flat fee for water use, which results in inefficient water use since the marginal cost of consuming more water is zero. By pricing water on a per unit basis, the District could alleviate some of the growing water supply problems in the Vancouver area.

Taxes and Charges

Taxes and charges can be used to discourage certain behavior, while providing revenue for the government. Impact fees are taxes on activities that have undesirable social or environmental impacts. Real estate taxes can be used to discourage urban sprawl. The information needed by agencies in order to administer appropriate taxes or charges may be substantial, but the use of an imperfect charge is surely more valuable than no charge at all.

Undesirable behavior by firms, such as noise, can be discouraged using charges or taxes. The Netherlands has an industrial noise pollution tax, and several countries levy noise charges on aircraft (Jacobs 1993). An alternative to taxing an undesirable output is taxing an undesirable input. Taxes on the use of natural resources are a method of encouraging firms to try to minimize resource use in production processes. It makes sense to tax more the undesirable things (e.g., noise, pollution) and to tax less the desirable things (income, labor) (Rees 1995a, 1995b).

Subsidies and Tax Incentives

Many of the available policy instruments could be labelled generally as subsidies. It is important to identify many of these instruments as subsidies explicitly, and justify them as such. Economists may argue that subsidies create inefficiencies in markets, but this is not necessarily the case. Social and environmental externalities are not taken into account by conventional market economics, and financial mechanisms used to encourage desirable or environmentally-friendly behavior are actually attempts to make the market more efficient in these ways.

In both Greece and Germany, road taxes are reduced for drivers according to the emissions from their cars (Nieuwenhuis 1994). In Greece, taxes are set according to the engine size in a car, under the assumption that smaller cars have lower emissions. In Germany, taxes are set according to the type of engine; between 1984 and 1986, lower taxes on diesel-engine cars allowed them to move from 13.4 percent to 22.3 percent of the total market in Germany.

Subsidies may be offered to local governments by federal or provincial governments. Local governments in the Australian state of New South Wales save a U.S.$1.50-per-ton surcharge if they have recycling programs.

Grants and Loans

Direct financial awards to researchers or firms are a useful way to encourage the development of particular industries and technologies. Seed money for firms to start up are a common form of financial grants. For example, the City of St. Paul, Minnesota gave money to a nonprofit recycling program that was then able to expand throughout the whole city (Osborne and Gaebler 1993). Although grants are more likely to encourage behavior, since they do not have to be repaid, they are also much more costly.

The City of Kingston, Ontario used low-interest loans as a mechanism to convert obsolete downtown buildings into residential units. This attempt to revitalize the downtown core required an initial allocation of just $250,000, which served as a revolving fund.

Rebates, Rewards, and Surety Bonds

Another type of financial incentive, rewards can be made to firms that are most successful at behaving in a particular way. For example, firms that build the most energy-efficient housing complex in a municipality in a given year can be rewarded financially for their achievement. Similar to rewards, surety bonds are deposits of money made by a firm before an activity is undertaken. If the activity (e.g., successful pollution reduction) is successful, the deposit can be refunded; otherwise it is spent by the government agency for the same purpose.

The German City of Saarbrücken (with a population of 128,000) rewards citizens who use solar energy by allowing them to sell excess power back to the municipal utility. The city buys back solar power at a price of about U.S.$.15 cents per kilowatt hour.

Vouchers

Consumer behavior can be influenced drastically by providing vouchers that effectively make a particular product cheaper. Vouchers for public transit passes would likely encourage people to try switching from cars to public transit. It is recognized that people perceive discounts off of regular prices as more of a benefit than a financially equivalent reduction in the regular price (Kahneman et al. 1986). This psychological tendency can be used by policy-makers in order to encourage certain behavior.

CONSTRAINTS ON IMPLEMENTATION

As noted previously, many policy instruments could fall into more than one category. In some cases there might be an overlap between regulations and financial incentives; it is also possible to have elements of two or more categories (e.g., expenditures and voluntary instruments) in the same policy measures. The critical challenge, however, is not in sorting the instruments by category, but rather in determining those situations and circumstances in which it is appropriate to employ particular instruments.

An additional challenge is determining the efficacy of various instruments over longer time frames than are yet known for most of the examples discussed here. Organizations such as the International Council for Local Environmental Initiatives, as well as various local government associations in several countries, can serve a valuable role in monitoring and evaluating progress over time (see Appendix).

Although it is beyond the scope of this chapter to examine whether or not each of the instruments could be utilized in specific circumstances at the local level, some general considerations can be made. In many situations, some of the instruments perhaps may be used best only at a federal or state/provincial level, while others may be used best by local governments. In cases where jurisdictional limitations prevent local governments from taking essential actions, state/provincial governments can be lobbied to use their jurisdictional power to carry out initiatives that will benefit multiple communities.

The principle of subsidiarity maintains that policy-making should occur at the lowest or most local level possible while maintaining effectiveness (Osborne and Gaebler 1993). Community planners should not simply copy the policy objectives of neighboring communities (Alexander 1991), but instead realize that each community has its own unique environmental, economic, social, historical, and cultural circumstances.

Local governments in recent years have been particularly innovative in initiating sustainability policies (ICLEI et al. 1996; Roseland 1996, 1997). In the U.S., although there is some power at the local level to take actions to pursue local objectives, some local planning initiatives have been viewed by the courts as inconsistent with state policies (Stone and Freilich 1991). Local governments in Canada can also expect to be constrained by jurisdiction. Some analysts argue that the division of powers in Canada does not delegate enough power to communities, and prevents them from looking after their own affairs (M'Gonigle 1991). Still, an instrument that is not feasible in one set of circumstances may work in another, so local policy-makers should consider all alternatives.

A system of government that does not give adequate legal power to local governments, and does not allow local governments considerable flexibility in the use of funds, cannot be expected to achieve all community objectives (Osborne and Gaebler 1993). Central governments must give local governments permission to take measures towards sustainable community planning, even though that requires giving them power to address broader issues. At the same time, when issues that should be addressed at national and international levels are not addressed, local governments may be able to take action individually. For example, the cities of Irvine, California and Newark, New Jersey passed comprehensive bans on ozone-depleting compounds in 1989-90 when international agreements would have allowed their use for another decade. Community leadership helped ensure that atmospheric change was put high on the agenda of senior governments.

It is interesting to speculate on the efficacy of economic instruments vis-a-vis other kinds of policy instruments in promoting sustainable community development (for example, in comparison with some of the social policies described in Chapter 11: Housing and Community Development). However, given the general reluctance (and perhaps inability) of governments at all levels today to consider non-economic and, particularly, non-market policy instruments, it is wise as well as timely for citizens to improve their understanding of economic policy instruments for sustainable communities.

Advantages of Subsidiarity

Compared to centralized institutions, decentralized institutions are more flexible, more effective, more innovative and generate higher morale, more commitment, and greater productivity. In their influential **Reinventing Government**, Osborne and Gaebler (1993) explain the principle of subsidiarity with this rule of thumb: "Unless there is an important reason to do otherwise, responsibility for addressing problems should lie with the lowest level of government possible. The closer a government is to its citizens, the more they trust it. The closer it is, the more accountable its officials tend to be."

REFERENCES

Alexander, N. 1991. "Fifteen Ways to Make Growth Management Work." *In Balanced Growth: A Planning Guide for Local Government*, ed. J.M. Degrove. Washington, D.C.: International City Management Association.

Brooks, D. B., and R. Peters. 1988. *Water: The Potential for Demand Management in Canada.* Ottawa: Science Council of Canada.

Gilbert, R., D. Stevenson, H. Giradet, and R. Stren. 1996. *Making Cities Work: The Role of Local Authorities in the Urban Environment.* London: Earthscan.

International Council for Local Environmental Initiatives (ICLEI), International Development Research Centre (IDRC), and United Nations Environment Program. 1996. *The Local Agenda 21 Planning Guide.* Toronto: ICLEI and Ottawa: IDRC.

Jacobs, M. 1993. *The Green Economy.* Vancouver: University of British Columbia Press.

Kahneman, D., J. Knetsch, and R. Thaler. 1986. "Fairness as a Constraint on Profit Seeking: Entitlements in the Market." *American Economic Review* (September): 728-41.

Kenworthy, J. 1990. "The Land Use/Transit Connection in Toronto: Some Lessons for Australian Cities." In *Transport Energy Conservation Policies for Australian Cities: Strategies for Reducing Automobile Dependence*, eds. P. Newman, J. Kenworthy, and T. Lyons. Perth, Western Australia: Institute of Science and Technology Policy, Murdoch University.

Leithe, J. L., and J. C. Joseph. 1991. "Financing Alternatives." *In Balanced Growth: A Planning Guide for Local Government*, ed. J.M. Degrove. Washington, D.C.: International City Management Association.

Local Government Commission. 1989. *Local Government Procurement and Market Development.* Sacramento, Calif.: Local Government Commission.

M'Gonigle, M. 1991. "Recasting the National Debate." *Canadian Forum* 802 (September): 11-15.

Newman, P. 1993a. "Sustainable Development and Urban Planning: Principles and Applications in an Australian Context." *Sustainable Development* 1(1): 25-40.

Newman, P. 1993b. Towards an Urban Bruntland. Prepared for London into the Next Century: An Agenda for the Responsible City, London, Ontario, 27-29 October.

Nieuwenhuis, P. "Emissions Legislation and Incentives in the USA and Europe," in Nieuwenhuis, P., and P. Wells, eds. 1994. *Motor Vehicles in the Environment: Principles and Practice.* London: John Wiley and Sons.

Osborne, D., and T. Gaebler. 1993. *Reinventing Government.* New York: Plume.

Plous, K.F. 1994. "Off the Road, Vehicles." *American Planning Association* 60(9): 8-12.

Planning and Management Consultants (PMC). 1990. The Regional Urban Water Management for the Metropolitan Water District of Southern California. Prepared for the Metropolitan Water District of Southern California, Carbondale, Illinois.

Rees, W.E. 1995a. "More Jobs, Less Damage: A Framework for Sustainability, Growth and Employment." *Alternatives* 21(4): 24-30.

Rees, W.E. 1995b. "Taxing Combustion and Rehabilitating Forests: Achieving Sustainability, Growth and Employment through Energy Policy." *Alternatives* 21(4): 31-35.

Roseland, M. 1996. "Economic Instruments for Sustainable Communities." *Local Environment* 1(2): 197-210.

— — — . 1997. *Eco-City Dimensions: Healthy Communities, Healthy Planet.* Gabriola Island, B.C.: New Society Publishers.

Roseland, M., and M. Jacobs. 1995. *Sustainable Development, Economic Instruments, and the Sustainable Management of Aquatic Resources and Ecosystems: A New Framework for Water Management in the Fraser River Basin.* Burnaby, B.C.: School of Resource and Environmental Management, Simon Fraser University.

Stone, K.E., and R.H. Freilich. 1991. *Balanced Growth: A Planning Guide for Local Government*, J.M. Degrove, ed. Washington D.C.: International City Management Association.

Wackernagel, M., and W.E. Rees. 1996. *Our Ecological Footprint: Reducing Human Impact on the Earth.* Gabriola Island, B.C.: New Society Publishers.

PART 2

SUSTAINABLE COMMUNITY
BUILDING BLOCKS

T*he framework introduced in part 1 proposes that applying the concept of sustainable development to North American communities requires unprecedented and simultaneous emphasis on the efficient use of urban space, minimizing consumption of essential natural capital, multiplying social capital, and mobilizing citizens and their governments toward these ends.*

This section of the book, part 2, is a set of sustainable community "building blocks." Each chapter provides an overview explaining the topic and its relevance to sustainable communities, followed by a set of "Tools and Initiatives," and "Resources." These building blocks are a set of planning tools, practical initiatives, and associated resources that have helped citizens and their governments move toward sustainable communities. While not every tool will "fit" every community, many of them will fit quite well.

Since the powers of municipal and local governments vary considerably, proponents of sustainable community initiatives must research their issues and fashion an approach that works within the specific legal framework of their jurisdiction. For example, a creative municipal solid waste management bylaw will have to fit the specific municipal situation, as well as the legislative framework of the province or state.

4

GREENING THE CITY

Greening the city refers to strategies and techniques that protect and restore ecology within urban communities. It means a fruit tree-lined street, a creek meandering through an urban neighborhood, geraniums and basil adorning a window box, wildflowers blossoming amid rows of houses, and tomato plants growing in a community garden. It means combining urbanism and nature to create healthy, civilizing, and enriching places to live (Hough 1995).

Greening the city is a manifestation of bioregionalism (Berg et al. 1989). The central idea of bioregionalism is place. Bioregionalism comes from *bio*, the Greek word for life, as in "biology" and "biography," and *regio*, Latin for territory to be ruled. Together they mean "a life-territory, a place defined by its life forms, its topography and its biota, rather than by human dictates; a region governed by nature, not legislature" (Sale 1985).

A bioregion is about the right size for human-scale organization: it is a natural framework for economic and political decentralization and self-determination. The primary social unit of a bioregional society is a human-scale, sustainable settlement based on ecological balance, community self-reliance, and participatory democracy (Bookchin 1987). Bioregional practice is oriented toward resistance against the continuing destruction of natural systems, such as forests and rivers; and toward the renewal of natural systems based on a thorough knowledge of how natural systems work and the development of techniques appropriate to specific sites.

Many urban areas lack green space, especially in lower income neighborhoods. However, simply creating more "green" — flowers, grass and trees — does not necessarily lead to a more sustainable environment. In fact, conventional greening can be wholly unsustainable in its design. Although playing fields, parks and sod strips along boulevards add aesthetic or recreational value, they demand costly amounts of water, fertilizer, herbicides, maintenance, and contribute little in terms of wildlife habitat and food self-sufficiency.

Urban ecology strives to create, preserve and restore green and open spaces *sustainably*. It uses climate- and region-appropriate plants, xeriscaping to minimize the need for fertilizer and water, and uses land for multiple functions such as food production, wildlife habitat, recreation *and* beautification. Urban ecology provides many environmental benefits: it reduces the urban heat island effect, minimizes our use of pesticides, conserves energy, cleans urban air, and absorbs carbon dioxide from the atmosphere.

Urban ecology offers much more than environmental benefits. It offers an opportunity to foster a greater understanding and connection with nature. Conventional urban design and city living causes alienation between humans and the natural world. Many urbanites think food comes from supermarkets, water comes from faucets, and wastes are simply taken "away." Environmental awareness and activism often focuses on issues outside the city. We support endangered species campaigns or oil spill cleanups, while neglecting the ecological health of our urban spaces. Yet cities and towns are where most of us live. Getting involved in community gardens, planting trees, or participating in stream stewardship projects can improve our health, protect our ecosystem, foster local-self reliance, build community, and even provide some of our food needs. Who doesn't enjoy a fresh, home-grown tomato?

RETHINKING URBAN GREEN SPACE

Urban Parks and Open Space

Creating sustainable green spaces can begin with parks, as they offer a host of ways to reduce the environmental impact of cities. The restoration and preservation of open spaces is another target for sustainable green initiatives, as is the desire to incorporate greening into private outdoor spaces. Many urban neighborhoods need more green space, period. Other communities are struggling to overcome the "parks as ornaments, something to look at but not use" problem. Conventional parks are designed and managed by parks departments or professionals who lack experience in ecological landscaping. Often they also fail to appreciate the range of community needs and wants. When space is a premium in urban areas, diversity is key. Naturalized parks are multifunctional, offering a wide range of opportunities for recreation, education, naturalist activities, wildlife habitat, community gardens, and indigenous species planting.

For example, the Queen's Park Xeriscape garden in Toronto, Ontario, developed by the Ontario Ministry of Natural Resources, features 140 drought-resistant plants that are well suited to the regional climate. Local residents, university students, and faculty conduct projects and experiments in the garden. Plants and clippings are available for sale, and the ecological design reduces maintenance, operating, and water costs of the garden by about 70 percent (Chaplin 1994). Planners, local governments and developers are getting the message — sustainability in urban green space is not only possible, but profitable too.

Citizens and non-government organizations in some communities are also taking initiatives to develop, maintain, and use local open spaces such as vacant lots, traffic islands, rooftops, and abandoned industrial lands to address the unique recreational and ecological needs of their neighborhoods. These open spaces, created by community members, reflect local values because their own sweat and labor are the impetus for implementation.

> *"Our best crop is concrete. Our diesel buses chug along emitting black clouds like mechanical squids. And our rivers turn into toilet bowls every time heavy rains cause our sewage system to overflow. No wonder, come weekends, any New Yorker with a really disposable income heads for the Hamptons of Long Island or the north woods" (Nixon 1991).*

A naturalized back yard

Integrated pest management is a non-chemical alternative for pest control. There is no one fix-all, so the key is to think holistically and use many techniques together. Some strategies include: planting pest resistant species, encouraging beneficial critters like toads and ladybugs, and planting marigolds, garlic, onion, and pansies, which all naturally deter insects.

Greening Private Spaces: In My Backyard Please

Backyards, corporate parks, and private gardens share many of the same opportunities for urban ecology as parks and public spaces. Local governments can foster change by implementing bylaws and regulations restricting use of turf and pesticides on private property, or encouraging change by offering education and incentives. Voluntary programs, such as British Columbia.'s Naturescape BC, provide pointers on inexpensive ways to increase wildlife habitat at home (and yes, there is wildlife in cities!). Pamphlets explain how to get squirrels, birds, and butterflies to frequent balconies and backyards.

In addition to government and private homeowner initiatives, a growing number of enlightened developers and landscape architects are going green. Recognizing a growing market for environmentally responsible real estate, some developers are incorporating trails and nature preserves, and protecting existing vegetation in residential housing projects. In an urban redevelopment project on Chicago's eastside, one developer converted dreary alleys into courtyards with gardens, park benches and places for people to gather (see Chapter 11: Housing and Community Development). Companies are also joining in by revolutionizing the concept of corporate office parks. AT&T converted the manicured lawns at two of their corporate campuses in Illinois into prairie wildflowers, saving about $75,000 in maintenance, fertilizer and irrigation costs, and UPS protected creeks and woodlands at their headquarters building in Atlanta, Georgia (Rocky Mountain Institute). Boeing incorporated jogging trails and restored a wetland in Renton, Washington, and Patagonia planted fruit trees at their new headquarters in Nevada.

Golf courses are another private land use in and around our cities, and they're notoriously unsustainable. Conventional golf courses carve fairways out of forests and deserts; guzzle massive amounts of water for irrigating miles of Kentucky blue grass, fertilizers, and pesticides; and require endless labor in raking each sand trap to perfection. "What was once accepted as a benign form of open space is under attack for its impacts on water quality, wildlife habitat, and land use," explains Paul Parker of the Center for Resource Management. However, a number of golf courses are going green. Audubon International and other agencies now have programs to assist golf-course designers and maintenance staff create ecologically responsible golf courses. Boardwalks at Squaw Creek Golf Course in Squaw Valley, California have carried golfers over marsh and meadow areas since its opening in 1992. Design firm Robert Trent Jones Jr. restored acres of native grasses and enhanced natural filtration ponds that feed Squaw Creek. Audubon certified Squaw Creek as a "cooperative sanctuary" and, apart from using small amounts of nitrogen, the golf course is maintained organically to protect the aquifer it sits upon.

Benefits of Functional Green Space

Decrease Energy Costs: The U.S. Renewable Energy Laboratory, Department of Energy reports that properly positioned trees provide shade, wind-breaks, and evapotranspiration (lowering ambient temperatures), and save about 20 percent to 25 percent of average annual residential energy costs, compared with the costs for the same house in an unsheltered area.

Reduce Urban Heat Island Effect: Urban areas are significantly hotter than surrounding rural areas. The difference in temperature ranges from as little as 1.1º to 4.4ºC (2ºF to 8ºF) in St. Louis Missouri, to 5.6ºC (10ºF) in New York City, to as much as 10ºC (18ºF) in Mexico City. The heat island effect occurs as urban surfaces, such as concrete, asphalt, and brick absorb the sun's heat and radiate it out, causing increased urban temperatures. Highrises create an "urban canyon," also reducing heat loss to the atmosphere. In contrast, plants absorb and metabolize solar energy, helping to moderate hot temperatures. As well as discomfort, urban heat islands costs money. About 3 percent to 8 percent of air conditioning use in the U.S. is for compensat-

A rooftoop lawn

ing for the heat island effect. Scientists at the Lawrence Berkeley Laboratory estimate the country's total electricity costs for offsetting the effects of summer heat islands at more than $1 billion per year (MacPherson and Rowntree 1994).

Decrease Water Use: Indigenous species or native plants are adapted to local climates so they require less irrigation than non-native species. Xeriscaping gardening practices use native plants and drought-tolerant species which require less water and chemicals. The term is derived from the Greek word for dry, *xeros*.

Increase Absorption of Pollutants: Plants act as a "sink" for pollutants, absorbing carbon dioxide and other deleterious substances. A Douglas-fir is capable of removing 18 kilograms (39.6 pounds) of sulfur dioxide from the atmosphere a year without harm to itself (Haughton and Hunter 1994).

Increase Urban Wildlife Habitat: Urbanization has radically altered both natural and wildlife communities. Urban land use has fragmented forests and other ecosystems, and created isolated islands of habitat. Ideally, critical habitat is identified before development, and urban activities can accommodate or integrate areas for birds and animals. Maintaining vegetation diversity helps provide for breeding, cover, and food sources.

Improve Drainage: Often close to 50 percent of urban areas are paved over. High percentages of impervious surfaces regularly lead to storm water run-off problems. Properly planted land absorbs the rain that falls on it, eliminating excessive run-off that otherwise requires expensive storm sewers that often overflow and flood. (See also Chapter 5: Water and Sewage.)

Act as Indicators of Ecological Health: The vigor and robustness of native animals and plants indicate how clean the air and water are, and can help us assess the health and life-supporting capacity of the entire ecosystem.

Increase Community Space and Aesthetics: Aside from all of the ecological benefits identified above, there are many social and psychological benefits associated with thoughtful urban ecology. Green spaces can provide places to play, meditate, gather, rest, and rejuvenate.

Create More Livable Cities and Connect with Nature: Green space in cities can enhance our connection with ecological processes. "These strong ties between people and trees cannot be explained by increased property values, reductions in air pollutants, and moderation in temperature" (Dwyer, Schroeder, and Gobster 1994). Getting involved brings you closer to the natural environment and strengthens communities by creating opportunities to know your neighbors. Plant a tree! Restore a stream!

Save Money: Sustainable landscaping and gardening saves money. Simply by planting trees and using alternative ground cover to sod, citizens and their municipalities can enjoy lower water, energy, and maintenance costs.

TOOLS AND INITIATIVES

Policy and Regulatory

Bioregionalism considers people to be part of a place, as dependent on nature as native plants and animals (Aberley 1993, 1994).

Municipal governments play an integral role in the sustainable management of green space, and citizens can influence their local officials to act. Efforts can take the form of government policy, bylaws, or regulations, and/or be driven by NGOs, citizens, or private initiatives. Governments can conduct Environmentally Sensitve Area (ESA) studies and inventories to determine which areas are in greatest need for protection and/or reclamation, and use official community plans and development permits to dictate substantial leave strips, setbacks, and protection of green space and watercourses. Conservation commissions and environmental advisory boards can partner with local organizations and other municipal governments to initiate local greening initiatives. The list is long once the political will is in place.

ESA Strategy: In 1994, Burnaby, B.C. City Council adopted an initial ESA strategy, applying environmentally sensitive planning and management principles to protect public green lands. The city also engages in annual State of the Environment Reporting, has enacted a watercourse protection bylaw, and partners with local NGOs and other levels of government on a variety of initiatives from streamkeeping to land management plans.

Natural Planting Ordinance: In a critical aquifer district in the town of Southampton on Long Island, New York, a natural planting ordinance requires that at least 80 percent of each lot remain in its natural state, and no more than 15 percent of any lot can be planted in fertilized lawns or plants. These restrictions still leave landowners with ample landscaping choices; sites are left in woodland vegetation or planted in meadow grasses, perennial wildflowers, ivy, or other dense plantings that need little or no fertilizing (Lowe 1991).

Green Roofs: The German Cities of Mannheim and Frankfurt grant planning permission for structures with flat or gently sloping roofs only if they are designed to be of the "living" variety. According to the German League of Cities, flat green roofs save energy and increase residents' comfort by limiting the temperature spread, and reduce heating and air conditioning requirements. Green roofs have 60 percent less run-off than gravel or asphalt tiles, reducing the costs of drainage systems and, in sufficient numbers, improving the urban micro-climate (*Public Innovation Abroad* 1990).

Xeriscape Bylaw: In 1991, Florida passed the first state xeriscape bylaw in the U.S. Xeriscaping is required on all newly developed public properties, and existing properties are being phased into the program according to a five-year plan. All local governments that operate water supply systems have adopted water conservation ordinances. Anyone who buys automatic lawn sprinklers must also install a rain sensor to ensure the system shuts off when it begins to rain.

Land Trusts and Conservation Trusts

These are effective tools for preserving land, and are typically funded by government, citizens or NGOs. Land is put into trust protecting it from development for an agreed purpose — typically for parks, preserves, or community gardening. Trusts employ a variety of strategies: obtain title to land; obtain conservation covenants; buy land, place a covenant and resell; or buy land and develop it in a limited way to pay for preserved area; encourage private philanthropists to buy and preserve land; and/or help individuals or governments manage land. (See also Chapter 11: Housing and Community Development.)

Education and Promotion Programs

Water Efficient Landscaping: There are numerous examples of communities promoting water efficient landscaping. A study comparing conventional and water-efficient landscapes in Northern California found savings of 54 percent for water, 25 percent for labor, 61 percent for fertilizer, 44 percent for fuel, and 22 percent for herbicides (Rocky Mountain Institute). The City of Palm Desert, California installed low water using landscapes and low-volume drip irrigation systems in some of the city's median trips. Compared to conventional medians, both maintenance costs and water use were significantly lower.

Cool Communities: American Forests, a leading force in the protection, wise management, and enjoyment of urban and rural forests in the U.S., started the Cool Communities program in 1992 to collect information from different geographical areas on the costs and benefits of planting trees for cooling. Eight communities are currently monitoring results.

Land Trust Success Stories

• Over 1000 local U.S. land trusts protect over 4 million acres. National U.S. organizations protect an additional seven million acres.

• From 1988-92, San Francisco Bay Area land trusts acquired 80,000 acres — 56 percent of the new open space in the region.

• About 25 percent of Maryland's Protection Open Space programs involve land trusts.

• In Vermont, land trusts and affordable housing groups have leveraged $60 million in state government grants to produce $235 million in conservation and affordable housing projects.

• Recognizing that greenways are part of the transportation system in sustainable cities of the future, the Netherlands devotes 10 percent of gas taxes for greenways and related initiatives.

• In over 30 states, taxpayers can simply check a box if they want to send their tax refund to a habitat acquisition fund (Sandborn 1997).

A community garden in East Vancouver

"Community Food Security means that all people have dignified access to food which is safe, nutritious, and culturally appropriate, and which has been produced in a manner which is environmentally and socially sustainable" (Kneen et al. 1997).

Trees for Tucson: This Tucson, Arizona program is affiliated with the American Forests' Global ReLeaf Program. It provides information to homeowners, neighborhood groups, and schools on low-water plants and trees appropriate to the local environment. According to the city's calculations, each tree will save more than $20 in air conditioning costs by providing shading and evapotranspiration, saving a total of $236.5 million in the next 40 years. Officials also estimate that planting 500,000 trees will save the city $600,000 in storm drainage management in 40 years (Centre of Excellence 1996; MacPherson 1994).

Volunteer / NGO Urban Greening Projects

Turn a Lot Around: This Chicago Resource Center focuses on vacant lots as the centerpieces of community renewal efforts. Volunteer work includes the clearing of debris, garden creation, and building playgrounds.

Green Guerrillas: This organization began in 1973 with a group of neighbors on the lower east side of Manhattan in New York City. Tired of the destruction of their community, they cleaned and greened a vacant lot in an area known as Bum's Row. Today that lot has meandering paths, a grape arbor, a pond, and all kinds of flowers, fruits, and vegetables; and the metasequoia tree they planted is now 12.2 meters (40 feet) tall. Anything that will grow in an urban environment is there — it even has a bee hive. That the garden is in an area known for its urban blight is significant (Keller 1990). The group now helps neighborhoods green lots throughout New York City.

Greening the Great River Park: Since 1995 in St. Paul Minnesota, over 2,500 volunteers have planted 9,500 native trees and shrubs, more than 1,500 wildflowers, and .8 hecatare (2 acres) of native prairie along a 4.8-kilometer (3-mile) industrial stretch of the Mississippi River. "The real innovation in our project is doing ecological restoration in an urban area that crosses political and private property boundaries," says Greening the Great River Park's Executive Director Rob Buffler. Eighty percent of the 486-hectare (1,200-acre) river front is privately owned. A volunteer design team including a landscape architect, a community representative, and an ecologist drafts a plan for each parcel of land and reviews it with the owner. The state's Reinvest in Minnesota program funds the plant purchases (*GreenClips* 1997).

La Société de verdissement du Montreal metropolitain (Greening Society of Metropolitan Montreal): This program recaptures the diversity of the original hardwood forests in the greater Montreal, Quebec region. The society grows and provides native trees and shrubs which they make available to individuals, community groups, schools, and businesses to plant around Montreal. The goal is to plant two million trees by 2010. They also distribute information on care and planting of trees and shrubs.

URBAN AGRICULTURE

Most urbanites pay little attention to where food comes from, or how much waste and environmental damage is associated with its production and transportation. On average in the U.S., food in a supermarket travels about 2,000 kilometers (1,300 miles)

between its point of production and its point of consumption. "The principle of proximity is simple: food should be consumed as close to the point and condition of production as possible" (Kneen, 1993). Agribusiness pumps chemicals onto fields and farmworkers. Processing, packaging, and shipping, wastes energy and materials, and freshness, nutritional value, and good taste are often lost somewhere along the way.

A just and sustainable food system protects the land which produces the food; supports the local economy through local production; empowers communities through self-reliance, and gives them increased food system security; enhances community well-being through increased health, decreased illnesses; increases sense of community; and increases environmental health because of reduced transportation of food. Local food systems are inherently tied not only to the health of individuals, but to the short and long-

Urban agriculture can be beautiful as well as nourishing

term economic, social, and environmental health of communities. Where food systems become unjust and unsustainable due to state/provincial, national, and international forces, it is communities that bear the burden (Kneen et al. 1997).

Urban agriculture can address many of these problems. It can take the form of community gardens, locally-supported farms on the fringe of cities, or backyard plots, greenhouses, and balconies full of beans and herbs. Small-scale food growing efforts are often organically-managed, and permaculture techniques can reduce the need for labor and materials.

Communities are growing food in every location imaginable — in parks, vacant lots, abandoned industrial lands, rooftops, and on vertical surfaces — but they often face challenges. Health bylaws prevent farmers' markets within city limits; other bylaws restrict park use for growing food; codes and covenants favor lawns and parking lots; and real estate development competes for land tenure. But the benefits outweigh the challenges, as people reconnect with one of nature's most basic processes, save money on food bills, and enjoy greater local self-reliance.

There are many other environmental and social benefits of urban agriculture. Local farms and gardens can use the city's organic wastes for compost, helping to reduce burden on local landfills (organic wastes account for about 30 percent of household waste), and home-grown food reduces packaging waste and energy consumption. Edible planting and permaculture also exposes the public to environmentally sound alternatives to conventional urban landscaping, and it expands opportunities for people to have access to personal green space.

Perhaps the greatest benefit of urban agriculture is the provision of affordable food supplies for lower-income people. North America is touted as having one of the most abundant food systems in the world, yet more than two million people (including 800,000 children) visited over 400 food banks across Canada in 1993. In the same year,

A community garden in East Vancouver

the number of U.S. residents participating in federal food stamp programs rose to more than 27 million, representing nearly 10 percent of the population (Kneen 1993). Urban food production can help feed the poor. On the east side of Vancouver, locals share the fruits of their labor with homeless people, and low-income residents rely on the seasonal bounty of Strathcona community garden for much of their food supply.

TOOLS AND INITIATIVES

Community Gardens

City of Seattle's P-Patch Program: In conjunction with the nonprofit P-Patch Advisory Council, this program provides community garden space for residents of 35 Seattle neighborhoods. Over 1,600 plots serve 4,500 urban gardeners. Special programs serve refugees, low-income, disabled, and youth gardeners, and the Lettuce Link project delivers 8-10 tons of fresh produce to food banks every year. All gardening is organic; no insecticides or herbicides are permitted. Since its inception, 10 community gardens have been started at four sites, and a Community Shared Agriculture (see below) program has also been initiated.

Gardening Angels: In Detroit, Michigan, the Gardening Angels aim to use the power of planting to heal a city ravaged by declining industry, depopulation, and narcotics wars. About 60 local people have planted over 200 gardens on derelict sites throughout Detroit. They've managed to drive off drug gang and crack house activity, encourage youth participation and entrepreneurship, and partner with a diverse group of folk including residents, churchgoers, inmates from a nearby prison, drug and alcohol rehabilitation patients, the Hunger Action Coalition, and city council. The gardens feed the homeless, and tentative steps are being made to market their fruit and vegetables. Many people in the city see the gardens as a metaphor for recovery as well as a practical means to it (*Urban Ecologist* 1996).

Community Shared Agriculture

Many urban dwellers across North America are benefiting from community shared agriculture, a means of feeding people that allows both growers and consumers to share responsibilities for growing food. Typically, local farmers on the urban fringe grow food for a pre-determined group of consumers (guaranteed market), with whom they enter into an agreement (usually money in exchange for produce) before a season begins. By keeping money in the community, this form of agriculture secures the livelihood of local family farmers, supports the local economy, fosters greater self-reliance for food supplies, and helps people remain connected with the food they consume.

Prairie Crossing: In a new residential community outside Chicago, Illinois, the

"Community gardens provide a means for gardening and growing together with friends and neighbors. Gardens range in size, location, and participation; they can be small, local neighborhood gardens in vacant lots or parks, communal rooftop gardens, or municipally maintained allotment gardens" (Guberman 1995).

developers of Prairie Crossing clustered much of the housing development to preserve agricultural lands. Realizing that farmers on the urban fringe are often struggling to survive, the developers are organizing community shared agriculture to encourage new residents to support local farmers.

Food Policy Organizations

Food policy organizations are community, city, or regional groups that aim to improve the security of the local food system. They are essentially vehicles for food activists to undertake projects and programs that move toward sustainable food policy. Such organizations initiate, support, and connect community projects and programs with policy-making. They are holistic, dealing with both the causes and effects of hunger, and work for short and long-term change on issues of food production, processing, distribution and access, public education and research, waste reduction, and policy. Examples may include hospital and institutional

The Living Wall Garden Project in Vancouver, B.C.

buy-local policies, community shared agriculture, farmers' markets, school breakfast and hot lunch campaigns, community kitchens, breastfeeding support programs, and community gardens.

Food Policy Action Coalition and Food Share: Food policy organizations range in structure from informal volunteer groups such as Peterborough's Food Policy Action Coalition to established nonprofit organizations such as Toronto's Food Share; the latter has an executive director, 10 paid staff, a volunteer board, and upwards of 500 volunteers involved in making projects work (Kneen et al. 1997).

Training and Mentoring to Learn Gardening Skills

Living Wall Garden Project: This Vancouver, B.C. project aims to create, beautify, mentor, educate, promote self-sufficiency, celebrate possibility, and improve the city for it's future inhabitants. At-risk youth research and practice vertical gardening techniques, and volunteer community mentors, such as master gardeners, landscape architects, and youth counsellors help with site design, construction, and youth training. The longer-term goals are to establish a youth-owned vertical gardening cooperative, and encourage similar urban agricultural projects throughout the inner-city.

From the Ground Up: A local urban gardening organization in Washington, D.C., grows organic vegetables for shareholders and provides produce for farmstands. Low-income residents involved in the program learn business skills, and inner-city youth are taught about nutritional, environmental, and food security issues. In 1996, the group's 3-hectare (8-acre) farm on the outskirts of the city produced over 50,000 kilograms (110,000 pounds) of fresh vegetables (Nelson 1996).

InSightOut's Youth Employment and Education Project: Another Vancouver, B.C. project organized a small group of young adults to work with a herbalist to plant med-

"New York City has 2.6 million street trees, and 700-800 community gardens, from pocket parks to small farms such as one in the South Bronx that produces 8,000 pounds of fruit and vegetables a year." (Nixon, 1991)

icinal herbs on the roof of the cancer treatment center at Vancouver General Hospital. What better place for plants to bring their healing powers?

URBAN AQUATIC SYSTEMS

Urban aquatic areas — streams, ponds, beaches and marshes — are often filled-in, neglected or manipulated beyond recognition. Protection and restoration of streams and other aquatic systems revitalize neighborhoods and commercial areas, and give us a place to find the child again (who loved to play by them). Healthy aquatic systems are full of life and offer communities a place for art, science, and a celebration of nature. Conceiving restoration projects in this way can infuse community activism with a creative and inspirational dimension that has profound implications for grassroots efforts to revitalize our cities.

Stream corridors, creeks, and marshes are vehicles for education about local history and ecology, and places for rest, recreation, and neighborhood beautification. Preservation and restoration projects in urban areas also have numerous ecological benefits. They can increase biodiversity, provide habitat for fish and wildlife, restore native vegetation, act as a natural filtration system for greywater, and accommodate storm water run-off.

Creek "daylighting" is another restoration strategy. It involves returning creek beds to the surface from their current underground, culverted state. This is an expensive endeavor in terms of up-front costs, but the benefits are many. Stream corridors represent one of the most varied ecosystems, and streams are effective in storing and absorbing storm water run-off over their vegetated and riparian surfaces.

TOOLS AND INITIATIVES

Developer- and City-run Stream Restoration and Preservation Projects

Watercourse Protection Bylaw: Communities that have raised and restored their creeks include San Luis Obispo and Berkeley, California (Steere 1990). Burnaby, B.C. passed a resolution in 1972 that its streams must be preserved and conserved, and passed a watercourse protection bylaw in 1988. Housing developments must incorporate existing streams into their landscaping, and individual homeowners are not allowed to build right down to the bank (setbacks are required).

Creek Daylighting Project: El Cerrito, California recently undertook a creek daylighting project and restored a strip of long-culverted creek as part of a city-wide storm drain renovation program. The Urban Creeks Council suggested that the Waterways Restoration Institute become involved. This nonprofit agency uses hands-on educators to work with local governments and citizens to develop alternatives to traditional flood control. They created gentle meanders, and pools and riffles to diversify flow, increase water quality, and halt erosion. Banks were stabilized with native plant species (*Urban Ecologist* 1997).

Watershed Restoration: The Wheaton Branch restoration is the first phase of a larger, ongoing watershed restoration of Sligo Creek by an interdisciplinary team composed of staff from public agencies, including the Maryland National Capital Park and Planning Commission. Located in a highly urbanized area, 55 percent of Wheaton Branch's watershed is covered by impervious surfaces. The project is addressing everything from controlling run-off at the headwaters of the stream to bank stabilizing and fish restocking (Thompson 1996).

Stream Stewardship Programs

Once stream restoration projects are complete, there are many more activities to be done. Volunteer community groups can organize clean-up and education programs, or partner with local governments and others to obtain funding for monitoring programs. Citizens can lobby for stricter ordinances protecting riparian zones (through Official Community Plan policies, zoning and environmental protection bylaws, development permit areas, comprehensive development and density bonusing, conservation covenants, ESA studies, and the list goes on.) These measures involve individuals interested in moving from private to participatory citizenship, taking responsibility for the local ecosystem in our urban areas. (See Chapter 5: Water and Sewage for examples of initiatives.)

River Stewardship: The Virginia River Conservation Society in St. John's, Newfoundland has worked to return the river to its original condition and encourage river stewardship. With foundation funding, members cleaned up the river banks and restored sensitive fish habitat in areas where urban development had damaged the river's ecology. In one eroded area they made a lattice-work of logs, covered them with soil and peat, and planted native plants to stabilize the ground.

RESOURCES

Center for Watershed Protection publishes a quarterly journal, *Watershed Protection Techniques;* the summer 1995 issue focused specifically on urban stream restoration. The Center also offers a bibliography of useful sources and courses on a range of topics, such as the design of best-management practices.

8737 Colesville Road, Suite 300
Silver Spring, Maryland
USA 20910
Tel: 301/589-1890

City Farmer is touted as "Canada's Office of Urban Agriculture." The group's web site offers information on almost every aspect of urban agriculture, and maintains a large list of links to other relevant sites.

318 Homer Street, Suite 801
Vancouver, B.C.
Canada V6B 2V3
Tel: 604/685-5832
E-mail: cityfarm@unixg.ubc.ca
Web site: www.cityfarmer.org/

Green City Project is a volunteer network linking over 425 San Francisco Bay Area environmental groups. The network provides a point of entry for residents, schools, companies, and other organizations to become active with these groups.

P.O. Box 31251
San Francisco, California
USA 94131
Tel: 415/285-6556
Fax: 415/285-6563
E-mail: planetdrum@igc.apc.org

Department of Fisheries and Oceans and the B.C. government created a stewardship series of documents to provide tools and information for citizens, planners, and municipal governments to protect local streams and fish habitat. The series includes *Stream Stewardship: A Guide for Planners and Developers and The Streamkeepers Handbook: A Citizens Guide to Stream Stewardship.*

Department of Fisheries and Oceans
Communications Branch
555 W. Hastings
Vancouver, B.C.
Canada V6B 5G3
Tel: 604/666-8675

Waterways Restoration Institute is a nonprofit agency whose hands-on restoration projects educate agency personnel and citizens about alternatives to traditional flood control. The Institute's creek projects have become models for saving blighted urban areas across the country.

1250 Addison Street, Suite 107
Berkeley, California
USA 94702
Tel: 510/848-2211

REFERENCES

Aberley, D. 1993. *Boundaries of Home: Mapping for Local Empowerment.* Gabriola Island, B.C.: New Society Publishers.

— — — , ed. 1994. *Futures By Design: The Practice of Ecological Planning* (Gabriola Island, B.C.: New Society Publishers.

Berg, P., et al. 1989. *A Green City Program for San Francisco Bay Area Cities and Towns* San Francisco: Planet Drum Books.

Bookchin, M. 1987. *The Rise of Urbanization and the Decline of Citizenship.* San Francisco: Sierra Club.

Centre of Excellence for Sustainable Development. 1997. "Cooling Our Cities." <www.eren.doe.gov/cities_counties/coolcit.html>.

Chaplin, S. 1994. *Water Efficient Landscaping: A Guide for Utilities and Community*

Planners. Water Efficiency Implementation Report No. 6. Denver, Colo.: Rocky Mountain Institute.

Dwyer, J., H. Schroeder, and P. Gobster. 1994. "The Deep Significance of Urban Trees and Forests." In *The Ecological City: Preserving and Restoring Urban Biodiversity,* R. Platt, R. Rowntree, and P. Muick, eds. Amherst: University of Massachusetts Press.

Greenclips. 1997. <GreenClips@aol.com>.

Guberman, C. 1995. "Sowing the Seed of Sustainability: Planning for Food Self-Reliance." In *Change of Plans: Towards a Non-Sexist Sustainable City,* M. Eichler, ed. Toronto: Garamond Press.

Haughton, G., and C. Hunter. 1994. *Sustainable Cities.* Regional Policy and Development Series 7. London: Jessica Kingley Publishers.

Hough, M. 1995. *Cities and Natural Processes.* New York: Routledge.

Keller, T. 1990. "The Greening of the Big Apple." In *Green Cities: Ecologically Sound Approaches to Urban Space.* Montreal: Black Rose Books.

Kneen, B. 1993. *From Land to Mouth: Understanding the Food System.* Toronto: NC Press Limited.

Kneen, B., C. McDougall, and C. Kneen. 1997. *A Baseline for Food Policy in British Columbia.* Vancouver: Farm Folk/City Folk Society.

Lowe, M.D. 1991. "Shaping Cities: The Environmental and Human Dimensions." Worldwatch Paper 105. Washington, D.C.: Worldwatch Institute.

MacPherson, G., and R. Rowntree. 1994. "Energy Efficient Landscapes." In *Urban Forest Landscapes: Integrating Multidisciplinary Perspectives,* G. Bradley, ed. Seattle: University of Washington Press.

Nelson, T. 1996. "Closing the Nutrient Loop." *WorldWatch* 9(6): 10-17.

Nixon, W. 1991. "The Greening of the Big Apple: If It Can Happen Here, It Can Happen Anywhere." *E- The Environmental Magazine* II:5.

Public Innovation Abroad. 1990. 14(5) May.

Rocky Mountain Institute. In press. *Green Development: Integrating Ecology & Real Estate* New York: John Wiley and Sons Publishers.

Sale, K. 1985. *Dwellers in the Land: The Bioregional Vision.* Gabriola Island: New Society Publishers.

Sandborn, C. 1997. *The Green Zone Priorities for Tomorrow Conference Workbook.* Burnaby, B.C.: Greater Vancouver Regional District.

Steere, J. 1990. "Creeks Alive!" In *Report of the First International Ecological City Conference.* Berkeley, Calif.: Urban Ecology.

Thompson, J.W. 1996. "Down by the Creekside." *Landscape Architecture* 86(10): 82-93.

Urban Ecologist. 1996. 3.

— — —. 1997. 1

5

WATER AND SEWAGE

North America is abundant in lakes and rivers yet, in many regions, water resources are in critical supply. Even the moist Pacific Northwest has begun to feel the pinch as drier seasons and urban growth overwhelm infrastructure and water supplies. Despite some conservation initiatives, especially in California and other arid regions, Canada and the U.S. consume more water per capita than any other countries in the world.

Citizens also bear the burden of exorbitant costs for expansion of infrastructure for dam and reservoir construction, and chlorination plants. Costs for operating, maintaining and expanding sewage treatment facilities continue to compete for our tax dollars, while water pollution and the rapid rate of water extraction is causing damage to fish stocks as well as other environmental degradation. Water consumption and treatment also influences energy demand, as energy is required to pump and process water supplies and wastewater. Even more energy, such as natural gas and electricity, is used to provide domestic hot water and heated water for commercial and industrial needs.

Some communities are addressing these problems by seeking solutions that satisfy people's needs while reducing or minimizing environmental and financial costs associated with supply and sewage treatment infrastructure expansion. Demand-side management, alternative sewage treatment, wastewater reclamation and integrated resource planning are some of the most significant and successful strategies used currently for sustainable stewardship of this critical resource.

SUPPLY AND DEMAND

We waste our water because we think it's cheap, but is it? In most places in North America, a portion of our water supply and sewage treatment costs are paid through general tax revenue or property taxes. Apart from industrial customers, most users pay a flat rate rather than pay per volume, so we don't realize the actual cost of our consumptive patterns. These low costs and hidden subsidies have a significant impact on the amount of water we use, and several studies indicate that increasing the cost of water and enforcing user pay (per volume) rates on customers will encourage conservation (NRTEE 1996).

True cost pricing may be the simplest solution, but faced with population growth and soaring demand, many cities are seeking physical and financial ways to expand water supply. Yet, by encouraging and even demanding more *efficient* use of existing resources, communities can satisfy their needs while *saving* money and conserving existing water supplies.

From simple faucet aerators and low-flush toilets to sonar leak detection units and computerized water modeling for decision-making, there are a host of low- and high-tech solutions for reducing waste and improving water-efficiency. The challenge is to reduce our consumption without compromising our comfort, and it can be done if communities use water-efficient products and devices, and adopt strategies or techniques that foster water conservation. Some of these approaches can be employed by individual homeowners, tenants, building owners or occupants; others can be implemented by builders or developers; and others require participation of local or regional governments, water service departments or public works departments.

Financial benefits include direct savings from lower water usage, and reduced sewage costs resulting from less wasted water. Additionally, the city and its taxpayers avoid the cost of treatment and supply for each gallon, liter or cubic foot of water conserved. While consumers may not realize it when they leave a tap dripping, or a lawn sprinkler running, efficient use of water may also help avoid the huge capital cost of constructing reservoirs and expanding treatment plants. These demand side management strategies make sense from an environmental and financial perspective, yet municipal governments may need to introduce incentives or policies for water conservation, and restrictions or penalties encouraging water conservation initiatives. (See Chapter 7: Energy Efficiency and Renewables for more discussion of demand side management.)

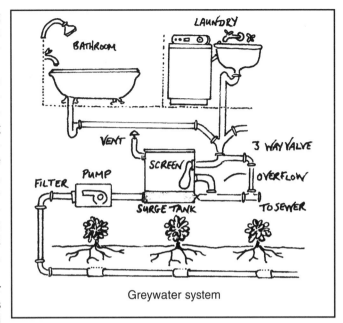

Greywater system

TOOLS AND INITIATIVES

There are many ways to achieve water efficiency in communities. Perhaps the most common solutions are voluntary and mandatory curtailment programs, requesting or requiring customers to water their gardens only at certain times or on certain days. These programs work best if accompanied with education and promotional programs, helping customers understand the financial savings and environmental benefits, as well as local supply issues associated with water consumption. Incentive programs and education about efficient hardware and techniques can also promote customer participation in water conservation programs, as can bylaws and ordinances requiring efficient plumbing and irrigation products and techniques.

Audit Programs
Often, the first step to water conservation is awareness of the opportunities for savings. Many local governments, water utilities, water service companies, and even volunteer

organizations offer water audits to residents and/or businesses.

Home Audits and Upgrades: Dartmouth university student volunteers perform home energy and water audits and provide basic efficiency upgrades, including installation of high-efficiency showerheads and insulating blankets around water heaters.

Rebates and Replacement Programs

Toilet and showerhead Incentive Program: The New York City Department of Environmental Protection initiated in March, 1994 a program for property owners to replace their old toilets and showerheads with water-efficient models. The popular toilet rebate program is budgeted to replace as many as 1.25 million toilets, providing savings estimated between 189 million and 378 million liters (50 and 100 million gallons) of water per day.

Low-Flow Toilets Distributed Free: The Mothers of East Los Angeles-Santa Isabel buys low-flow toilets at bulk discounts, distributes them free to low-income residents, and collects rebates of $100 per toilet from the local water district in California. The rebate money pays for the toilets and nine salaries for local residents who distribute the toilets, assist in installation, and conduct follow-up inspection. Since the program began, more than 2,000 toilets have been installed and most of the old toilets have been recycled into road construction material. Households, which also receive energy-efficient lights and high-efficiency showerheads, save from $30 to $120 in water and energy bills per year (Roseland and Jacobs 1995).

Rebates for Water-Efficient Landscaping: Homes and businesses receive rebates from the local water utility for installing water-efficient landscaping in Mesa, Arizona. These properties use an average of 40 percent less water than similar sites with turf-intensive landscapes.

Upgrades and Subsidies: A broken water main required mandatory lawn-watering restrictions in Delta, B.C. in the summer of 1997. But the city also offered water-efficiency upgrades to toilets and faucets and subsidies so that local residents could purchase low-cost rainwater collection barrels.

Grants, Loans, and Tax Credits

Connection Fee Discount and "Cash for Grass": The North Marin Water District in California discounts the connection fee for developers who conform to the district's water conservation criteria for landscaping and irrigation systems. They also offer "cash for grass" rebates or credits to owners who limit turf areas to less than 20 percent of the total landscape for single family units, as well as to multi-unit residential developments.

Grants from Water Wholesalers: The Metropolitan Water District of Southern California pays grants to its retail agencies for water savings. Several towns, such as Pasadena and Santa Monica, have seized this incentive to implement water conservation programs.

Education and Demonstration Programs

All over North America, cities such as Denver, Palo Alto, Tucson, Vancouver, and New York City have education and information programs providing literature on water-efficient products and appliances, and water-efficient landscaping. (See also Chapter 4: Greening the City for more water-efficient gardening initiatives.)

Annual Contest: The El Paso Water Utilities and the Council of El Paso (Texas) Garden Clubs sponsor an annual contest, Accent-Sun Country. Homes with water-conserving landscapes compete for cash prizes and publicity, and people are invited to tour the gardens to get ideas about how to beautify their gardens while saving water, time, and money.

Toilet Demonstration Program: The Massachusetts Water Resources Authority implemented a municipal toilet demonstration program installing a thousand 6 liter- (1.6 gallon-) per-flush toilets in municipal buildings in 28 communities. The goal was to familiarize the public with ultra-low-flow toilets, and to monitor the water savings and toilet performance. The Authority also sponsors workshops, trade show presentations, and provides printed information to educate plumbers, building facilities engineers, and maintenance personnel to increase acceptance of water-conserving products and devices.

Leak Detection and Repair Programs

Community Services and Environmental Education Program: As part of New York City's Community Services and Environmental Education program, school children are given badges and designated "New York Drip Control Inspectors." Students learn to search for, and encourage repair of leaks in their homes. The city's Bureau of Water Register also conducts door-to-door programs inspecting residential, commercial and industrial interior plumbing systems. In the first 15 months of the program, 70,000 inspections led to 10,000 lead repairs, saving a total of 12 million liters (3.2 million gallons) of water per year.

Leak Detection Program: Boston and New York conduct Leak Detection Programs. Thousands of leaks have been discovered in the cities' water mains and, in New York City alone, the loss of an estimated 337 million liters (89 million gallons) of water per day has been avoided. Additional benefits are protecting the sewer lines from leakage infiltration and increasing wastewater flows.

Rate Restructuring, Metering Programs, and User Fees

Surcharge: Irrigators of large turf areas (i.e., in excess of 1.2 hectares or 3 acres) in Los Angeles must reduce their outdoor water use by 10 percent compared to water consumption rates in 1986. Those who do not comply are charged a surcharge which increases by 10 percent monthly to a high of 100 percent. Most people have complied.

Ten-Year Program to Install Meters: Starting in 1988, this program focused on all buildings in New York City. By mid-1995, more than 60,000 meters per year were installed as part of a plan to make customers economically accountable for the amount of water they consume.

A naturalilzed fountain

Increasing Block Rates: In the late 1970s, the City of Tucson, Arizona began charging increasing block rates for customers' water supplies. Rates increase with higher volumes of water consumption. Coupled with a public-education campaign called "Beat the Peak", rate increases resulted in a 94.7 liter- (25 gallon-) per-capita per day reduction in water use (13 percent).

Sliding-Scale Hookup Fee Program: This program is underway or being considered by electric utilities in several U.S. states, including Massachusetts, Idaho, Iowa, Washington, Oregon, and Montana. Developers or new customers are charged fees for hook-up proportional to the anticipated water use. Those who install less-efficient plumbing fixtures are charged more, and the others installing water-conserving toilets and faucets, etc., may receive rebates.

Permits, Bylaws, and Ordinances

Many communities have established standards for water-efficient building products, fixtures, and water offset requirements for new development. In some places, city policies dictate efficient landscaping and irrigation practices.

Developers Required to Replace Old Toilets: In existing buildings in San Luis Obispo, Santa Barbara and Santa Monica, California, developers must replace old toilets with low-flow models to offset the amount of water that will be required by new buildings.

Water-Wasting Ordinance: Clark County, Las Vegas Valley (Nevada) Water District adopted a water wasting ordinance that makes it illegal to allow water to flow into a gutter or storm drain for more than 20 consecutive minutes. On the first day of the ordinance, the city reported 310 water wasters.

Model Water-Efficient Landscape Ordinance: In 1992, the California Department of Water Resources adopted a Model Water-Efficient Landscape Ordinance. Development projects use a water budget approach to designing, installing, maintaining and evaluating the water efficiency of landscaping. Cities and counties may adopt this state model or develop an ordinance based on this model.

Land-Use Planning for Water Conservation

Comprehensive Plan: The County of Santa Barbara established a policy within its Comprehensive Plan that requires development applicants to demonstrate an adequate supply of services and resources, including water. If any improvements or expansions are needed in order to cope with increased demand, the developer must finance those improvements. This encourages developers to look beyond their own subdivisions to realize the impact of growth on water supplies, and to seek ways to minimize new demand. The county also assesses potential environmental impacts, such as groundwater recharge rates, of proposed developments.

Regulatory and Incentive Programs

Audits, Restructured Rates, Rationing, and Education: Goleta, California and its Water District combated their problems of drought and water shortage by providing free on-site water-efficiency audits identifying more efficient outdoor watering methods and other water savings opportunities. They also gave 35,000 free high-performance showerheads to community members, and encouraged installation of other water-efficient fixtures and irrigation methods. They re-structured rates, added surcharges, metering, and an imposed mandatory rationing plan in conjunction with public education, and established targets for water savings per sector. They exceeded their targets, achieving a 50-percent reduction in water consumption in the residential sector, and an overall savings of 30 percent (including commercial, agricultural and industrial customers).

WATER QUALITY AND SEWAGE TREATMENT

The quality of water affects the quality of the life it touches. Both groundwater and surface water systems have deteriorated in quality in many urban areas. Water pollution in combination with a too rapid rate of water extraction can cause serious harm to hydrological systems. Wastewater treatment is a particular concern in many communities, and conventional wastewater treatment technologies are major environmental polluters on at least three fronts:

- they produce an often-toxic byproduct called sludge which is difficult to dispose of;
- they use hazardous compounds in the treatment process that end up in the environment; and
- without massive federal subsidies, most communities cannot afford to build and operate advanced wastewater treatment facilities.

In many North American cities, storm water and sewage are combined and sent to wastewater treatment facilities. Often during heavy rains, such systems overflow, sending raw sewage directly into rivers and streams. Efficient use of water can also improve water quality by helping reduce loads on sewage treatment plants. Treatment plants and septic tanks work better with reduced flows because detention time can be increased if plants aren't overburdened. Efficiency can further benefit water quality by avoiding a draw on water supplies, which can cause seepage of saltwater or soil contaminants from agricultural pesticides or fertilizers, landfills, toxic-waste sites, or sewage lines.

Water quality is also affected by pollution from agriculture, industry, households, automobiles, and sedimentation from cleared land. Reducing pollution and preventing degradation to the quality of our water is the most sustainable way to preserve this precious resource, which requires changes in our patterns of land use, auto dependency, and economic activities. While there are many efforts in this direction, this section will primarily discuss "end of the pipe" strategies for wastewater treatment.

Sewage treatment plants themselves are major contributors to water pollution, as

---

Water Quality and Land Use

"While it is commonly recognized that specific activities such as sewage treatment or paper processing can be notorious water polluters, it is less widely understood that whole categories of land use are also inherent threats to water quality. For example, car-dominated urban areas contaminate stormwater runoff with salt, oil, and toxic fluids from roads and parking lots. Suburbs allow large amounts of chemical fertilizers and pesticides to runoff golf courses and large lawns. Construction sites from which trees and other natural vegetation are stripped add large amounts of eroded soil to runoff. Often, stormwater from cities and suburbs — together with agricultural runoff containing chemicals and animal wastes — constitute a greater hazard to water quality than factories and other specific sources do" (Lowe 1991).

GREENHOUSE

CLARIFIER

CLARIFIER

HEAD WORKS ①

EQUALIZATION ②

③

④

SOLAR SILOS

⑥

⑦

UNDERFLOW

REED BED FOR PASSIVE COMPOSTING

⑤

MARSH ⑧

⑨

UV LIGHT

SURFACE DISCHARGE

A Solar Aquatics System

many cities only have primary treatment (settling tanks removed two-thirds of suspended solids and one-third of the biological oxygen demand) of waste, so contaminants are discharged in local waterways causing degradation of aquatic systems and fish. Other urban areas provide secondary treatment, removing most of the biological oxygen demand and suspended solids. However, very few plants conduct tertiary treatment to purify wastewater before discharge. The high monetary cost of treatment precludes these efforts, yet the true cost of degradation to the ecosystem and deteriorating water quality and fish stocks may be greater to communities. Sustainable water management aims to treat effluent at its pollution source, thus the polluter is responsible for avoiding or eliminating water contamination. The goal is also to treat wastewater so that it is as high or higher quality than water coming into urban water systems.

Many strategies are available for reducing wastewater and improving water quality through reclamation and reuse of treated wastewater (instead of discharging it to waterways). There are more than 1,000 wastewater reuse projects in the U.S. alone, in which water is reused for irrigation, industrial cooling and processing, and groundwater recharge (Rocky Mountain Institute 1991). In some cases, treated wastewater is applied directly to the land with treatment standards less stringent than is required for drinking water. The nutrient-rich wastewater can be used as fertilizer and applied to forests, agricultural crops, parks, or golf courses. Water is filtered as it is stored in the vegetated soils and woodlands, and percolates through the ground to recharge water tables. Another strategy for minimizing demand for potable water supplies is to use seawater for industrial processes, such as cooling.

Use of aquatic plants, marshes or wetlands is an effective, yet little known way of processing wastewater. Marshland is effective at absorbing nitrates and phosphates, and sedimentation and filtration also help to purify water. Some developers and communities are using existing marshes, or constructing artificial wetlands or solar aquatic systems (SAS) for wastewater treatment.

SAS is a biologically integrated technology that treats sludge, sewage, and industrial process wastewater to high quality specifications at low cost. It uses plants and microorganisms in greenhouses to filter and consume contaminants. SAS mimic wetlands in processing waste, but are typically more compact so more waste can be processed in a smaller area. The water is purified and could be reused, but in North America, fear of system failure precludes reuse of SAS-treated water, so the clean water is typically discharged or used for irrigation.

Inside the solar aquatic waste treatment facility in Providence, Rhode Island

In addition to providing ecologically responsible ways of processing sewage without toxic chemicals, wetlands and SAS can serve as recreational amenities, bird sanctuaries and tourist attractions. Other ecological water management strategies can also be integrated into urban design and landscaping. Pavement and other impermeable surfaces increase run-off in urban areas. In some communities, instead of using culverts or underground storm drains, run-off is managed through permeable surface drainage and overland flow in creeks and swales (vegetated surface channels for runoff). Water quality is improved as percolation through soil and vegetation helps to purify water before it reaches rivers and reservoirs, and it can also help reduce erosion and sedimentation. Another economical way of controlling and purifying run-off is through retention ponds and lakes. Pollutants from rain, paved surfaces, and rooftops settle out, and flow is modified, helping to avoid "shock loads" during periods of wet weather (Hough 1995).

TOOLS AND INITIATIVES

Water monitoring programs

Hot Spots Remediation Project: The Baynes Sound Hot Spots Remediation Project involves dozens of local volunteers conducting stormwater monitoring program of drains around Comox and Courtenay on Vancouver Island, B.C. Concern over water pollution impacting residents as well as shellfish promoted the cooperative initiative between community members and government ministries. In Courtenay,

The Solar Aquatic System™, or SAS, mimics the natural water purification processes of freshwater wetlands

the tests discovered excessively high fecal counts were caused by 10 household sewer lines that had mistakenly been connected to storm drains.

Education and Information Programs

Stewardship Initiative: The Baynes Sound Stewardship Initiative began with provincial and local government agencies, but grew to include more than 60 volunteers from the community who help clean up water contamination in the local watershed. Volunteers distribute information on septic system care, and educate citizens about what should enter storm drains. One local group, Citizens for Action on Recycling and the Environment, organized "septic socials." Local residents attended summer barbecues hosted by neighbors that mixed a party atmosphere with informal talk about septic system management. Says group member Dick Drake, "If we called it a workshop, we'd lose 90 percent of the audience. The socials have become so popular, sometimes we have trouble getting people to go home."

Nature Interpretive Centre: The Toronto Board of Education established the Nature Interpretive Centre at the Boyne Conservation Area in Ontario. A small SAS in the building functions both as a treatment system for the center's wastewater and a learning tool for students.

Pollutant Reduction: By reducing the amount of pollutants needing treatment, the small town of Alekulla, Sweden was able to avoid expansion of their near capacity sewage treatment plant. In spring 1989, each resident was given free samples of low phosphate cleansers and detergents, and the local shop began selling those same products. As a result, the phosphate levels in the domestic wastewater was reduced by more than 50 percent.

Bylaws, Ordinances and Performance Standards

WastewaterBylaw: Standards for maximum acidity levels and concentration of certain toxic substances discharged into the treatment system are set by the Greater Vancouver Sewage and Drainage District. The bylaw requires any operation that discharges more than 10,000 liters (2640 gallons) per day to have a permit specifying allowable concentration levels of various substances. Violation of the bylaw is a violation of the federal Waste Management Act (WCERLRF 1994).

Industrial and Commercial Standards: Standards for industrial and commercial polluters have been set by a program in Stockholm, Sweden since the 1960s. The standards have forced many industries to introduce new technologies for treating pollutants at source. For example, the graphics industry and photo processing must separate and treat all fixing solutions and other chemical solutions instead of discharging into sewage system, and dentists must use amalgam separators to remove mercury from their waste streams.

Taxes and Charges

Run-off Charge: The Storm and Surface Water Utility in Bellevue, Washington manages storm and surface water systems to protect water quality and wildlife habitat. They believe water quality is determined by run-off quantity, so they charge land owners for the amount of runoff. Calculations are based on development intensity and impervious surface area (vegetated and unpaved land areas have less run-off than impervious areas with the same activities on site.) (B.C. Municipal Waste Branch 1992).

Public/Private Partnerships

Wastewater Reclamation Plant: The East Bay Municipal Utility District and Chevron USA Inc. partnered to build a wastewater reclamation plant. East Bay financed construction of the $17 million treatment plant in North Richmond, while Chevron financed improvement of pipelines and associated facilities to convey reclaimed municipal wastewater to the company's refinery in Richmond, California for use in industrial cooling.

Treated Wastewater for Farming: About 72 million liters (19 million gallons) of treated wastewater is delivered to 769 hectares (1,900 acres) of city-owned farmland every day in Tallahassee, Florida. The city contracts out the farm operations to a private operator who grows and markets a variety of crops.

Land-Use Planning for Water and Wastewater Management

Grass Paving: The city required developers to manage run-off for their shopping mall and parking area development in Hartford, Connecticut. The projected cost for construction of a retention pond was more than $1 million, so instead the developers chose grass paving which cost about $500,000. This was more expensive than conventional paving, but the permeable surface parking lot (made of grass interspersed with paved sections) accommodated run-off effectively, thus eliminating the need to construct a detention pond.

Swales Instead of Culverts: In the early 1970s, developers Michael and Judy Corbett struggled to get approval for swales instead of culverts for storm water run-off at the subdivision they were developing in Davis, California. They incorporated the swales (permeable surface open drainage channels) into the landscaping, saving $800 per lot (in 1981 dollars). The swales at Village Homes also proved more effective than conventional storm sewers in neighboring developments when a 50-year storm flooded other parts of the Davis area a few years later.

County Land Purchase: To protect a sensitive groundwater recharge area from development, Suffolk County, Long Island, New York spent $118 million to acquire 3,400 hectares (8,398 acres) of open space. The groundwater feeds the county's potable water supply (Brown 1993).

Master Plans and Programs for Wastewater Management and Reclamation

Dual Distribution System: Palo Alto, California developed a Water Reclamation Master Plan which calls for a dual distribution system for large turf areas (such as golf courses and parks) that uses a blend of treated and reclaimed water. This system saves millions of gallons of treated water per year as the reclaimed water provides a portion of irrigation needs.

Reclaimed Water for Golf Courses: The City of Tucson, Arizona irrigates all of its golf courses and some parks with reclaimed water. According to Mike Tubbs, Director of Tucson Water, "By continuing to remove large public turf irrigation demands from the potable water system we are not only conserving our precious groundwater, we are lessening peak demands on our drinking water system" (Rocky Mountain Institute 1991).

Biological Sewage Treatment Facility: Denham Springs, Louisiana runs its processed sewage through two shallow 16-hectare (40-acre) ponds that have been lined, carpeted with stones, filled with water, and planted with lilies and other plants. Although it looks like a flower farm in summer, the biological sewage treatment facility can treat over 11 million liters (3 million gallons) of sewage per day. Compared with conventional processing, the city saved $1 million in initial construction costs and saves approximately $60,000 per year on operation and maintenance (MacLeish 1990; Marinelli 1990).

Wastewater for Community Economic Development

SAS Greenhouse: Bear River, Nova Scotia constructed a 303,030-liter (80,000-gallon) SAS providing sewage treatment for the local hospital, and discharging tertiary treated water to the local river. Instead of hiding the wastewater treatment plant on the edge of town, they located it right next to the tourist bureau in the heart of town. The SAS has become a popular tourist attraction, drawing 1,500 new visitors to Bear River each year.

INTEGRATED RESOURCE PLANNING

Water-efficiency and ecologically responsible ways of managing water quality and wastewater are key to sustainable urban development, but there are a number of barriers to progress. One of the greatest barriers is the departmentalization of city, municipal or regional water and wastewater services. In many communities, water and wastewater treatment departments are totally separate; their staff, boards, billing, budgets, and goals should be coordinated so that mutual goals can be achieved while saving costs and reducing impact on the ecosystem. A planning department may issue building permits, while the water and sewage departments are worrying about water supply infrastructure, water quality and capacity for sewage treatment.

Integrated Resource Planning or Integrated Water Planning is a nontraditional planning and management strategy for long-range water resource issues that considers all water uses and water-related activities, within whatever political, administrative, economic, or functional boundaries they are defined (Child and Armour 1995). It requires inter-governmental cooperation and strives for multiple-purpose and multiple-means projects including: use of zoning and other land-use management strategies; regulations; incentive programs; taxation; and whatever else works to achieve multiple goals for provision of water and sewage services, and other objectives (such as energy-efficiency, recreation, flood control, wildlife preservation, irrigation, and even economic development).

Integrated resource planning opens the door for community economic development and job creation associated with sustainable development. For example, while reducing operating and infrastructure costs for communities, many water-efficiency programs can create jobs and stimulate markets for water conserving products and technologies. An SAS can offer other opportunities for jobs and economic benefits from tourism and educational programs; and it is possible to combine production of flowers, plants and herbs with greenhouse operations of an SAS.

TOOLS AND INITIATIVES

Public Involvement in Decision-Making: In the early 1980s, the Denver (Colorado) Water Board began plans for a large dam on the South Platte River. Environmentalists and citizens groups balked at the plans, and eventually persuaded the federal government to veto the project in favor of more cost-effective and environmentally benign water-efficiency initiatives. Today the Board uses an integrated resource planning process, publishing a public information newsletter, conducting workshops, participating in public forums and receiving input from a citizens advisory council as well as stakeholder groups. According to Peter Johnson, former Director of the Bonneville Power Administration, "By involving the public in the decision-making process itself, we gained authority and legitimacy, avoiding costly lawsuits and political challenges, and arrived at creative solutions to seemingly intractable problems" (Jones 1994)

Conservation Avoids Dam Construction: Ashland, Oregon also used conservation to avoid construction of a new dam. The town of 20,000 people is saving almost 507,575 liters (134,000 gallons) of water per day as a result of high-efficiency showerheads and other aggressive initiatives. In addition to avoiding the cost of a $12-million dam, the program saves residents 500,000 kilowatt hours of electricity annually and reduces the burden on wastewater treatment facilities.

RESOURCES

American Water Works Association has issued several publications of interest, such as *Integrated Resource Planning: A Balanced Approach to Water Resource Decision Making and Water Conservation* (1987), the latter written by William O. Maddaus (the "father of water conservation"), Chair of American Water Works Association's Conservation Division, Integrated Resource Planning Subcommittee. To order a copy of Maddaus' book, call 510/820-1784 in Alamo, California. To review case studies on Integrated Resource Planning in U.S. cities, see the Subcommittee's web site: www.waterwiser.org/books/irp.html.

American Water Works Association
6666 West Quincy Avenue
Denver, Colorado
USA 80235
Tel: 303/794-7711
Web site: www.awwa.org/catframe.html

From Eco-Cities to Living Machines: Principles of Ecological Design, by Nancy Jack Todd and John Todd (Berkeley: North Atlantic Books, 1994), discusses SAS, biotechnologies, renewable energy, and systems based on natural cycles in agriculture, aquaculture, fuel resources, and general design.

Canadian Water Resources Association is a national organization of individuals and organizations interested in the management of Canada's water resources.
P.O. Box 1329
Cambridge, Ontario
Canada N1R 7G6
Tel: 519/622-4764
Fax: 519/621-4844
E-mail: cwranat@wchat.on.ca
Web site: www.cwra.org/cwra/Welcome.html

Center for the Protection and Restoration of Waters @ Ocean Arks International is a not-for-profit global center for water awareness and action founded in 1989. Dr. John Todd of Ocean Arks originally developed the SAS. Membership in OAI is available from:
1 Locust Street
Falmouth, Massachusetts
USA 02540
Tel: 508/540-6801
Fax: 508/540-6811

Ecological Engineering Associates purchased the rights to the SAS technology and markets the system. They provide wastewater treatment plant design, engineering, construction and operating services. For further information, contact:
13 Marconi Lane
Marion, Massachusetts
USA 02738
Tel: 508/748-3224
Fax: 508/748-9740

Environmental Protection Agency's Office of Water has an Internet site that provides information on water quality and management with links to other sites.
401 M Street, S.W.
Washington, D.C.
USA 20460
Tel: 202/260-5922
Fax: 202/260-6257
E-mail: OW-General@epamail.epa.gov
Web site: www.epa.gov/watrhome/

Environmental Protection Agency's National Small Flows Clearinghouse gathers and distributes information about small community wastewater systems.

National Small Flows Clearinghouse
617 Spruce Street
PO Box 6064
Morgantown, West Virginia
USA 27505
Tel: 800/624-8391

[U.S.] **National Drinking Water Clearinghouse** can be reached at 800/624-8301 for water quality questions.

WaterWiser is a partnership between the government and private sector to be the preeminent resource for water efficiency and water conservation information.
6666 West Quincy Avenue
Denver, Colorado
USA 80235
Tel: 800/559-9855
E-mail: bewiser@waterwiser.org
Web site: www.waterwiser.org/

REFERENCES

B.C. Municipal Waste Branch. 1992. Urban Run-off Quality Control Guidelines for the Province of British Columbia, Environmental Protection Division, B.C. Environment, June.

Brown, L. 1993. *State of the World 1993*. New York: W.W. Norton and Co. Pp.35-41.

Child, M, and A. Armour. 1995. "Integrated Water Resource Planning in Canada: Theoretical Considerations and Observations From Practice." *Canadian Water Resources Journal* 20(2).

Hough, M. 1995. *Cities and Natural Processes*. London/New York: Routledge.

Jones, A. 1994. *Public Involvement In Water Management*. Rocky Mountain Institute.

Lowe, M.D. 1991. "Shaping Cities: The Environmental and Human Dimensions." Worldwatch Paper 105. Washington, D.C.: Worldwatch Institute.

MacLeish, W.H. 1990. "Water, Water, Everywhere, How Many Drops to Drink?" *World Monitor* (December): 54-58.

Marinelli, J. 1990. "After the Flush: The Next Generation." *Garbage* (Jan/Feb): 24-35.

National Round Table on the Environment and the Economy (NRTEE). 1996. *Water and Wastewater Services in Canada.*

Rocky Mountain Institute. 1991. *Water Efficiency: A Resource for Utility Managers, Community Planners and Other Decision-makers.*

Roseland, M., and M. Jacobs. 1995. "Sustainable Development, Economic Instruments, and the Sustainable Management of Aquatic Resources and Ecosystems: A New Framework for Water Management in the Fraser Basin." Burnaby, B.C.: Science Council of B.C.

West Coast Environmental Law Research Foundation (WCERLRF). 1994. "Municipalities Have Resources to Implement Source Control." WCELRF Newsletter 17(8).

6

WASTE REDUCTION AND RECYCLING

Despite a growing awareness of the three "Rs" — reduce, reuse, recycle — North Americans produce an embarrassing amount of solid and hazardous waste. The U.S. alone produced over 22 trillion kilograms (50 trillion pounds) of solid waste in 1996 (Hawken 1997). Until recent years, the conventional method of managing our waste stream was to bury it in a local dump or sanitary landfill located on the fringe of a community. In the late 1960s, higher regulatory standards and public resistance to facility siting began to create problems in accessing affordable landfill space (Blumberg and Gottlieb 1989; Young 1991). Solid waste management responded to these issues with "end-of-the-pipe" solutions such as incineration and export of wastes. Efforts focused on waste diversion, which simply cleans up the mess rather than preventing it in the first place. This approach neglects other options in the principles of waste management, which actually includes four Rs in a hierarchy of preferred options: reduce, reuse, recycle, and recover (RCBC 1994b). Recovery and recycling are ranked as the lowest priorities, yet energy recovery (incineration for use as a fuel supply) and recycling programs have blossomed across the continent, while little has been done to promote source reduction or materials reuse.

The irony of the waste diversion strategy is that it only delays the onset of landfill crises in communities across the continent (RCBC 1994b). Reuse and reduction offer the greatest opportunities for eliminating pollution and depletion of natural resources, yet they are often perceived to be at odds with economic development. How does a community (or business or individual) prosper by reducing and reusing? This may require a paradigm shift in perceptions of wealth, economic development, and quality of life, or at the very least, a more comprehensive means of measuring costs and benefits. Let us explore some of the elements of the waste management hierarchy.

SOURCE REDUCTION

The best way to reduce waste is by not creating it in the first place. Arguably, "re-think" should be at the top of any waste management hierarchy. As a society we need to re-think our indicators for quality of life. Current measures of success can be summed up in a bumpersticker: "the one who dies with the most toys wins." However, there is a vast difference between standard of living and quality of life. New indicators, such as how much time we spend with our friends and families, and how many walks we take per week, can replace our consumer-oriented lifestyles while enhancing our quality of life. By re-thinking our consumer habits, we may realize we just don't need so much *stuff!* This may be the ultimate way to achieve source reduction.

More typically, the definition of source reduction refers to reducing the amount of waste and byproducts that enter the waste stream. This can be done by: industries modifying processes and procedures to reduce the amount of waste associated with product manufacture; government offices and businesses choosing to double-side photocopy and correspond electronically; and consumers avoiding packaging at the store.

Source reduction strategies are available in all categories of the waste stream: agriculture, construction and demolition, industrial hazardous, industrial non-hazardous, mining, oil and gas, and municipal solid waste. Municipal solid waste is what most citizens and local governments think of when considering community-based action because it is the most visible (OTA 1992) waste. Municipal solid waste typically consists of consumer discards such as durable and non-durable goods, containers and packaging, food scraps, yard trimmings, and miscellaneous organic and non-organic items; it flows from households, commercial establishments such as stores and restaurants, institutions, and office and support operations in industrial sectors. However, a large percentage of solid waste produced in the

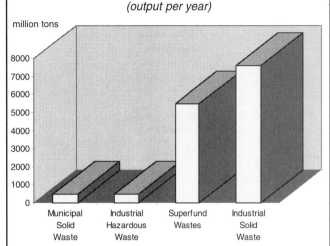

U.S. Solid Waste and Its Sources
(output per year)

Source: Council on Environmental Quality, *United States of America National Report* (prepared for the United Nations Conference on Environment and Development, 1992). Exhibit 6h.1, p.333 — from World Resources Institute (1993), *The 1993 Information Please Environmental Almanac*

Note: Superfund (Resource Conservation and Recovery Act) wastes include discards from oil and gas operations (1.5 billion tons), mining (3.6 billion tons) cement kiln dust (4 million tons), and electric utility wastes (8.5 million tons)

U.S. and Canada is not directly generated by consumers. Despite being the focus of much public concern, municipal solid waste represents less than 2 percent of all solid waste regulated under the Recycling and Resource Recovery Act (OTA 1992; World Resources Institute 1993). However, much of waste production originates in the manufacturing and distribution phases of production of consumer products. Therefore opportunities for source reduction in municipal solid waste begin before products are even manufactured — citizens can choose to reduce the amount of waste they produce by changing their consumption choices and patterns.

For cities and towns, source reduction translates into lower costs for municipal waste management services and less burden on local landfills. For business and industry (and even government offices), source reduction can mean thousands, even millions, of dollars in savings by avoiding disposal costs. In an era of downsizing and budget cutbacks, businesses simply cannot afford to waste resources, and source reduction may be the most cost-effective means of reducing waste.

Hierarchy of preventive options

From Hirschhorn, J., T. Jackson, and L. Baas, "Toward Prevention: The Emerging Environmental Management Paradigm," in T. Jackson, Ed., *Clean Production Strategies*, Ann Arbor: Lewis Publishers, 1993

Product life-cycle and cradle-to-grave management are two systemic approaches to encourage source reduction. Conventional waste management is designed as if solid and hazardous wastes emerge out of nowhere, with no connection to previous actions and decisions, except those of the final consumer. Yet every product has a life history which remains generally unknown to the consumer, *and* unaccounted for by our economy. A product's life has many stages, beginning on the drawing board of the industrial designer, and continuing through resource extraction, manufacturing, retailing, purchase or consumption, and disposal. At each of these stages wastes may be produced, compounding the total ecological impacts of the product. Life-cycle analysis reveals the opportunities to reduce waste at each of these stages.

Cradle-to-grave management is a way of assigning responsibility for a product so the producer considers the pollution and waste associated with the product after it leaves the manufacturing plant. Responsibility for solid and hazardous waste starts at the beginning of the product's life when brand owners and designers make choices to determine the extent of environmental impact a product will have throughout its life cycle. They decide, for example, on the composition of the product, its durability, toxicity, and potential for reuse and recycling. Cradle-to-grave management is yet to gain widespread acceptance in North America, but the business sector may benefit from this approach in two significant ways: through enhanced public image as conscientious members of their community and through cost savings.

Life-cycle analysis reveals the benefits of more durable goods for source reduction. If products last longer, we don't throw them away and replace them with another. Responsible product stewardship will encourage design and manufacture of products that have extendable lives, by being durable as well as reusable, repairable, and remanufacturable (or recyclable). It also reveals the true cost of using hazardous substances as manufacturers will bear the burden of disposal or diversion. Faced with reclamation, producers may find alternative ways to manufacture products. Communities can use regulatory measures, education programs, or technical assistance programs to help industry reduce toxic wastes.

REUSE

Reuse is another under-used component of the waste hierarchy. By considering waste a resource and seeking opportunities for reuse, either for the same purpose or service, or for other purposes, the life of products, packaging and other materials can be extended, thereby reducing waste. The possibilities are endless and so is the potential to link job training with reuse and repair businesses. Local governments can provide special zoning, financial incentives, and information to encourage reuse, lease and

"We are far better at making waste than at making products. For every 100 pounds of products we manufacture in the United States, we create at least 3,200 pounds of waste" (Hawken 1997).

rental businesses.

Recognizing the potential savings — both financial and environmental — some businesses are starting their own initiatives to reuse products and materials. For example, while over 90 percent of all manufactured goods are shipped in corrugated cardboard boxes that are discarded after being used only once, Toyota Motor Manufacturing, U.S. saves millions of dollars per year since adoption of a modular reusable packaging system for transportation of goods (Fishbein and Saphire 1992).

By identifying the *service* needed instead of the *product,* many businesses have leased and rented their office equipment, recognizing savings in maintenance, repair, and upgrading costs. Reuse also offers business opportunities. Urban Source, a Vancouver arts and crafts supply store, collects discards from local industries and businesses to sell as art supplies. The REstore in Bellingham Washington sells used building materials, and provides trade-ins and tax-deductible receipts for donations of used building materials.

Reused, repaired, and rental goods are important players in facilitating a shift from a product-based economy to a service-based economy; not only does the local economy expand, but waste destined for the landfill diminishes. Using the example of businesses leasing office equipment, is it unreasonable to imagine widespread support for leasing/rental options for other goods? The Interface company leases all its carpets in tile form, then recycles the materials; they aim to be using entirely recycled fiber by 2000.

Bottle-deposit legislation provides a powerful mechanism for reuse and recycling. The beer industry has been doing it for years. On average, a beer bottle is reused 15-20 times before being reprocessed into a new bottle. The resulting energy savings are enormous. Bills requiring refillable bottles for certain types of beverage containers emerged in the early 1970s. Despite the environmental benefits of bottle reuse, industry has promoted and proliferated disposable bottles, rendering refillables out of style. As a result, many bottle-deposit systems simply recover materials to be recycled. As packaging and products have become increasingly diverse, a second generation of bottle-deposit legislation is needed to encompass a broader range of beverage containers.

Bottle-deposit legislation has the potential not only to create a financial incentive for industry to return to refillables, but also to boost local economies. For example, over 1200 jobs were created in Maine as the result of a bottle deposit law (RCBC 1992b). The logic of deposits/refund can apply to almost anything (e.g., large appliances, batteries).

While reuse of consumer goods is an important waste management strategy, industrial reuse eliminates pollution and other byproducts of manufacturing processes. Many industries have long had symbiotic relationships where wastes and

Community-level struggles for change can be severely hindered by the power of the players in the waste industry. In the past three decades, a handful of hauling and disposal corporations have dominated the industry. Big business has taken on the roles of ownership and management of landfills and incinerators, garbage collection, and more recently, recycling collection and processing. These companies make money through waste production, not waste reduction (Crooks 1993). Community-based efforts to encourage waste reduction through product and package design, and use of recycled materials, or to prevent landfill and incinerator expansion are often in direct opposition to corporate and industry Goliaths.

BEVERAGE CONTAINER LITTER REDUCTIONS WITH DEPOSIT STRATEGY

Mich. 41%
Calif. 45%
Iowa 79%
Maine 86%
Vermont 76%
Oregon 83%
N.Y. 75%

Courtesy of the Recycling Council of British Columbia

A neighborhood recycling center

materials are transformed internally or by others. For example, metal industries use scrap materials in the production process, and the growth of rubber, plastics, paper, and glass recycling industries has generated demand for previously discarded goods. "Industrial ecology" is the term used to describe a strategy for modeling industrial systems after ecological systems. In natural systems, very little is wasted. Industrial ecology strategies use one industry's wastes as another's raw materials. The goal is cost-savings and ecological responsibility through reuse to eliminate waste. Industrial waste exchanges are already in existence, and some communities in North America are planning eco-industrial parks where complementary businesses operate in the same industrial park to share byproducts and close the loop on industrial waste. (See also Chapter 12: Community Economic Development for more discussion of eco-industrial parks).

RECYCLING AND RECOVERY

It is easy to become confused about recycling given the barrage of information and media surrounding it. The term "recycling" is often used when only recovery or even collection are the activities taking place. Recovery refers to finding some way to extract energy or utility from waste materials. Waste-to-energy facilities that burn wastes for fuel to produce heat or power for manufacturing processes or electrical generation are a popular option. However, while these facilities may reduce the use of fossil fuels, they often waste valuable resources, sending economic opportunities right up their smokestacks. Collection of recyclable materials, such as the Blue Box program, is the first step in a recycling program. Other mechanisms for capturing and collecting recyclable products and materials include bottle deposits, take back programs, and eco-industrial parks. Ensuring cost-effective and environmentally sound recycling is another vital step in the waste management hierarchy.

Anti-recycling arguments are plentiful and deserve exploration. One argument, often supported by corporate interests, suggests that as more technologies become available for waste disposal, we will not need to go through the trouble or incur the costs of source separation and collection. This contention neglects to acknowledge benefits associated with recycling, including: reducing the extraction of virgin raw materials; creating new industries and jobs in local communities; and cost-savings. For example, in the area of paper manufacturing, mills recycling waste paper for newsprint, boxes, cartons, and other products may have lower capital and operating costs than new mills using virgin wood. Recycling also saves energy. At the current national rate of about 26 percent, recycling saves enough energy to supply the needs of nine million U.S. households (Denison and Ruston 1996).

It is also argued that viable markets for recyclables do not exist. Recycling and

If you're not buying recyclables, you're not recycling!

remanufacturing industries are still young in North America, and like any industry, price fluctuations and trial and error present challenges to success. However, as the real costs of disposal (such as pollution and remediation) are recognized, recycling and recycled goods will become competitive. Although recycling is a growth industry, cost-effective collection and transportation of materials is another challenge. This is another argument for source reduction, but innovative new ways to reuse and recycle products and materials within the community will also generate employment and local economic activities.

Curbside recycling programs and other collection programs are both a benefit and a hindrance to the recycling industry. By focusing on only four categories — paper, plastics, glass, and metal — communities and industry may be neglecting opportunities for more creative and cost-effective waste management. Co-mingling of construction waste, for example, renders many potentially valuable byproducts useless or less available for reuse or recycling.

Given the hidden subsidies for disposal, local governments will benefit by encouraging commercial, institutional and industrial recycling efforts. In addition, by supporting industries that manufacture and distribute recycled goods, governments and consumers will stimulate demand for recycling programs as well as recycled products. There are numerous barriers, such as the fiercely competitive nature of raw materials markets in which subsidies support the continued dominance of virgin-materials suppliers.

COMPOSTING

Organic wastes are often seen as a stand alone component of waste management, but they too should be subject to the waste hierarchy. Where organic food wastes cannot be avoided or reduced, then redistributing food wastes to those in need should be a priority. Each *day* in New York City, 4545 kilograms (10,000 pounds) of food that restaurants, corporations and cafeterias would otherwise throw away is brought to homeless shelters, daycare centers, and other social service facilities by City Harvest (Fishbein and Saphire 1992). Only after reduction and reuse options are exhausted should composting be considered.

Local governments are finding that composting is a recycling technology that offers an avenue to significantly reduce waste management costs and volumes. While some communities are offering curbside pick-up of yard wastes and food scraps, others are recognizing it is more cost-effective to provide low-or no-cost recycling bins for on-site recycling. Backyard composting has proven to be a successful option for recycling organic household wastes, and for those without a backyard, vermiculture (worm composting) is an effective way of breaking down wastes held in small containers stored on balconies or under kitchen sinks. Multi residential on-site composting units and community composting depots are other options (RCO 1993).

Restaurants, grocers, food manufacturers, breweries, and universities are only a sample of the kind of businesses and institutions that can reduce disposal volumes and costs through composting or other organic waste diversion strategies. Mid-scale in-

The Blue Box has become the focus of attention over the past few years. It has become a convenient means for people to feel like they are doing something good for the environment. Although the Blue Box has increased the rate of diversion from local landfills, it has done little to promote source reduction or address over consumption. In addition, we must consider the distance the materials collected by Blue Box programs must travel to be processed (and associated impacts).

Who pays for curbside programs is also an important issue. Currently, most municipal recycling programs are funded by taxpayers, not industry. When local governments are forced to pay for recycling programs, recycling offers a hidden subsidy to industry, as they are able to continue making products without concern for the costs of disposal.

situ composting technologies are offering options that were not previously available or affordable. Middlebury College in Vermont saves $25,000 annually on disposal costs alone since it introduced an on-site composting program, and the New York Department of Correctional Services saved more than $1 million in 1995-96, a result of the 31 compost sites it operates (*Biocycle* 1997).

A study of 10 states found recycling added $7.2 billion in value to recovered materials through processing and manufacturing activities, employing approximately 103,000 people (Denison and Ruston 1996). Results from a study conducted by the Institute for Local Self-Reliance indicate that one job is created for every 15,000 tons of solid waste land-filled each year. When considering the jobs created per million tons of material, this amounts to 67 jobs for waste landfilling, 467 jobs for composting, and 600 jobs for recycling (Institute for Local Self-Reliance 1995).

TOOLS AND INITIATIVES

Education and Information

Guide and Directory: In an effort to promote reuse, the Greater Vancouver Regional District, B.C. published *101 Uses for your Old Shoes 'n Other Stuff* (1996), a guide that includes tips on reusing and repairing household goods, and a resource directory of businesses and organizations that reuse, repair, and rent goods in the region.

Waste Reduction Awards Program: The California Waste Reduction Awards Program provides an opportunity for California businesses to gain public recognition for their outstanding efforts to reduce waste. The logo is used on products, in advertising, and on public educational materials to recognize waste-reduction efforts (California Integrated Waste Management Board).

Eco-Labelling: Labeling that identifies the percentage of recycled content (or the use of non-toxic ingredients, etc.) helps consumers make informed choices about the products they purchase. Canada, Germany, Japan, and the Nordic countries have government-sponsored programs, while the U.S. has two private label programs (OTA 1992).

Precycle Program: Berkeley, California has a Precycle Program to encourage people to consider waste *before* they buy.

Master Composter Program: Interested citizens are trained in the art of household composting in Seattle, Washington. Participants receive their "masters" in composting and go out into the community to pass on the information. This model has proved very effective at increasing both community awareness and involvement in composting.

Responsible Care Guidelines: The Chemical Manufacturer's Association adopted the *Responsible Care Guidelines*, which are based on the product stewardship model. By requiring adherence to the guidelines, the Association has formalized an age-old tactic — peer pressure — to ensure environmental responsibility in their field (*Chemical Engineering* 1995).

Collaboration and Partnerships

Scrap Lumber Collection: The City of Aberdeen, Maryland set up a demonstration project to collect scrap lumber at curbside. In addition to diverting a significant amount of waste from the landfill, the city worked with community volunteers to make birdhouses and backyard composters. Wood was also given to local nonprofit organizations for trail building and other purposes (*Biocycle 1996*).

Newspaper Deposit Charge: The *Observer Newspaper* in Quesnel, B.C. added a five-cent deposit charge to their daily newspaper price (RCBC 1994a). When residents are finished reading the paper, they can return it to be recycled for a three-cent refund. The deposit income supports a community-run association that operates the collection depot.

Community Composting: Zurich, Switzerland's community composting program consists of nearly 600 neighborhood composting sites. Suitable sites, educational information, and support is provided by the city. Maintenance for the compost piles is shared by the participating households. Nearly 10 percent of the city's population participate in the program (RCO 1993).

Vehicle Recycling Partnership: Durable goods could be designed to be easily disassembled for recycling. Automobile makers, Chrysler Corporation, Ford Motor Company, and General Motors Corporation formed the Vehicle Recycling Partnership in 1991 to research the potential to increase vehicle recycling through design for disassembly, and to encourage upstream suppliers to use recycled materials in new parts.

Economic Instruments

The most useful financial instruments, applied by national, provincial/state or local authorities, are those that target the production, manufacturing, and design stage of the products. At the other end of the waste cycle, disposal charges (tipping fees) aid in reflecting the real cost of disposal and recycling, and act as financial incentives for businesses to reduce.

Unit Charges: Charges can be levied to manufacturers to internalize recycling and disposal costs, or discourage use of certain products. British Columbia applies a $3-levy to used tires, in part to fund research and development for new uses for the discarded materials (RCBC 1992a).

Tax credits: Financial incentives such as tax credits can encourage businesses to base their production on secondary (used or recycled) materials. California's Recycling Market Development Zones offer tax breaks to recycling-based businesses.

Deposit/Refunds: Deposits and refunds have been successfully used for beverage bottles for years, however the concept can be applied to other materials and products. Michigan recently passed legislation requiring a deposit system for nickel cadmium and mercury batteries. Consumers pay a $2-deposit, refundable when they return the battery, and retailers are responsible for delivering used batteries to an authorized disposal facility. A deposit on batteries helps rechargeable batteries become more cost-competitive.

In-House Waste Disposal Charge: Businesses and government can encourage waste reduction and recycling by implementing more accurate tracking of waste production and accounting for disposal costs. The City of Santa Monica (1996) charges each of their departments independently for waste disposal, creating an in-house incentive to decrease waste. Waste audits are an important tool that enable businesses and institutions to evaluate current practices and develop plans to minimize waste.

User Pay: Consumers can be required to "pay as you throw" — the less you throw out, the less you pay. For example, some communities have begun charging households per bag (or garbage can) picked up at the curbside; there may be an extra charge for disposal of large consumer goods. Research indicates some barriers to user pay, such as public acceptance, illegal dumping, and financial burdens to lower-income residents, but these barriers can be overcome with creative management strategies (Kutzmark and Canturbury 1996).

Waste Taxes: Isolating the cost of disposal and recycling on tax bills highlights the costs to users and may provide an incentive to reduce. The City of Tulsa, Oklahoma developed a user-pay system charging waste taxes based on the amount of wastes generated. Waste taxes are charged monthly along with water/sewer taxes. If the waste portion of the bill is not paid, water service is halted. This provides an effective means of enforcement.

Flexible Variable Rates: A simple shift in the fee structure to charge one price for waste, and a lower price for recyclables not only encourages recycling, but also source reduction. The town of Hope, B.C. charges businesses $25 per ton to collect garbage, and $15 per ton to collect recyclables (RCBC 1992a,b). Iowa, Minnesota, Washington, and Wisconsin also require variable-rate pricing at the community level (Kutzmark and Canterbury 1996).

Regulations and Legislation

Recycled Content Laws: Minimum recycled content requirements, such as those required by several states for certain paper products, create market opportunities for recyclables. In 1991, Germany passed a "refill law," whereby 72 percent of beverages must be sold in refillable containers (Fishbein and Saphire 1992).

Materials Ban for Landfill: Municipal governments can ban certain materials from local landfills to encourage recycling or avoid contamination of landfills by toxic wastes. The Greater Vancouver Regional District, B.C. banned gyprock (wallboard) from local landfills because under wet, oxygen-starved conditions it generates a toxic gas, hydrogen sulfide. Because extra charges are levied for disposal of this toxic waste, new local businesses have sprung up that recycle gyprock into new wallboard.

Post-Consumer Paint Stewardship Program: North America's first completely industry-funded collection program for paint began in British Columbia in 1994. A provincial regulation requires any company that sells paint to provide a stewardship program for old paint by providing return depots.

Germany's Green Dot System: Implemented in 1993, this system requires manufacturers, users, and distributors of packaging to take back used packaging from consumers for recycling. In order to sell in Germany, manufacturers *must* reduce the amount, weight, and dimensions of packaging to make less do more, reuse where possible, and make packaging easier to recycle. Even though packaging waste is presently down to 5 percent compared to 30 percent in 1990, Germany exports a large amount of its packaging waste to other countries because its recycling facilities cannot keep up (Dragicevic 1997).

Environmentally Acceptable Packaging: Research has proven that mandatory recycling bylaws increase participation substantially (Institute for Local Self Reliance 1995). St. Paul, Minnesota has adopted an ordinance on environmentally acceptable packaging, controlling the use of non-biodegradable packaging products within the city (Olson 1989).

Guidelines, Policies, and Other Programs

Procurement Policies: Purchasing policies can create reliable markets for reused or recycled products. A legislated procurement preference for compost helped launch statewide composting programs and businesses in Minnesota and Florida (Anderson and Burnham 1992).

Development Permits and Building Codes: Permits and codes provide mechanisms to ensure builders and real estate developers incorporate waste reduction into their plans. Developers in Boulder, Colorado seeking residential building permits must score at least 20 points among several categories of conservation measures. For example, designing homes and buildings that accommodate recycling (such as built-in recycling boxes in homes) earn two points. In tendering a contract for demolition of a prison outside Vancouver, B.C., the province required submissions of bids for salvage (or deconstruction) as well as demolition. The winning bid was for deconstruction. Despite requiring more labor (creating two additional jobs), the contractor saved money by avoiding disposal costs and selling salvaged materials.

Materials Waste Exchange: Ventura County, California operates a materials waste exchange that matches companies and individuals seeking to dispose of wastes or surplus materials with those seeking to acquire used goods or materials. The exchange posts listings of materials available and materials wanted on their web site and in a quarterly publication. Staff also use a database to seek immediate matches that may be critical for certain wastes (such as organics). The service is free and includes collection of materials needed for the county's schools, food for the needy, and building materials for low-income housing construction.

Toxic Round-Ups: In New Jersey, yearly or bi-annual "toxic round-up" events provide a central drop-off location for hazardous household wastes, and "toxic taxis" cruise neighborhoods for collection. If well advertised, such programs are very effective (Association of New Jersey Household Hazardous Waste Coordinators).

Resourceful Economic Development

Dishwasher on Wheels: Boeblingen, Germany (with a population of 42,000) has a new "dishmobile" for use at public festivals to prevent the use of millions of disposable plates and utensils. Equipped with a commercial-size dishwasher and enough plates and cutlery to serve 600 guests, the mobile facility is also available for a modest user charge to serve clubs and other groups. The dishwasher on wheels, with its associated plates and equipment, costs approximately U.S.$15,000 (*Public Innovation Abroad* 1990).

Conservation and Job Creation: Materials for the Future Foundation in San Francisco links resource conservation and waste reduction with job creation and local empowerment. The Foundation works with youth organizations to establish computer reuse, repair, and recycling programs, and an affordable housing project in which youth are trained in deconstruction of old buildings and construction using the salvaged materials. Also, grants are offered for development of businesses based on waste reduction (*Resource Recycling* 1996).

Recovery and Re-Sell: The City of Berkeley, California developed a comprehensive strategy to reduce and manage municipal waste. A nonprofit organization (the Ecology Centre) runs curbside collection of recyclables, and a network of for-profit businesses are clustered around the transfer station. Businesses include a building materials exchange, a general store selling used and salvaged merchandise, an antique building material and parts store, and a composting company making an organic soil amendment. Program participants recover about 83,000 tons of materials per year, creating 94 jobs, and circulating approximately $8.5 million annually through the local economy (Platt 1995).

Recycling Market Development Zones and Loans: The California Integrated Waste Management Board promotes the re-manufacturing industry through the development of Recycling Market Development Zones and Loans. Recycling is combined with community economic development to create new businesses and jobs. The Board offers low interest loans, financial assistance, product-marketing, and permit assistance to businesses located within a zone. Local governments offer additional incentives, such as relaxed building codes and zoning laws, streamlined local permit process, reduced taxes and licensing, and a reliable supplement of secondary material feedstock (California Integrated Waste Management Board). The Loan program provides direct loans to businesses who use recycled content feedstock in their manufacturing process and are located within a designated Recycling Market Development Zone; local governments in the zone are helped to finance public works infrastructure that directly supports businesses using post-consumer or secondary waste material.

Eco-Industrial Park: Kalundborg, Denmark is home of the world's first Eco-Industrial Park. Several businesses, including a power station, pharmaceutical manufacturer, plasterboard factory, fish farm, and oil refinery are linked through an innovative symbiotic relationship. Byproducts, such as water, steam, surplus gas, and other waste materials, are redistributed as fuel or resources for other businesses in the Park. The exchange of wastes provides mutual commercial benefits. (See also Chapter 10: Land Use and Urban Form.)

RESOURCES

Association of New Jersey Household Hazardous Waste Coordinators
Web site: www.njhazwaste.com/

California Integrated Waste Management Board: Business Waste Reduction Assistance
Tel: 916/255-INFO
E-mail: wpinfoex@ciwmb.ca.gov
Web site: www.ciwmb.ca.gov/mrt/wpw/wpbiz/wpbiz4.htm

City Farmer
318 Horner Street, Suite 801
Vancouver, B.C.
Canada V6B 2V3
Tel: 604/685-5832
Fax: 604/685-0431
E-mail: cityfarm@unixg.ubc.ca
Web site: www.cityfarmer.org

Cornell Composting
Department of Agricultural and Biological Engineering
New York State College of Agriculture and Life Sciences
Riley Robb Hall
Cornell University
Ithaca, New York
USA 14853-5701
Web site: www.cals.cornell.edu/dept/compost/

U.S. Environmental Protection Agency Solid Waste Hotline
Tel: 800/424-9346
Web site: www.epa.gov/epaoswer/non-hw/recycle/index.html

REFERENCES

Anderson, D., and L. Burnham. 1992. "Towards Sustainable Waste Management." *Issues in Science and Technology.*

Biocycle 1996. 37(3).

Biocycle 1997. 38(1).

Blumberg, L., and R. Gottlieb. 1989. *War on Waste: Can America Win its Battle With Garbage?* Washington D.C.: Island Press.

Chemical Engineering. 1995. 102(1).

City of Santa Monica. 1996. *Sustainable City Progress Report.* Santa Monica: Task Force on the Environment.

Crooks, H. 1993. *Giants of Garbage — The Rise of the Global Waste Industry and the Politics of Pollution Control.* Toronto: James Lorimer and Co.

Denison R.A., and J.F. Ruston. 1996. *Anti-Recycling Myths: Commentary on "Recycling is Garbage."* Washington D.C.: The Environmental Defence Fund.

Dragicevic, M. 1997. "German Waste Exports." Trade and Environment Database, American University, School of International Service, Washington, D.C. <gurukul.ucc.american.edu/ted/GERMWSTE.HTM>.

Fishbein, B., and D. Saphire. 1992. "Slowing the Waste Behemoth: Source Reduction is Overshadowed by Recycling's Success." *EPA Journal* 18 (3): 47-49.

Hawken, P. 1997. "Natural Capitalism." *Mother Jones* (March/April): 40-62.

Hirschhorn, J., T. Jackson, and L. Baas. 1993. "Towards Prevention — The Emerging Environmental Paradigm." In *Clean Production Strategies — Developing Preventive Environmental Management in the Industrial Economy,* T. Jackson, ed. Ann Arbor: Lewis Publishers.

Institute for Local Self-Reliance. 1995. *Manufacturing from Recyclables: 24 Case Studies of Successful Recycling Enterprises.* U.S. Environmental Protection Agency, Solid Waste and Emergency Response, Grant No. EPA530-R-001.

Kutzmark, T., and J. Canterbury. 1996. "Pay as You Throw: One Step Closer to a Sustainable Future." *Public Management* 78:4.

Office of Technological Assessment (OTA), U.S. Congress. 1992. *Green Products by Design: Choices for a Cleaner Environment.* Washington D.C.: U.S. Government Printing Office.

Olson, A. 1989. "Legislation on Non-biodegradable Packaging." *Challenge and Change: The Newsletter of the Canadian Healthy Communities Project* 1(3).

Platt, B. 1995. "Recycling Boosts the Local Economy." *Biocycle* 36 (8).

Public Innovation Abroad. 1990. 14(5) May.

Resource Recycling. 1996. (15)11.

Recycling Council of British Columbia (RCBC). 1992a. "The Cost Of Recycling." *Reiterate: The Newsletter of RCBC* (May).

— — —. 1992b. "Deposits, Curbside and the Second 'R'." *Reiterate: The Newsletter of RCBC* (October).

— — —. 1994a. "B.C. Debates the Regulation of Plastics." *Reiterate: The Newsletter of RCBC* (February).

— — —. 1994b. "Why We Must Reduce our Waste." *Reiterate: The Newsletter of RCBC* (May).

Recycling Council of Ontario (RCO). 1993. *Multi Residential Composting.* Toronto: RCO.

World Resources Institute. 1993. *The 1993 Information Please Environmental Almanac.*

Young, J.E. 1991. "Reducing Waste, Saving Materials." In *State of the World 1991, Worldwatch Institute.* New York: W.W. Norton.

Energy Efficiency and Renewables

Energy production is big business, and its consumption fuels our economy just as it fuels cars, heats and cools our homes, and lights our office buildings. Yet what is the price to our communities, our ecosystem, and to the world around us?

Canadians and Americans consume more energy per capita than any other nation. Environmental impacts of our consumptive lifestyles include ozone layer depletion, acid rain, smog, potential climate change, and other forms of pollution and environmental degradation. Our addiction to energy also manifests itself in congested roads, urban sprawl, excessive heating, cooling, lighting, and ventilation expenditures in buildings, costly inefficiencies in commercial and industrial equipment, weaker local economies, and excessive taxes.

Citizens and their governments hold tremendous power to change our patterns of consumption and support sustainable ways of using energy resources. Designing more energy-efficient buildings, and retrofitting existing homes, office and civic buildings saves millions of dollars in energy expenditures, and frees up money for investment in schools, hospitals, community economic development, and a more secure future.

Reducing consumption is usually more cost-effective than expanding supply. By increasing efficiency, the same amount of electricity can serve more users without requiring massive capital investments to expand power plant capacity. If additional supply is needed, renewable energy production, such as wind power and photovoltaic (solar) power, as well as cogeneration are more sustainable options. For heating options, technologies such as ground-source heat pumps and district heating, are more efficient and environmentally responsible than most conventional heating systems.

By encouraging energy efficiency and clean, renewable or efficient energy supply strategies, communities foster local self-reliance and economic diversification. This is not science fiction — these are "off-the-shelf" technologies and techniques that are available today. All that is required is public and political will.

ENERGY EFFICIENCY

Energy-efficiency simply means "more bang for your buck." It implies use of products, such as refrigerators, lightbulbs, washing machines, computers, printers, copiers, industrial motor systems, air conditioners, space heaters, and ventilation systems that deliver the same service as other units, but with a fraction of the energy or electricity demands. Energy-efficient buildings use strategies and technologies, such as passive solar design, light shelves, light-tubes, and high-performance windows, to reduce energy consumption by minimizing or even eliminating the need for heating, cooling, ventilation systems, and day-time lighting.

To a homeowner this can mean hundreds, even thousands of dollars in savings every year from reduced utility bills. To a large commercial building owner or industrial operations this can translate into millions of dollars in energy savings. To a utility company, reductions in energy consumption can mean loss of revenues, but doesn't have to mean loss of profits.

Supply and Demand

Population growth, economic development, and increasing demands for electricity require costly expansions to energy-supply infrastructure. Faced with the cost of constructing multi-billion dollar power plants, and the uncertainty in planning future capacity needs, many utilities support initiatives to improve customer energy efficiency. Helping a customer reduce demand for electricity is often more profitable than building a new power plant. While the latter expands revenues, it is accompanied by long-term debt, higher operating expenditures, and the risk that an economic slump may reduce consumption, leaving an excessive supply.

Energy efficiency means doing more with less.

This strategy was termed "demand-side management" (DSM), referring to the focus on managing customer demand instead of simply expanding supply. Today, it is often referred to as energy productivity strategies or energy services.

Most electric utilities in Canada are Crown corporations (owned by the provinces), however, there are a few regionally-owned electric generators and a growing number of independent power producers. In the U.S., the Department of Energy owns and operates several large power generators, but there are also hundreds of larger shareholder-owned utilities, independent power producers, and many municipal-owned power generators as well. Regardless of whether a community owns its utility or purchases power from a large provider, investment in cost-effective DSM strategies is simply good business.

Energy and Local Economies

For many towns, 75 cents of every dollar spent on energy (electricity and fuel) leaves the community to pay generators, refiners and the coffers of large electric or gas utility companies. When a dollar is saved on energy, it can be re-invested in the local economy and circulate several times over. This strategy is termed "economic multipliers." (See Chapter 12: Community Economic Development for examples and discussion). "Plugging the leaks" in local energy expenditures saves individual homeowners and tenants money, and helps businesses reduce operating costs to increase their economic competitiveness (Hubbard and Fong 1995).

Many individuals and companies are realizing these opportunities. They're purchasing more energy-efficient products and devices, retrofitting buildings, or requiring high standards of energy efficiency for new buildings. Citizens and local governments can play a strong role by organizing education and information campaigns, and by influencing equipment standards or policy and codes for energy-efficient building design and operations.

Governments can also save taxpayer dollars by reducing energy expenditures in libraries, hospitals, schools, community centers and civic buildings. Money saved on a school's utility bills can be spent on books and teachers' salaries instead, and savings in electricity and heating costs for public buildings can translate into lower taxes or re-direction of tax dollars to community economic development, affordable housing programs, or environmental, cultural, or sports programs that enhance the quality of life for residents of the community.

Economic multipliers and government energy efficiency programs directly and indirectly create jobs for local citizens, and DSM initiatives address the regressive nature of low income people's energy use. Low income people tend to live in the worst housing stock, often characterized by drafty rooms, inefficient heating systems, and energy-guzzling refrigerators. DSM programs improve the comfort of homes and reduce utility bills, thereby increasing the standard of living for those who need it most.

> ### Reducing the Heat Island Effect
>
> Dark, heat absorbing materials, such as concrete and brick, absence of tree cover, waste heat from buildings, industry and automobiles all contribute to increasing temperatures in cities. In addition to exacerbating effects on public health, this urban heat island effect leads to significantly higher demand for air conditioning (Torrie 1997). Cities can counteract the heat island effect by planting more trees, increasing vegetated land within the city, and by using lighter color paints and building materials to reduce absorption of solar radiation. The U.S. National Academy of Sciences estimates that strategic use of white surfaces and vegetation could save $2.6 billion in energy costs (Lowe 1991).

TOOLS AND INITIATIVES

Public Education and Information Programs

Conference and Trade Show: The Energy 2000 committee, formed by residents of Roaring Fork Valley around Aspen, Colorado, organizes an annual "town hall" meeting and celebration, followed by a two-day conference and trade-show to educate and inspire locals to pursue energy efficiency issues. The group solicits sponsorship from local government, utilities and businesses, to pay for speakers and other costs of the event. Local newspapers run a full section promoting the event, the sponsors, and the local energy-efficient businesses, and feature articles describe success stories about energy-saving initiatives.

Interfaith Coalition on Energy: Since 1980, the Interfaith Coalition on Energy has helped religious congregations in Philadelphia reduce their energy use. The Coalition sponsors workshops to help congregations of any faith make their buildings more energy-efficient, and they publish a newsletter providing tips on energy-efficient strategies. The newsletter also offers information on where to buy products and services, and how to finance building retrofits and efficiency upgrades.

Workshops for Homeowners: The City of Fort Collins, Colorado offers workshops on energy efficiency for homeowners. The series includes workshops on city conservation programs, tips for controlling home energy costs, and lectures on home renovations.

Builder and Architect Education Programs

Green Builder Program: The Austin Green Builder Program in Texas provides training in energy-efficient and environmentally-responsible construction techniques. Participants receive guidebooks, product and service source books, and attend workshops and training seminars. Builders and developers can apply the Austin Green Builder rating system, awarding one to four stars to their houses. The program is so popular, it has generated greater participation among builders, architects, engineers, and building-products suppliers.

Innovative Design and Energy Analysis Service: San Jose, California runs an program called IDEAS (Innovative Design and Energy Analysis Service) to encourage energy efficiency in new commercial and industrial buildings. It is a free service providing information on efficient building technologies and design. In addition to working directly with architects, builders, developers and engineers in the early stages of projects, the program offers energy consultant referrals and case studies of successful energy-efficient buildings.

Audits and Retrofit Programs

Audits and Upgrades: Sacramento Municipal Utility District in California promotes audits and arranges complete residential efficiency upgrades for their customers. An inspector recommends an appropriate package of measures to improve efficiency, typically including: improved insulation, weather stripping, insulating the hot water tank, installing compact fluorescent fixtures, and replacement of electric resistance heating with a heat pump. For simply agreeing to the audit, the utility provides the homeowner with a free compact fluorescent light bulb, a high performance showerhead, and two trees (which can reduce air conditioning energy requirements). If the customer decides to proceed with the retrofit, part of the cost is an outright grant (about $800) from the utility, and the rest of the cost (typically $3400) is put on the customer's utility bill, amortized over 15 years. This extra charge is less than the immediate reduction in energy costs, so the customer comes out ahead with lower power bills (Millyard 1992).

Energy Policy: In April 1990, the City of Portland, Oregon adopted an energy policy with the goal of "increasing energy efficiency in all sectors of the City by 10 percent by the year 2000 so as to enhance the livability, economic strength and well-being of the City's residents and businesses and reduce environmental problems, such as air pollution and emissions that contribute to global warming." By 1992, the city's Energy Office had already helped to weatherize thousands of apartment units and homes, including more than 1,300 of residences of the city's poorest families. (ICLEI 1991).

Conservation Power Plant: Emerald People's Utility District in the Eugene-

Springfield, Oregon area signed an agreement with Bonneville Power Administration to build a "conservation power plant" to generate millions of kilowatt-hours of energy savings. The District offers residential weatherization programs, and helps local businesses retrofit buildings and upgrade industrial motor systems. Bonds are issued through the Oregon Department of Energy's Small Scale Energy Loan Program to finance program costs; the Power Administration pays the principal and interest on the bonds, recognizing the benefits in avoided cost of new power-plant construction. Customers pay a small levy to offset revenue losses to the utility, but these charges are more than offset by the savings accrued from retrofits (*Conservation Monitor* 1993a).

Codes, Bylaws, and Ordinances

Building Code: Osage, Iowa established higher-than-state standards of energy efficiency in their local building code. If, for example, commercial or residential buildings do not meet the city's standards for insulation levels, the building will not receive utility service. Since 1984, every building has complied with the energy-efficient standard.

Retrofit Ordinance: San Francisco, California enacted a comprehensive residential energy conservation retrofit ordinance in 1982. The ordinance requires all existing residential buildings, including apartment buildings, to be brought up to an energy-efficiency standard at the time of sale. The cost of the measures can be included in the financing of the residential unit. San Francisco also has a commercial energy conservation retrofit ordinance, which saved San Francisco businesses over $50 million in energy costs in the first five years (Local Government Commission 1990).

Solar Access Ordinance: Many local governments have adopted and implemented solar access ordinances. Carbondale, Colorado has one that protects buildings from interference with solar access to the south face of buildings. This means new building or renovation projects, trees or other objects cannot block the sun (and the view of Mount Sopris).

Setting Examples with Public Buildings

What better way to demonstrate the benefits of resource conservation than through building and retrofiting more efficient schools, libraries, hospitals, and civic buildings. The U.S. government set a grand example with the Greening the White House program, which started in 1993. Energy upgrades were just one of the many initiatives, and in 1997, the U.S. Department of Energy announced plans to renovate 500,000 more federal buildings by 2005. Through a program called Financing Renewable Energy and Efficiency, the U.S. government will cut its energy bills by one quarter while supporting private industry. Energy service companies will install energy-efficient lamps, motors, air conditioning systems, and heating equipment in federal buildings. The government will pay no money up-front as payment will come from a portion of the savings from the lower electricity bills for a designated number of years (*Green Business Letter* 1997).

Passive Solar Building: The school board of Johnston County, North Carolina, realized they spend more taxpayer dollars on utility bills and building maintenance over the life of a building than they spent on constructing the building itself. They invested in better design at Four Oaks Elementary School where the passive solar building uses half the energy of a typical school and has low maintenance costs as well.

Enery Conservation and Savings Plan: The City of Phoenix, Arizona has saved several million dollars since they began auditing and retrofiting civic buildings in the late 1970s. As an incentive for participating in the energy efficiency program, departments and city agencies get to keep all (or a predetermined percentage) of the money they save from using energy more efficiently, and a professional energy manager monitors and documents all savings. In 1984, city council established the Energy Conservation Savings Reinvestment Plan. Under this plan, the city reinvests 50 percent of all documented energy savings (up to $500,000) to finance energy efficiency capital projects (DOE 1992a).

City of Phoenix Yearly Utility Cost Savings from Energy Efficiency Projects

Facilities	Costs Before Retrofit	Costs After Retrofit	Savings in Dollars
Civic Plaza	$1,465,627	$1,046,748	$418,879
Parks	884,714	508,709	376,005
Municipal	923,796	609,744	314,052
Fire Stations	453,328	243,381	209,947
Cultural Centers	719,908	524,719	195,189
Plaza Municipal	565,568	399,591	165,977
Police and Public Safety	1,008,358	886,748	121,610
Branch Libraries	344,750	173,934	170,816

Guidelines, Certification, and Rating Systems

Certification Benefits: The Home Builders Association of Kitsap County introduced a self-certification checklist for rating new buildings in the Bremerton, Washington area. Builders participating in the Build a Better Kitsap program receive a handbook to assist them in building or remodeling homes to improve energy and environmental performance, and a certificate of merit, useful as a marketing tool. Similar programs exist in other cities and states in the U.S. Some home energy rating systems, such as one developed by Energy Rated Homes of America, enable homebuyers to receive preferred mortgage rates.

Power Smart Home Award: BC Hydro's Power Smart division offers a variety of energy efficiency services. One of their most successful programs is their Power Smart Home award. Home builders earn this certification by upgrading windows, lighting and other features to reduce energy loads in new and renovation projects. Participants range from individual home builders to large construction companies building subdivisions and high-rise apartment complexes. In a newer program, BC Hydro awarded the Westin Bayshore with a Power Smart certification for reducing energy and water consumption in a downtown Vancouver hotel.

Grants, Loans, Mortgages and Bonds

Upgrade Financing: When a development firm was constructing a multi-unit building for low-income residents, it approached the locally-owned utility company, Emerald People's Utility District in Eugene, Oregon for support. Realizing that people with lower incomes have a harder time paying their bills, the developer requested a lower rate for electricity supply for residents of the new building. Instead, the utility kept rates the same, but financed upgrades to the building's windows, lighting, and heating system so that occupants would enjoy lower monthly energy bills.

Zero Interest Loans: Some municipal utilities, such as Fort Collins, Colorado have made zero-interest loans available for residential energy efficiency improvements or installation of solar hot-water heaters. Fort Collin's program initially started with a Community Development Block Grant and the utility contributed by buying down the interest rates on the loans.

Municipal Bonds: Many local governments can also issue bonds to raise money to construct public buildings, bridges, or to repair roads. The City of Ann Arbor, Michigan issued $1.4 million in municipal bonds to finance energy improvements to 30 public buildings.

Home Energy Improvement Financing: The Vermont Energy Investment Corporation, a Community Development Corporation, offers loans and other financing for home energy improvement to low- and middle-income Vermonters. They also provide technical assistance and energy efficiency consultation for public housing projects, nonprofit developers, owners, and tenants of low-income housing.

Energy-Efficient Mortgages: Neworld Bank in Massachusetts is one of dozens of financial institutes in North America offering energy-efficient mortgages for home purchase or renovation. Typically homes are rated (see above) or there are a list of energy efficiency requirements that qualify a home for a reduced mortgage rate of 1 percent to 2 percent below prime. Energy-efficient mortgages may be supported directly by the financial institute, or backed by local governments, Community Development Corporations, or state, provincial, or federal energy-conservation programs. In the U.S., national secondary mortgage institutes offer energy-efficient mortgages, but few lenders and mortgage applicants are aware of the opportunity.

Rebate Programs

Energy Bucks: Waverly, Iowa's municipal utility has been encouraging energy efficiency for several years now. In an effort to support the local economy as well, the city gives out "Waverly bucks," which can only be used for purchasing energy-efficient appliances and products in local stores. Local stores cooperate by accepting the local currency and stocking energy-efficient products and brands. It's a win-win program as customers save money while supporting a sustainable, local economy.

Utility Company Rebates: For years many utility companies (municipal and others), such as BC Hydro, Ontario Hydro, and Bonneville Power Authority, have offered rebates on energy-efficient lightbulbs, refrigerators, and other appliances. Several of these programs have been abandoned as utilities try other strategies and services or slash DSM budgets. Pacific Gas and Electric in California, is one utility which continues to offer rebates. The utility pays up to $300,000 to commercial customers for upgrades of lighting, air conditioning, motors or refrigeration appliances; 100 percent equipment financing is also provided if needed. In 1995, the program saved enough electricity to power more than 40,000 homes.

Community Energy Services

Community Energy Services Corporation: The City of Berkeley, California established a Community Energy Services Corporation offering energy services, such as audits and project management to commercial, residential and public building projects. The nonprofit corporation also helps people find financing for energy-efficiency initiatives.

ENVIRONMENTALLY RESPONSIBLE ENERGY SUPPLY

Energy efficiency is clean, cost-effective and widely available, but we still need some source of power supply. What are the options? Ecological impacts of large-scale hydro electric dams are no longer acceptable to the public, and its been more than a decade since the last power plant was built in North America. Utility companies and communities in Canada and the U.S. recognize nuclear power generation is simply too expensive and short-sighted. (Where do we put the radioactive waste kept in "short-term" storage at nuclear facilities across North America?) Rising concerns about local and global pollution and climate change is spurring review of fuel choices and operating efficiencies of oil, coal and gas-fired conventional power plants. Pollution-abatement technologies and combustion efficiencies are improving some plants, but renewable energies offer opportunity for local-self reliance in energy production for electricity needs. Community-scale projects, using efficient technologies such as cogeneration or district heating, are other options to minimize consumption and reduce dependency on fossil fuels.

Renewable Energy Supply

Renewable energy sources are often regarded as new or exotic, but in fact they are neither. Until quite recently, in historical terms, the world drew most of its energy from the sun, either directly from sunlight or indirectly through the natural processes that generate winds, rivers, and plants. The advantages of renewable energy sources — particularly wind, solar, and biomass (plant) energy — are, if anything, more compelling today than ever before (Brower 1990).

While renewable energies have not enjoyed the massive subsidies of the fossil fuel and nuclear power sectors, great strides in technological improvements, operating efficiencies and equipment costs have been made in recent years. In many parts of the U.S., wind technology is now directly cost-competitive with new supply costs for conventional power plants. In fact, all renewable technologies are cost-competitive, and even more economical when long-term operating costs and the financial benefits of environmental protection are factored into the equation. Thousands of Canadians and Americans use solar hot water panels or photovoltaic (solar electric) panels to provide domestic hot water and electricity for their homes, yet few utility companies or communities recognize the opportunity. Rooftops all over North America are ideal for installation of solar panels to provide sustainable energy supplies.

District Heating

District heating pipes heat, hot water, or steam generated at a central facility to each building in a community. By constructing systems to serve a large customer base, such as a whole neighborhood or community, energy-efficient heating systems, such as co-generation and ground-source heat pumps can compete with cheaper inefficient heating systems. District heating requires a certain level of density to be effective. For example, in Britain, 44 dwellings per hectare is considered the minimum density for economical operation (Lowe 1991).

The source of district heat is often a hospital, university, hotel, or factory, that has its own cogenerating system. Cogeneration systems make electricity and steam together to power and heat buildings with one-third less fuel than is needed to produce each on its own; they are also well-suited to sophisticated pollution control equipment. Industries that generate excessive heat, such as pulp and paper mills, can harness waste heat for cogeneration; and industrial wastes, such as wood chips and sewage sludge may also be used as fuel sources. Some wastes are better suited than others for fuel; while burning wastes is still not without environmental impact, it may be more advantageous to burn than dump.

Ground-source heat pumps use heat pump technology to extract heat from the earth to heat buildings, swimming pools, or domestic hot-water supply. Water-source heat pumps use water sources such as ponds as a source of heat. The technology can also work in reverse to cool buildings or keep ice rinks frozen. Ground-source heat pumps use a series of closed-loop pipes containing heat-absorbing fluid that absorbs heat from the surrounding earth. These are not to be confused with geothermal systems that extract heat from hot springs or hot rock areas in the earth. While geothermal systems are effective, there are few places with suitable geology for this technology. Ground-source and water-source heat pumps work effectively with only the moderate temperature increases found below the earth's surface or in bodies of water.

Ground-source heat pumps deliver three to five times more heat (or air conditioning) per unit of energy consumed than conventional space heating systems, so

---

Renewable Energy Options

• *Photovoltaic (solar electric) power.* Photovoltaic panels produce electricity for independent systems with batteries for storing energy, or supply electricity to the power grid.

• *Solar thermal energy.* Solar hot-water systems typically provide water for showers and baths, heating swimming pools, hot tubs, or radiant heating (space heating). Some solar thermal projects are designed to convert heated water into electricity.

• *Wind power.* Stand-alone turbines supply electricity for homes, farms, small communities. Wind farms are clusters of wind turbines generating power for the electrical grid.

• *Micro-hydro:* Unlike large-scale hydro electric projects, micro-hydro exerts minimal disturbance of waterways. Small turbines typically use springs, creeks or municipal water supply lines to generate enough electricity for a single building or an entire town.

• *Biomass:* Agricultural plants or organic wastes provide fuels, such as methanol or ethanol, which can be used as an alternative for most oil or gas needs. Biomass still contributes to air pollution and greenhouse gases. While not strictly a renewable technology, hydrogen gas is a clean, efficient technology that will soon be used in vehicles, and may be adapted for building and community heating and power generation.

Ground source heat pump

operating efficiencies are high. The mechanical heat pump action can be powered by electricity or natural gas, and the cost to install piping is the biggest expenditure. The capital cost is prohibitive for most homebuyers, but for community-scale projects, or large buildings, such as schools, nursing homes and housing complexes, the operating savings offset the investment.

TOOLS AND INITIATIVES

District Heating Programs and Cogeneration

Cogeneration: Helsinki, Finland's district heating program uses cogeneration to reduce Helsinki energy demand to 30 percent of early 1970s levels (Helsinki Energy Board 1989).

Local Energy Supply Program: Saarbrücken, Germany has an aggressive Local Energy Supply program that requires conservation, district heating, and local energy supplies. Over 40,000 homes are served by district heating, and the homeowners can receive subsidies to install rooftop solar-energy panels.

District Heating: The City of Toronto requires new downtown buildings to install connection infrastructure for district heating in the event the technology becomes cost-effective in the future.

Ground-Source Heat Pump Public Projects

Ground source heat pumps are used residentially in North America, but not so for public buildings and large-scale projects, which could benefit cost-wise. According to one study, a heat pump system in a recreation center could save $25,000 per year in energy bills by efficiently cooling an ice rink; the heat extracted could be used to heat hot water for showers or a swimming pool.

School System: A $150,000-ground source heat pump provides two-thirds of the heating requirements for Gulf Islands Secondary School on Salt Spring Island, British Columbia. Along with energy-efficiency initiatives, the system is saving the school about $50,000 per year in heating costs.

Renewables Demonstration Programs

Numerous communities and utilities are testing reliability and compatibility of various solar and wind power products. In a program called the Photovoltaic Utility Group, a cooperative effort of 50 utility companies in the U.S. are supporting hundreds of solar electricity programs.

Wind Turbine: The municipal-owned utility of Waverly, Iowa, purchases most of its power from a major producer. In order to promote local self-reliance, the city encourages energy efficiency. They are also exploring clean energy supply options, and the first step is a wind turbine that contributes to the local grid. By working with a local college, the cost of the pilot project is reduced because engineering technology students provide maintenance and collect data to monitor operating costs and efficiencies.

Green Power Programs

Green power programs are cropping up all over. Community-scale power production, typically using renewable energy supplies, is fostering local self-reliance and greater environmental responsibility.

Cooperative Wind Turbines: Groups of families in Denmark cooperatively own and operate wind turbines scattered throughout the country. Typically, each family pays for its share of the project, financed by bank loans, and sells excess electricity back to their utility. More than 100,000 families are involved.

Methane Gas Extraction: As part of their ongoing efforts to reduce dependency on power purchased from Bonneville Power Authority, Emerald People Utility District in Oregon is tapping into the local landfill to extract methane gas for small-scale electricity production. While not a renewable resource, methane gas is seemingly inexhaustible, being a byproduct of decomposing garbage.

Photovoltaic Rooftop Program: Sacramento Municipal Utility District is running a photovoltaic rooftop program. Participants in the program lend their home's rooftop to the utility for installation of photovoltaic panels for solar electric power generation fed into a grid.

Micro-Hydro Turbine: The small town of Cedaridge, Colorado tapped into their water supply pipeline for a low-cost source of clean, renewable energy. The town attached a micro-hydro turbine to the pipeline, providing a megawatt of power. Only the incremental cost of the turbine and power conversion equipment was required because the town had already paid for the pipeline. Apart from maintenance costs, their power supply is essentially free

COMMUNITY PLANNING AND MANAGEMENT ISSUES

While energy efficiency and green-power supply options offer many benefits for communities, greater benefits are possible if local governments integrate energy considerations into other planning decisions. Strategies and policies for land use, urban development, building sizes, architectural design and standards, transportation planning, environmental protection, air quality and economic development *all* influence energy issues. By integrating planning, communities can address multiple goals while maximizing cost-efficiencies. This requires cooperation among various governmental departments and non-governmental businesses and entities, and may require changes to conventional ways of planning and costing projects.

Least Cost Utility Planning

A number of cities in Canada and the U.S. are implementing Least Cost Utility Planning or Integrated Resource Planning. Such planning for electricity supplies allows investments for energy efficiency and DSM (as opposed to supply-focused) to

Sustainable Cities Project

With funds from the Urban Consortium Energy Task Force, the California Cities of San Jose and San Francisco, and Portland, Oregon developed sustainable energy plans. The cities collaborated but pursued independent courses to develop energy policies that meet their local needs and objectives. Key objectives were:

• to use energy effectively in achieving other municipal goals such as affordable housing, efficient transportation systems, economic development, and job creation;

• to protect and maintain the quality of life by reducing environmental problems associated with inefficient energy use; and

• to contribute to national security by reducing vulnerability to predicted oil shortages and price increases.

As part of the Sustainable City Project, the cities developed a planning guide to serve as a model for other communities. It describes a seven step process:

1. Conduct an environmental scan to identify the impacts of energy use and determine present and future energy resource needs.
2. Identify community goals and issues for policy planning.
3. Build support for a sustainable energy plan.
4. Identify and analyze options: costs, benefits, environmental effects, technological potential, and political acceptability.
5. Adopt policies and strategies to direct future actions.
6. Develop specific energy implementation plans.
7. Evaluate program success, including energy saved, positive environmental impacts, and specific lessons learned.

be on equal footing with investments for new generating capacity. Energy efficiency is treated as an alternative energy source (what Amory Lovins of Rocky Mountain Institute calls "negawatts" rather than "megawatts"), and substitution of non-conventional, decentralized, smaller generators for large, central generating plants is supported (a perfect application for renewable energy systems and cogeneration). Applications of this concept require close co-ordination among utility regulators, individual utilities and local governments. To ensure effectiveness, these programs commonly combine technical support and financial incentives for energy efficiency improvements targeted to residential, commercial, and industrial consumers.

Strategic Planning

Many local governments use strategic planning to identify, rank, and implement energy and environmental policies and programs. Strategic planning is a systematic way to identify and accomplish priorities. It goes beyond goal-setting to focus on implementation and allocation of resources. As part of the Sustainable City Project, sponsored by U.S. Department of Energy, Urban Consortium Energy Task Force (DOE 1992b), three cities (Portland, Oregon, San Francisco and San Jose, California) developed sustainable city plans on the strategic planning process, and published a guidebook for other communities (see "Resources").

Tools and Initiatives

Community Energy Management Projects

Local Advisory Committee: Faced with the decision to build another electric power plant, expand the existing diesel plant, extend a power line to hook up with the provincial utility grid, or pursue energy efficiency, Alberta Power collaborated with a local advisory committee to develop and implement goals for their energy-efficient project. The advisory committee, made up of the Jasper Chamber of Commerce, environmental groups, the school board, the local hospital, the Canadian Park Service, and Alberta Power, targeted all sectors including commercial, industrial and residential customers. Customers were offered audits, cash incentives, reduced prices on energy-efficient devices, and other options which helped the town achieve a 20-percent reduction in energy consumption in eight months (*Home Energy* 1994).

Energy Conservation Division: Ashland, Oregon integrates energy-efficiency initiatives with town planning. Since the early 1980s, the department of community development has included an energy conservation division offering audits and rebates for homes and businesses. They provide weatherization assistance and energy smart building design assistance, and they've upgraded the efficiency of area and street lighting. The city also influences energy efficiency by the codes, zoning and standards it enforces for building and land-use development. Energy issues are considered in all stages of planning, land use and building decisions, and the city promotes pedestrian-oriented urban planning to reduce vehicle energy consumption as well. The program saves about 8 million kilowatt-hours per year.

Comprehensive Energy Planning

Energy Office and Energy Commission: Portland, Oregon prepared a comprehensive energy conservation policy in 1979. As a result, the Energy Office and Energy Commission was established to coordinate programs dealing with energy efficiency, transportation, land-use planning and water conservation. Funded by the City of Portland, several staff work with utilities, services providers, state energy agencies and other local government departments to operate programs such as the Block-by-Block Weatherization Program. A one-percent fee on all city government energy bills generates some of the revenue to operate the Energy Office. In the first year alone, potential energy savings of $250,000 were identified.

Planning for Community Energy, Environment and Economic Sustainability: Modeling software and energy planning computer programs, such as Planning for Community Energy, Environment and Economic Sustainability help communities such as San Diego and San Jose, California, Portland, Oregon and Vancouver, B.C. include energy decisions in building design and urban planning. The program quantitatively measures integrated actions to evaluate energy, environmental and economic benefits of decisions about energy supply options, building design, orientation and lay-out, as well as neighborhood density and lay-out, transportation decisions, and other urban planning issues.

Bonds to Finance Sustainable Energy Management

Energy Resource Management Plan: In Eugene, Oregon, the Water and Electric Board is financing the city's Energy Resource Management Plan with a $150-million bond issue. After a citizen-based resource planning effort, residents voted overwhelming in support of this initiative, which includes financing for energy efficiency, renewables, cogeneration, and hydro power (*Conservation Monitor* 1993b)

RESOURCES

Alliance to Save Energy deals with various energy policy issues and provides publications on model building codes, energy education, updates on federal energy policy, and more.

    1200 18th Street, N.W., Suite 900
    Washington, D.C.
    USA 20036
    Tel: 202/857-0666
    Fax: 202/331-9588
    E-mail: info@ase.org
    Web site: www.ase.org/

Alternative Energy Resources Organization's mission is to promote safe alternative energy sources and conservation, sustainable agriculture, and community self-reliance.

    25 South Ewing, Room 214
    Helena, Montana
    USA 59601
    Tel: 406/443-7272
    Fax: 406/442-9120
    E-mail: aero@desktop.org

American Council for an Energy-Efficient Economy conducts research on energy efficiency to stimulate the adoption of energy-conserving technologies and practices.

    1001 Connecticut Avenue, Suite 801
    Washington, D.C.
    USA 20036
    Tel: 202/429-8873
    Web site: www.aceee.org/

American Solar Energy Society promotes education in fields related to solar energy and publishes a variety of information on solar-related topics.

    2400 Central Avenue, G-1
    Boulder, Colorado
    USA 80301
    Tel: 303/443-3130
    Fax: 303/443-3212
    E-mail: ases@ases.org
    Web site: www.sni.net/solar/

Building Sustainable Communities: An Environmental Guide for Local Government: Energy-Efficiency and Production Energy-Aware Planning Guide, by Cheryl Sullivan and Vincent Robinson, describes successful local government energy policies and programs.

Community Energy Workbook: A Guide to Building a Sustainable Economy, by Alice Hubbard and Clay Fong (Rocky Mountain Institute 1995), offers plans that promote the economy in an environmentally responsible manner.

Energy Efficiency and Renewable Energy Network has a clearinghouse for providing information. The publication, *Sustainable Energy: A Local Government Planning Guide For A Sustainable Future,* includes tips on building local government support and contains copies of the Cities of San Jose, San Francisco and Portland's energy policies and options.

Energy Efficiency and Renewable Energy Clearinghouse
P.O. Box 3048
Merrifield, Virginia
USA 22116-0121
Toll-free: 800/DOE-EREC
Fax: 703/893-0400
E-mail: doe.erec@nciinc.com
Web site: www.eren.doe.gov/

Energy Ideas Clearinghouse provides access to comprehensive and objective energy information, education, resources, and technical assistance for increasing energy efficiency in the commercial and industrial sectors.

925 Plum Street, S.E.
Olympia, Washington
USA 98504-3171
Tel: 360/956-2237
E-mail: webmaster@energy.wsu.edu
Web site: www.energy.wsu.edu/ep/eic

U.S. Green Lights Program promotes energy efficiency through investment in energy-saving lighting.

U.S. Environmental Protection Agency
Atmospheric Pollution Prevention Division
401 M Street S.W. (6202J)
Washington, D.C.
USA 20460
Tel: 202/233-9190
Toll Free: 888/STAR-YES
Fax: 202/233-9569
Fax-back system: 202/233-9659
Web site: www.epa.gov/greenlights.html/

REFERENCES

Brower, M. 1990. *Cool Energy: The Renewable Solution to Global Warming.* Cambridge, Mass.: Union of Concerned Scientists.

Conservation Monitor. 1993a. "Emerald PUD, PBA Reach Landmark Agreement." July/August.

— — —. 1993b. "EWEB Voters Seek More Resource Independence." July/August.

Department of Energy, U.S. (DOE). 1992a. "Energy Dollars Relieve Municipal Budgets." *Tomorrow's Energy Today for Cities and Counties*, NREL. December.

— — —. 1992b. *A Local Government Planning Guide For A Sustainable Future.* Urban Consortium Energy Task Force. December.

Green Business Letter. 1997. June.

Helsinki Energy Board. 1989. District Heating. Helsinki: Helsinki Energy Board.

Home Energy. 1994. "The Jasper Energy Efficiency Project." March/April.

Hubbard, A., and C. Fong. 1995. *Community Energy Workbook: A Guide to Building a Sustainable Economy.* Snowmass, Colorado: Rocky Mountain Institute.

International Council for Local Environmental Initiatives (ICLEI). 1991. *The Urban CO2 Project.* Toronto: ICLEI.

Local Government Commission. 1990. "Model Ordinances for Environmental Protection." Sacramento, California: Local Government Commission.

Lowe, M.D. 1991. "Shaping Cities: The Environmental and Human Dimensions." *Worldwatch* 105. Washington, D.C.: Worldwatch Institute.

Millyard, K. 1992. "A Preliminary Carbon Dioxide Inventory for the City of Ottawa." Ottawa: Friends of the Earth.

Torrie, R. 1997. Urban Energy Management and the Cities of APEC — Opportunities and Challenges (draft). Prepared for the National Round Table on the Environment and the Economy, March.

ATMOSPHERIC CHANGE AND AIR QUALITY

Many scientists believe that the context for thinking about sustainable development for the next several decades will be global atmospheric change. Put simply, we are changing the composition of the earth's atmosphere. If the change continues at current rates, the world's weather may be significantly altered by the middle of the next century. While scientists are unable to say conclusively that recent storms and floods are a result of human-induced climatic change, the insurance industry is expressing serious concern about its increasing weather-related losses (ICLEI 1997a).

Although atmospheric change is a complex technical issue, only a few basic concepts are required to comprehend its implications and design community strategies to reduce its threat. This chapter addresses the key areas of atmospheric change that concern communities — local air quality, potential climate change, and ozone layer depletion. Then the economic consequences of addressing climate change are explored.

LOCAL AIR QUALITY

Local air quality obviously varies according to local conditions, but shares causes and solutions with broader atmospheric change issues. The release of atmospheric pollutants by human activity results in two local phenomena: smog and acid rain.

The combustion of fossil fuels, primarily from motor vehicles, produces a yellow-brown layer of pollution known as smog. It is especially evident over cities in summer months. Smog results from the reaction of nitrogen oxides and hydrocarbon gases with sunlight to produce ozone and other trace gases. Ground-level ozone inhibits photosynthesis in plants.

Sulphur dioxide, emitted from cement works, oil refineries, and various industrial sources, is a primary cause of acid rain. It can contribute to plant, forest, and crop damage, and deteriorate structures and materials.

What are the health effects of atmospheric pollutants? While we don't know all the answers yet, those that we do know give cause for concern. Nitrogen oxides (a byproduct of fossil fuel combustion from motor vehicles) can increase susceptibility to viral infections such as influenza, irritate the lungs, and cause bronchitis and pneumonia.

"It is imperative that the insurance industry in the United States become cognizant of changes occurring in our climate and its causes." Franklin W. Nutter, President, Reinsurance Association of America (ICLEI 1997a).

Ground-level ozone (which reacts with nitrogen oxides in sunlight) irritates the lungs and respiratory system, reduces resistance to colds and pneumonia, can aggravate heart disease, asthma, bronchitis, and emphysema, and is associated with the symptoms of dry cough, chest tightness or discomfort, sore throat, headache, and eye irritation. Sulphur dioxide and particulate matter concentrations can provoke or exacerbate cough, phlegm production, chest tightness and wheezing associated with asthma and chronic bronchitis. Low-level exposure to carbon monoxide from motor vehicles may exacerbate heart disease, and compromise brain function (French 1990; Kleinman et al. 1989).

CLIMATE CHANGE

Global warming is one possible consequence of atmospheric change. In essence, we might be giving the planet a fever by increasing the Earth's natural greenhouse effect. We know from personal experience that a fever allowed to rise unchecked poses serious health risks to the brain, the immune system, and many other key bodily functions. Likewise, an unchecked global fever poses serious health risks to food production systems (irrigation, growing seasons, crop failures, etc.) and many other key social and ecological functions that human civilization depends upon.

The greenhouse effect refers to heat retention in the earth's atmosphere. There has always been a natural greenhouse effect; without it the earth would be too cold for life. The problem now is what scientists call the enhanced greenhouse effect; in the last several decades we have dumped additional quantities of greenhouse gases into the atmosphere, which greatly increase its heat retention.

For the majority of North American communities, the most significant greenhouse gases to address are chlorofluorocarbons (CFCs), carbon dioxide, and methane.

OZONE LAYER DEPLETION

In the upper layer of the Earth's atmosphere, the stratosphere is a thin shield of ozone that limits the amount of ultraviolet radiation that can reach the Earth's surface. Depletion of the ozone layer causes an increase in ultraviolet radiation, which is expected to result in higher incidences of skin cancer, cataracts, immune system disorders, damage to crops and plant life, and destruction of marine phytoplankton.

Halocarbons

"There is now an effective consensus among the world's leading scientists and serious well-informed people outside the scientific community that there is a discernible human influence on the climate." John Browne, Chief Executive of British Petroleum (Clover 1997).

Ozone layer destruction is caused primarily by the release of a group of human-made chemicals known as halocarbons that have been used since the 1930s. CFCs, halons, and chlorocarbons including methyl chloroform and carbon tetrachloride drift up to the stratosphere where they destroy ozone molecules for 60-100 years. These gases also contribute to the greenhouse effect, trapping 20,000 times more heat, molecule for molecule, than carbon dioxide. Because it takes so long for ozone-depleting chemicals to reach the atmosphere, the ozone depletions now being observed are actually the result of releases prior to the 1980s. Most CFCs and related chemicals are still on their way up.

Ozone depleting chemicals are used as coolant materials in refrigerators, and in building and automobile air conditioners. They are also used as the blowing agent for foam products such as seat cushions, insulation, and foam containers, and they are used as cleaning solvents in the computer, aerospace, and metal products industries. Halon fire extinguishers and hospital sterilants also use ozone depleting chemicals (Local Government Commission 1990).

One pound of CFC-12 refrigerant, commonly known as R-12 and even more commonly as freon, can destroy 70,000 pounds of ozone. A 1994 United Nations Environment Program study estimated that every one percent decrease in the ozone layer results in at least a one-percent increase in the incidence of skin cancer (Sheff 1997). For these reasons, many communities have called for stricter actions. Making fast progress toward eliminating the release of ozone depleting chemicals is important since their ozone depleting capacity lasts for so long.

The cities of Irvine, California and Newark, New Jersey passed comprehensive bans on ozone-depleting compounds in 1989-90 when international agreements would have allowed their use for another decade. The leadership demonstrated by communities such as Irvine and Newark helped ensure that ozone depletion was put high on the agenda of senior governments.

On January 1, 1996, production of CFCs was to have ceased under the provisions of the Montreal Protocol of the Vienna Framework Convention on Ozone-Degrading Substances. Developing countries have a 10-year grace period before they must phase out production as well. The phase-out represents the culmination of diplomatic, scientific, and industrial work to forge an international consensus and to develop alternatives to these environmentally harmful substances (World Resources Institute et al. 1996). Consequently, communities no longer have to worry about taking a leadership role on ozone layer depletion, but they must concentrate on ensuring that these international agreements are enforced locally.

Carbon Dioxide

The recent progress witnessed in respect to ozone-layer depletion unfortunately does not apply to carbon dioxide (CO_2) emissions. Whereas phasing out ozone-degrading substances is essentially a technical problem, reducing atmospheric carbon dioxide emissions may require more fundamental long-term changes in how we organize our lives and our communities.

Carbon dioxide lingers for 100 years in the atmosphere and accounts for about half of the greenhouse effect. Carbon dioxide is fully integrated into our daily activities since it is released largely from fossil fuel combustion and from burn-

"Given the uncertainty associated with the effects of atmospheric change, should decision-makers act now or wait for more information? Global warming and the destruction of the ozone layer are essentially irreversible processes. If we wait to see the proof of these phenomena, the costs of dealing with changes in agriculture, forestry, and weather patterns will be much greater than if we act now to start reducing the likelihood of these events occurring" (City of Vancouver 1990).

CFC Smuggling

CFCs are invisible, the harm they do is both technical and abstract, and the service they provide is blandly and selfishly appealing. In the first three years since the domestic manufacture of chlorofluorocarbons began to be phased out as a result of the Montreal Protocol, an estimated 60 million pounds of illegal CFCs, with a street value of $1.5 billion, were smuggled into the United States. CFCs were replaced with relative ease in high-tech degreasers and solvents, refrigerators and home air-conditioning systems by 1993. However, while post-1993 vehicles use alternative chemicals in their air conditioners, some 80 million older Freon-spitting vehicles in the US alone must have their coolant replaced every two to three years. R-12 smugglers sell the coolant to auto-parts stores and various middlemen, who resell it to service stations and air-conditioning repair shops. These businesses can buy a 30-pound canister of R-12 for $400, charge a customer as much as $80 per pound, and pocket the $2000 difference. R-12 smuggling is a bigger business than gun-running or smuggling prescription drugs. The dollar value of intercepted CFCs is second only to that of intercepted drugs (Sheff 1997).

Global Warming as a Municipal Issue

The United Nations Intergovernmental Panel on Climate Change, a panel of world-renowned scientists, has concluded it is *certain* that "emissions resulting from human activities are substantially increasing the atmospheric concentrations of the greenhouse gases . . . resulting on average in an additional warming of the Earth's surface."

The major greenhouse gas forcing the rise in global temperatures is carbon dioxide (CO_2), produced largely through the burning of fossil fuels for energy use. The concentration of CO_2 in the atmosphere has risen about 25 percent since pre-industrial times and is continuing to rise at the rate of 0.5 percent annually due to human activities.

Critical scientific concerns about global warming are:

· Without action to reduce emissions of greenhouse gases from human activities, global warming may increase 2°C to 5°C, and sea levels may rise 30-100 centimeters (12-40 inches)over the next century.

· A continuous world-wide reduction of net CO_2 emissions of 1 percent to 2 percent per year would stabilize atmospheric concentrations of CO_2 by the middle of the next century.

· Many studies conclude that technical and cost-effective opportunities exist to reduce CO_2 emissions by at least 20 percent by 2005 in industrialized nations.

· These nations must implement reductions even greater than those required on average for the globe as a whole to allow for increased emissions from developing countries.

Cities, among the most energy-intensive ecosystems on the planet, are major producers of CO_2. As over half the world's population will live in urban areas by 2000, the reduction of fossil fuel use in cities will be vital to the implementation of an international climate change convention. Furthermore, many of the actions necessary to reduce CO_2 emissions — licensing, building codes, land-use planning, zoning, transit, and transportation plans — fall under the jurisdiction of municipal or regional governments (ICLEI 1991; IPCC 1996).

ing forests and plants. While deforestation may have contributed as much as 40 percent to the increase of carbon dioxide earlier in the century, *80 percent of today's carbon dioxide emissions are from fossil fuels* — coal, oil, and natural gas — and these will continue to be the most significant source (City of Vancouver 1990).

On a per person basis, Canada and the U.S. are among the world's largest consumers of fossil fuels and among the largest producers of carbon dioxide. For example, despite its relatively small population (one-half of 1 percent of the world's population), Canada is responsible for fully 2 percent of global greenhouse emissions. Other industrialized countries such as Japan and the U.K., with comparable standards of living, produce only half as much carbon dioxide per capita as do the U.S. and Canada (Flavin 1990). If North Americans are to help in reversing climate change, we must reduce our carbon dioxide emissions and contribute to the development of cleaner and more energy-efficient technologies. Transportation, land use, energy, and greening the city are all directly concerned with the challenge of reducing our carbon dioxide emissions.

The US Environmental Protection Agency has estimated that merely to stabilize atmospheric concentrations of CO_2 at the current level, carbon emissions must be cut by 50 percent to 80 percent by the middle of the next century. An important global action plan calls for the governments of all high- and medium-energy consuming countries to reduce their carbon dioxide emissions by 70 percent by 2030. Scientists and policy makers have offered short-term goals such as: cutting them by 20 percent by 2005 (Flavin 1990; IUCN et al. 1991; Toronto Conference Statement 1988). Yet while international bodies and national governments struggle to formulate policies to achieve these goals, *it is at the community level where most of these policies will be implemented.*

Despite commitments signed at the Rio Climate Convention in 1992 to stabilize greenhouse gas emissions at 1990 levels by 2000, U.S. emissions will probably have risen by 13 percent over that decade (*Economist* 1997). Canadian greenhouse gas emissions had risen 9.2 percent over 1990 levels by 1996, and current Environment Canada forecasts suggest that by 2010, Canadian emissions of greenhouse gases will be 18 percent above 1990 levels (Duffy 1997).

In the face of such challenges, many communities have started developing initiatives to address the root causes of environmental deterioration and to contribute solutions toward a sustainable future. They recognize that net fiscal, economic, and ecological benefits will accrue to those who get their environmental house in order.

Methane

Methane has received less media attention than other greenhouse gases, but it does play a significant role in local air quality and global atmospheric change. Methane, released from rotting organic matter such as bogs, wetlands, and landfills, is responsible for about 18 percent of the greenhouse effect. Although methane's lifespan in the atmosphere is approximately 10 years (versus up to 100 years for carbon dioxide and CFCs), methane's heat-trapping ability on a per-molecule basis is 25 times greater than carbon dioxide, and its presence is increasing in the atmosphere at a significantly faster rate than carbon dioxide (City of Vancouver 1990).

To initiate change, communities can construct methane gas collection systems for their landfills. When collected, methane can also be used as an energy source for the landfill or sewage plant, or sold to other users.

ECONOMIC BENEFITS OF ADDRESSING ATMOSPHERIC CHANGE

"No regrets" policies for reducing greenhouse gas emissions are policies which are either inexpensive (such as encouraging consumers to buy energy-efficient appliances) or worth implementing regardless of whether or not global warming proves to be a problem (such as reducing subsidies to fossil fuels). The Intergovernmental Panel on Climate Change calculates that cheap energy-efficiency measures could cut 10 percent to 30 percent of global energy consumption over the next decade (*Economist* 1997).

A number of economic benefits arise from policies that reduce atmospheric and air emissions. These include:
- lower energy costs that come from conservation and energy efficiency;
- growth of businesses that sell energy-efficient technologies;
- growth of renewable energy businesses;
- more disposable income from increasing taxes on the inefficient use of energy and using that money to reduce taxes on income and capital; and
- reduced repair costs for damage to the environment and human health caused by climate change and other pollutants.

As stated in a declaration signed by over 2,000 economists across North America, including six Nobel laureates:

> There are many potential policies to reduce greenhouse-gas emissions for which the total benefits outweigh the total costs . . . For the United States and Canada, sound economic analysis shows that there are policy options that would slow Climate Change without harming North American living standards, and those measures may in fact improve productivity in the longer run (*Economist* 1997; David Suzuki Foundation 1997).

Public Transportation and Greenhouse Gases

"Data from a study of 32 major world cities show that those cities with the highest public transport utilization (and these are virtually all rail-based systems) have the lowest greenhouse gas emissions. This is important as it is sometimes claimed that if we are going to use more public transport then it is not much better than the automobile when it comes to emissions per capita. However, this is because simplistic assumptions are being made about changing from one mode to the other. It is not just a matter of one trip by car being replaced by one trip on public transport. Once a mode is provided that can adequately compete with the automobile, then a range of other changes also occur. Only by considering these kinds of changes is it possible to do justice to the full benefit of rebuilding our cities around non-automobile modes.

The study data show that the cities with highest CO2 emissions have the greatest provision for the automobile in terms of roads and car parking. The data also show that the cities with the lowest CO2 emissions have the slowest moving traffic; this goes against the often stated theory that free-flowing traffic saves fuel and reduces emissions due to greater vehicle efficiency. A more realistic explanation is that congestion does indeed reduce vehicle efficiency but it also facilitates other modes, and most of all it keeps a city from sprawling and hence building in extra travel distances. The conclusion has been applied in the US, where the Environmental Protection Agency has now requested all new highway applications to consider the effect of increased vehicle miles of travel (VMT) on emissions from new highways, not just the effect of improved vehicle efficiency. This is an important step in recognizing the need for cleaner cities and not just cleaner cars.

In short, electric rail-based cities are clearly the way we should be heading in a greenhouse future" (Newman 1991).

Tools and Initiatives

Cities for Climate Protection Campaign

The International Council for Local Environmental Initiatives (ICLEI) Cities for Climate Protection Campaign is working with over 170 municipalities around the world to develop local strategies to reduce energy consumption and CO_2 emissions. The cities — representing perhaps 10 percent of global greenhouse gas emissions — have each pledged to develop a local action plan to reduce emissions.

North America: The Canadian cities of Vancouver, Victoria, Regina, Toronto, and others have set targets of freezing or reducing CO_2 emissions below 1988 levels by 2005. Canadian Cities for Climate Protection range from major urban centers such as Calgary, Edmonton, Toronto, and Vancouver to smaller towns such as Gondola Point, New Brunswick, and Port Alberni, B.C., and Fort Smith, Northwest Territories. U.S. Cities for Climate Protection range from major urban centers such as Atlanta, Chicago, Los Angeles, and Dade County, Florida to smaller towns such as Austin, Texas and Maplewood, New Jersey, and Chittenden County, Vermont.

Europe: Many European cities such as Frankfurt, Freiberg, and Hagen have set the more ambitious goal of halving CO_2 emissions by the year 2010. Hanover, Germany has proposed a comprehensive program that would include: switching fuels for electricity generation, retrofitting municipal buildings, strengthening energy performance standards in the building codes for new buildings, modifying land-use patterns, and improving waste management. Copenhagen has proposed a local energy tax and utility rate reform to reduce energy consumption (Sandborn 1996).

Urban Carbon Dioxide Reduction Plans

The International Council for Local Environmental Initiatives established The Urban CO_2 Project to help municipal governments develop effective strategies to reduce emissions of greenhouse gases. Twelve international urban jurisdictions participate in the program. Participating North American cities include: Portland, San Jose, Denver, Toronto, Minneapolis-St. Paul, and Dade County, Florida (ICLEI 1990, 1991, 1997b).

Minneapolis-St. Paul: developed a six-part strategy which includes a municipal action plan, diversification of the local transportation sector, expanded urban reforestation efforts, energy efficiency measures, energy supply measures (promoting renewables), and "precycling and recycling" (reducing product use and making products from secondary rather than raw materials).

Portland: also developed a six-part strategy which focuses on transportation, energy efficiency, renewable resources and cogeneration, recycling, tree planting, and lobbying for stronger federal actions with respect to vehicle fuel efficiency standards and tax incentives.

Toronto: "5 Best Measures" for action include: retrofitting city-owned buildings for energy efficiency and conservation; expanding the existing district energy system for heating and cooling, energy- and water-efficiency retrofits of all commercial and residential buildings; energy efficiency and conservation standards for new and existing buildings; and balancing employment and residential growth in the central area as part of an integrated land-use and transportation policy.

Dade County: The strategy focuses on four areas. Transportation objectives include improvements to mass transit, transportation demand management, promoting increased bicycle use, and increasing fuel efficiency. The land-use objective is to reduce vehicle miles traveled by 5 percent through mixed land use. Energy objectives include increasing efficiencies of county operations, decreasing residential sector energy use, expanding community tree plantings and white surfaces, and promoting public participation in energy conservation. Solid waste objectives include recycling 30 percent to 50 percent of the county's waste stream, recovering and utilizing landfill methane, and reducing the generation of solid waste by up to 5 percent.

Airshed Quality Management

For especially significant environmental problems, local governments have the ability and will to take significant corrective actions. The Los Angeles South Coast Air Quality District plan is the most drastic, comprehensive, and expensive effort to improve air quality ever drawn up locally in the U.S. While specific actions proposed were not mandated by the federal government, court decisions in response to the region's non-compliance with federal air quality standards were a major factor in the development of the local plan. Implementation of the plan will be a local responsibility (Cone 1997; OECD 1990; SCAG 1989; SCAQMD 1989).

Auto-Use Restrictions: In early 1989, an extensive three-stage program to substantially improve air quality was adopted for the metropolitan area of Los Angeles, California. The program's first stage (1989-93) includes tightening restrictions (at a cost of $2.8 billion per year) on the use of private automobiles and on pollution-causing industrial and household activities, including deodorants, hair sprays, perfume, nail polish removers, and bathroom cleaners.

Conversion to Cleaner Fuel: During its second stage (1993-98), all diesel buses, 70 percent of freight vehicles, and 40 percent of private automobiles will be required to convert to cleaner fuels, with an additional 50-percent reduction of industrial and consumer-related emissions. Smog-causing fumes from more than 3,000 consumer products — including automotive polishes, heavy-duty hand soaps, paint removers, metal polishes, spot removers, herbicides, lubricants, floor wax strippers, and hair shine sprays — must be cut in half. Although individually, household items add a miniscule amount of pollution to California's air, collectively they spew several hundred tons of hydrocarbons daily, which combine with nitrogen oxides in sunlight to form lung-irritating ozone.

Gasoline Prohibition: The final stage of the program anticipates the total prohibition of gasoline fuels in automobiles by the year 2007 — a prohibition that assumes the availability of new, perhaps unknown, technologies emerging as viable commercial alternatives to gasoline fueled vehicles. A key to the success of the plan is a redirection of development patterns, employment and housing locations, and a substantial reduction in travel from homes to employment centers. This redirection must be led cooperatively by communities within the Los Angeles metropolitan area.

RESOURCES

Alfonso Cipres Villareal, head of the Mexican Ecologists Movement, said his organization plans to put up 10 booths on street corners around Mexico City to sell clean air. Thirty-second shots of oxygen will sell for about CDN$2 (Reuter 1991).

The Changing Atmosphere: Strategies for Reducing CO2 Emissions, Volume One: *Policy Overview; Volume Two: Technical Volume* (Toronto: City of Toronto, Special Advisory Committee on the Environment, Report Number Two, March 1991) is available from:

Committees Secretary
City Clerks Department
City Hall
100 Queen Street West
Toronto, Ontario
Canada M5H 2N2
Tel: 416/392-6745
Web site: www.city.toronto.on.ca

Clouds of Change: Final Report of the City of Vancouver Task Force on Atmospheric Change (Vancouver: City of Vancouver, 1990) is available from:

Planning Department
City of Vancouver
453 West 12th Ave.
Vancouver, B.C.
Canada V5Y 1V4
Tel: 604/873-7344
Web site: www.city.vancouver.bc.ca/

International Council for Local Environmental Initiatives established the Cities for Climate Protection Campaign to help cities develop local action plans to reduce local emissions of toxic pollutants with special emphasis on CO_2 emissions. The Council also established The Urban CO2 Project to help municipal governments develop effective strategies to reduce emissions of greenhouse gases. For more information, contact ICLEI at:

New City Hall, East Tower, 8th floor
Toronto, Ontario
Canada M5H 2N2
Tel: 416/392-1462
Fax: 416/392-1478
Web site: www.iclei.org

REFERENCES

City of Vancouver. 1990. *Clouds of Change: Final Report of the City of Vancouver Task Force on Atmospheric Change.* Two volumes. Vancouver: City of Vancouver.

Clover, C. 1997. "Oil Firms Back Move From Fossil Fuels to Alternatives." *Daily Telegraph* (London), reprinted in *Vancouver Sun*, 23 May 1997, p. A1.

Cone, M. 1997. "California Takes Smog Fight Home." *Los Angeles Times.* Reprinted in *Vancouver Sun*, 25 July 1997, p. A17.

David Suzuki Foundation. 1997. "Preventing Climate Change." *Report* April.

Duffy, A.1997. "Canada Faces a Diminished Role." *Vancouver Sun*, 21 June, p. G4.

Economist, The. 1997. "Warm Words." *Economist* 343 (8021) 14 June pp. 89-90.

Flavin, C. 1990. "Slowing Global Warming." In *State of the World 1990: A Worldwatch Institute Report on Progress Toward a Sustainable Society*, L.R. Brown, ed. New York/London: W.W. Norton. pp. 17-38.

French, H.F. 1990. "Clearing the Air." In *State of the World 1990*, L. Brown, ed. New York/London: W.W. Norton.

International Council for Local Environmental Initiatives (ICLEI). 1990. The Urban CO_2 Project proposal. Cambridge, Mass.: ICLEI.

— — — . 1991. The Urban CO_2 Project. Toronto: ICLEI.

— — — . 1997a. "Cities for Climate Protection Campaign." *Campaign Update* 3 (Winter).

— — — . 1997b. Cities for Climate Protection Campaign, "Cities in Action." <www.iclei.org>.

Intergovernmental Panel on Climate Change (IPCC). 1966. IPCC Second Assessment Synthesis of Scientific-Technical Information Relevant to Interpreting Article 2 of the U.N. Framework Convention on Climate Change 1995, January draft. Geneva: World Meterological Organization/United Nations Environment Program.

Kleinman, M. T. et al. 1989. "Effects On Human Health of Pollutants in the South Coast Air Basin" El Monte, Calif.: South Coast Air Quality Management District/ California State University Fullerton Foundation.

Local Government Commission. 1990. *Model Ordinances: Addressing Ozone Layer Destruction.* Sacramento, Calif.: Local Government Commission.

Newman, P. 1991. "Greenhouse, Oil and Cities." *Futures* (May): 335-48.

Organization for Economic Cooperation and Development (OECD). 1990. *Environmental Policies for Cities in the 1990s.* Paris: OECD.

Reuter. 1991. "Mexico City Street-Vending Machines to Sell Oxygen." *Vancouver Sun*, 8 February, p. A8.

Sandborn, C. 1996. "Lessons From the Cities Summit: Toward Democracy and

Sustainability." In *Urban Green Governance: The Views from the United Nations Conference on Human Settlements*, M. M'Gonigle, ed. Victoria: University of Victoria Faculty of Law, Eco-Research Chair.

Sheff, D. 1997. "The Chilling Effect." *Outside* 22(8) August: 90-125.

South Coast Association of Governments (SCAG) and South Coast Air Quality Management District (SCAQMD). 1989. *Air Quality Management Plan: South Coast Air Basin.* Los Angeles: SCAG/SCAQMD.

South Coast Air Quality Management District (SCAQMD). 1989. *The Path to Clean Air: Attainment Strategies.* El Monte, Calif.: SCAQMD.

Toronto Conference Statement. 1988. Presented to The Changing Atmosphere: Implications for Global Security, Environment Canada, Toronto, 27-30 June.

World Conservation Union (IUCN), United Nations Environment Program (UNEP), and World Wide Fund for Nature (WWF). 1991. *Caring for the Earth: A Strategy for Sustainable Living.* Gland, Switzerland: IUCN/UNEP/WWF.

World Resources Institute, UNEP, United Nations Development Program, and World Bank. 1996. *World Resources 1996-97: The Urban Environment.* New York: Oxford University Press.

Transportation Planning and Traffic Management

Each second, another new car comes on the world's roads. Sixty cars a minute, 3,600 cars an hour, 100,000 cars a day. In 1950, there were 2.6 billion people on Earth and 50 million cars in the world. Nearly 50 years later, the human population has more than doubled, while the car population has increased *ten-fold* — to 500 million. The number of new cars is increasing by 38 million to 50 million cars per year (Elsworth 1995; Tunali 1996). Our obsession with the automobile is clearly unsustainable.

Unsustainable transport systems not only are a major contributor to atmosphere change, but also lead to increasing congestion, longer commuting times, increasing demands for shorter work hours to compensate for longer travel hours, and higher prices due to reduced worker productivity. In fact, the primary objective of conventional traffic management has been to move vehicles in and around communities as rapidly and efficiently as possible using strategies such as designation of one way streets, synchronization of traffic signals, road widening, and construction of left-hand turn bays.

Governments face increasing difficulties in funding expansion of transportation infrastructure to meet these continuous increases in demand. Even if the enormous financial challenge of meeting demand for such infrastructure could be met, our transportation dilemma would be far from solved. In the words of Whitelegg (1966): "If we build a freeway system or an extended airport system to meet some prediction of future demand, then we should not be surprised to discover that these investments hasten our progress in that direction. Our plans and analyses boomerang so that our efforts are rewarded by the return of the problem, usually with some force and destructive impact."

The term "automobile dependency" was coined in the 1980s by Australian researchers Peter Newman and Jeffrey Kenworthy to help define our transportation challenges. Rather than try to eliminate cars altogether, an idea which few people consider realistic, we should focus on breaking our addiction to, or dependence upon, the automobile. Cities in the U.S. have accelerated dramatically in their dependence on the automobile between 1980 and 1990, and have transit-use rates that are the lowest in the world by a significant margin (Kenworthy and Laube 1996). This chapter examines the costs, both environmental and social, of our current transportation system, the myths of technical fixes, and ways to move toward sustainable transportation.

TRUE COSTS OF DRIVING

Driving a car incurs more costs than gas, insurance, maintenance and parking. For the U.S. as a whole, the total costs from motor vehicles (e.g., air pollution, crashes, noise, time stuck in traffic, run-off into waterways, pollution from manufacturing vehicles, tires, and batteries, and pollution from disposing of them, etc.) include: $20 billion in taxpayer subsidies; $290 billion in social and environmental damage; and $415 billion in costs borne by drivers. The total cost is $725 billion annually (Komanoff 1995).

There is no clear relationship between the benefits of a car trip and the social costs incurred. Car-related taxes paid by motorists can add up to much more than government spending on roads, but the taxes are usually levied on the car itself, not on its use. One of the most significant barriers to more sustainable transportation systems is the manner in which motorists pay (or are subsidized) for their motor vehicle use. High fixed costs of motor vehicle acquisition combined with low incremental user costs (e.g., free parking, free roads, and in some countries like the U.S., very low motor fuel taxes) encourage rapid growth of motor vehicle use (Replogle 1996).

How Fast Are We Really Going?

There may be more costs involved in driving that most of us realize, but at least we get high-speed mobility for our pains, don't we? In 1997 the average American spent $6500 per year to operate a car, according to the American Automobile Association (Kay 1997). Over two decades ago Illich (1974) calculated that typical Americans devote more than 1,600 hours a year to their car:

> They sit in it while it goes and while it stands idling. They park it and search for it. They earn the money to put down on it and to meet the monthly installments. They work to pay for petrol, tolls, insurance, taxes, and tickets. They spend four of their sixteen waking hours on the road or gathering their resources for it. And this figure does not take into account the time consumed by other activities dictated by transport: time spent in hospitals, traffic courts, and garages; time spent watching automobile commercials or attending consumer education meetings to improve the quality of the next buy. The model American puts in 1,600 hours to go 7,500 miles; less than five miles per hour.

In countries deprived of a transportation industry, Illich (1974) observed that people manage to go the same speed, walking wherever they want to go. They allocate only 3 percent to 8 percent of their society's energy and monetary budget to traffic instead of 28 percent. "What distinguishes the traffic in rich countries from the traffic in poor countries," he says, "is not more mileage per hour of life-time for the majority, but more hours of compulsory consumption of high doses of energy, packaged and unequally distributed by the transportation industry."

We've come a long way since Illich's observations in 1974, right? Wrong. According

"Perhaps our age will be known to the future historian as the age of the bulldozer and the exterminator; and in many parts of the country the building of a highway has about the same results upon vegetation and human structures as the passage of a tornado or the blast of an atom bomb. Nowhere is this bulldozing habit of mind so disastrous as in the approach to the city. Since the engineer regards his own work as more important than the human functions it serves, he does not hesitate to lay waste to woods, streams, parks, and human neighborhoods in order to carry his roads straight to their supposed destinations" (Mumford 1964).

to the Canadian Automobile Association, Canadians spend about $7,000 a year on their cars for payments, repairs, gas and insurance to travel about 20,000 kilometers (12,420 miles. According to Roberts (1995), "Most of these cars can hit 120 kilometres an hour, but how fast do they actually go? To afford $7,000 clear, most Canadians have to work at least 12 weeks, 40 hours a week. That's 480 hours at zero kilometres per hour. Most drivers average less than 40 kilometres per hour, when traffic jams and speed limits are taken into account. That's 500 hours of less than pure enjoyment in the car. Total it up, and the typical driver takes 980 hours to drive 20,000 kilometres: a little less than 20 kilometres [12.5 miles] per hour."

Traffic and Social Networks

A landmark 1969 study by Donald Appleyard attempted to quantify for the first time how traffic levels and speed erode the social networks of a neighborhood. Residents on three San Francisco streets — one with light traffic, one with moderate traffic, and one with heavy traffic — were interviewed to measure how they were affected by their streets. The

> "Americans continue to own more cars and drive more miles in them [than their European or Japanese counterparts]: the average American car driver travels almost 20,000 kilometers (about 12,400 miles) a year, whereas the European one does only 14,000 kilometers. This does not have much to do with the size of the country: most trips are urban, with an average length of about 14 kilometers, the same as in Britain and somewhat less than in Germany. Part of the answer is that buses and trains in America account for barely 3 percent of travel mileage, whereas in Europe the figure is over 15 percent. The rest of the answer lies in the sprawling low-density structure of American suburbs, which involve greater distances between homes and shops, schools and other amenities" (Economist 1996).

housing type and population profiles were similar for each street, except that there were more families with children on the light traffic street. On the light-traffic street, residents were found to have three times as many local friends and twice as many acquaintances as those on the heavy-traffic street. Appleyard attributes this to two main factors: it was easier to cross the light-traffic street, and there were more children. People living on the light-traffic street felt a sense of ownership — that the street was an important part of their community.

In contrast, there was little social interaction on the heavy-traffic street: people seldom stopped to chat with neighbors, and there was a sense of loneliness among residents. As traffic conditions on their street deteriorated, residents were faced with three choices: adapt, withdraw, or move out. Families with children had more or less moved away from the heavy-traffic street. The residents remaining on the heavy-traffic street were those who could tolerate high traffic levels and those who were too poor or too old to move (Egan 1995).

An Australian study highlighted the vulnerability of the elderly in a car-dependent city by showing that they are less transport-independent due to a much higher proportion who do not drive; more isolated due to the physical distances and poor public transport in low density suburbs; and more prone to injury from vehicles while walking. The study suggests that the time to provide improved urban design options for the elderly (such as enhanced transit, traffic calming, and urban villages) is before the aging of the "baby boom" generation peaks in the early years of the new century (Newman 1991).

TECHNICAL FIXES

Ah, but soon we'll have electric cars, low- or zero-emission vehicles, alternative fuels, hydrogen buses, smart highways, mental telepathy, the transporter from Star Trek ("Beam me up, Scotty!").

Hypercars

Energy activist Amory Lovins of the Rocky Mountain Institute in Colorado is famous for showing utility companies how to produce "negawatts" from conservation rather than megawatts from new and expanded power plants. He is also trying to show the automobile industry that a new kind of ultralight, super-efficient vehicle he calls a "hypercar" could result in "negatrips." While a revolution in vehicle manufacturing could produce many desirable benefits in terms of fuel efficiency, safety, and costs, even Lovins acknowledges that hypercars cannot solve the problem of too many people driving too many miles in too many cars, "and could make it even worse by making driving cheaper and more attractive." Making cars seem environmentally benign "means only that we'll run out of roads and patience rather than air and oil," and further underscores the need for fundamental reforms in urban form and land use (Lovins 1996).

Indeed, the most worrying transport problems are not congestion, pollution and shortage of energy:

> [Instead, they are] the consumption of space for the means of travel, the despoliation of rural landscapes and historic towns, the growing disparities in access to opportunities between those who can drive and those who cannot, the danger that denies children their traditional freedoms, and the paranoia, anomie and social disintegration that result from a level of mobility that is creating a world of strangers. The principal barrier to a morally and politically sustainable transport policy is the belief that there are technical fixes for these problems (Adams 1996).

Telecommunications

Now that the era of electronic communications is in high gear, many large employers are implementing or considering options for telecommunications. Telecommuting has potential to substitute for some of the commuting that goes on in and between our communities, and so may lead to a reduction in vehicle trips generated. Telecommuting also has potential to *increase* vehicle trips in our communities. People working from home may need to make more trips per day than they would simply going to the workplace and having all their working requirements in one place. Working from the "electronic cottage" may also encourage flight from urban centers and thus promote further sprawl development of the countryside with its attendant problems.

Telecommuting poses special problems for certain kinds of employees. Working parents, especially of younger children, often find it much more difficult to find daycare services near their homes than near their workplaces (Gurstein 1996).

REDUCING AUTOMOBILE DEPENDENCY

Efforts to relieve traffic congestion alone do little to reduce polluting emissions or the amount of fuel consumed. Cities must now stress reduction of single-occupancy vehicle trips as the only sound way to achieve improved air quality, reduce energy consumption contributing to atmospheric change, and relieve traffic congestion.

Sustainable transportation planning and traffic management initiatives are usually motivated by goals to reduce the number of automobile trips; increase opportunities for non-automobile trips; increase opportunities for non-auto transportation including bicycles, walking, rail, buses, and alternative vehicles; and reduce the use of gasoline and diesel fuel in conventional buses, autos, and trucks.

The concept of "sustainable transportation" calls for a more holistic approach to community planning, policy, and investment to achieve a diverse and balanced mix of transportation modes and a sensible arrangement of land use that enables conservative use of energy and capital to fulfill mobility needs. In short, "sustainable transportation strategies are those that can meet the basic mobility needs of all and be sustained into the foreseeable future without destruction of the local or planetary resource base" (Replogle 1995).

To be acceptable to consumers, governments, and the private sector, sustainable transportation must meet several goals simultaneously: minimize costs; promote economic development; minimize environmental degradation and the resultant impacts on human health; minimize imports of oil; maximize safety; and maximize accessibility by all to the services provided by transportation. In other words, "the goals of sustainable transportation overlap substantially with the goals of achieving livable communities" (Bleviss 1996).

A comparison of global cities over the period 1980-90 reveals large differences in automobile dependence with strong implications for the future sustainability of cities in different countries. The study demonstrates there are significant statistical relationships between the key transport and land-use variables. First, urban density is a key determinant of auto and transit use, as well as the relative role of transit (auto use increases and transit decreases with decreasing density). Road provision, parking, and non-motorized mode use are all also strongly associated with the pattern of auto-dependence across cities. To reduce automobile dependence, the following directions should be pursued:

- *Land-use objectives*: more transit-oriented, higher density, mixed land uses which help to halt the growth in auto-based development;
- *Private transport objectives*: stabilized or lower car use and less emphasis on infrastructure for cars;
- *Public transport objectives*: higher quality transit systems, especially rail, which are more competitive with cars; and

- *Non-motorized mode objectives*: greater safety and amenity for walking and cycling and increased use of these modes (Kenworthy and Laube 1996).

In general, local initiatives should aim to encourage transit over personal automobile use by, for example, reducing the subsidies to private vehicles; identify means for managing transportation demands, especially of commuters; and emphasize bicycle and pedestrian networks as valid components of a regional transportation strategy.

Management Strategies

Transportation system management is one possible planning route in striving toward more sustainable transportation. It aims to affect the supply of transportation services by attempts to increase the person-carrying capacity of the road system without building additional road capacity, or by simply allowing congestion to become worse, thereby discouraging vehicle travel. Measures such as high occupancy vehicle (HOV) and transit-only lanes, queue jumpers, preferred parking for HOV vehicles and toll-free privileges for HOVs help to increase the person-carrying capacity of the road system without the need for additional road capacity.

HOV and transit-only lanes are the most common means of increasing road capacity. However in congested urban centers, transit-only lanes are more efficient since they have the capacity to carry far more people per hour. At freeway speeds, for example, a full bus or rail car can carry as many people as a lane of car-pool traffic up to a kilometer long (Leman et al. 1994). In 1982, New York established bus lanes covering a total of 19 kilometers (about 12 miles). These lanes increased bus speeds by 15 percent to 25 percent and have even allowed car traffic to move 10 percent to 20 percent more quickly (Zuckermann 1991).

However, all too often, transportation planning takes projected demand as a given and attempts to satisfy it rather than trying to reduce it. Growing traffic congestion, limited transportation budgets, and increasing opposition to roadway construction from environmental and community groups have led transportation policy makers to accept that accommodating growth solely by increasing transportation system capacity imposes greater costs on society than are warranted by the benefits (Wachs 1989). Policy makers now frequently admit that "we cannot build our way out of the problem."

While transportation system management strategies aim to affect the supply of transportation services, the goal of transportation demand management strategies is to influence people to shift to more efficient modes of transportation and to travel during off-peak hours. Since the 1980s, there has been a tremendous increase in the number and variety of demand management measures in use. Some strategies attempt to manage transportation demand with regulations and pricing schemes, such as parking management and time-of-day charges for roads; others manage demand by promoting alternative-mode choices, such as ridesharing and telecommuting. The most successful policies integrate supply and demand strategies to create a transportation network that promotes efficient, low-polluting choices.

Walking and Cycling

For distances under two kilometers (1.2 miles) pedestrian traffic can play a large role if provided with safe and attractive conditions. Pedestrian improvements should not be limited to small islands in the form of pedestrian zones, but rather should be included as part of the area-wide road network. The City of Boulder, Colorado even hosts an annual Pedestrian Conference.

Bicycles are ideal for use in highly congested urban centers and thus can play an important role in sustainable transportation strategies. They avoid air pollution and high levels of fuel consumption associated with low-vehicle operating speeds and short distance, cold start trips. Bikes also help reduce congestion since they demand far less space than motor vehicles. Experience in Davis, California and Toronto suggest that where cycling facilities are improved, the number and frequency of cycling trips increases dramatically (Toronto City Cycling Committee 1994).

Many cities have comprehensive bicycle plans that encourage cycling by recommending improved street design, educating cyclists, and enforcing cycling regulations. However, these plans often cater largely to those who already cycle. Depending upon local geography and other place-specific circumstances, they generally propose that bicycles and cars should travel on the same arterial roads in traffic ("integration"), or that bikes should travel in bike lanes (if the streets are wide enough), or that bikes should have separate paths or rights-of-way ("segregation"). Rarely has either integration or segregation led directly to a significant increase in transportation (versus recreational) cycling, nor are they likely to.

The rationale for the integration approach came mainly from a controversial California bicycle enthusiast and engineer named John Forester. Unlike most international cycling specialists, Forester has argued it is safest to "integrate" bikes with cars on main streets. He believes "segregated" routes for cyclists cause accidents when cyclists and cars meet at intersections. Although Forester has not changed his opinion, he has acknowledged that his "theory" is impossible to prove with existing quantitative data (Vancouver Bikeway Network Group 1991). Even if one were to adopt Forester's view that main roads are safe for everyday cycling, most people still don't see it that way. Perceptions are powerful. To encourage more people to cycle regularly, a network of bicycle routes that are perceived as safe must be provided.

Many communities have narrow streets and therefore bike lanes are not a viable option. Bike paths are nice for recreation, but are not a serious transportation alternative unless they go where people need to travel.

It is a daunting challenge for many communities to find the space or finances to build separate bicycle paths. But many communities have a large network of quiet residential side-streets running parallel to main arteries. They offer the potential for a compromise solution that will satisfy both the integrationists and the segregationists. These residential streets can provide the basis for a network of bicycle routes that will be both safe and perceived as safe — leading to a significant increase in cycling.

Tools and Initiatives

Automobile Restrictions

Taming the Automobile: Freiburg, in former West Germany has shown that it is indeed possible to virtually stop the growth of car use, even when car ownership is growing. Car use in Freiburg remained virtually constant between 1976 and 1991, while transit passengers have increased 53 percent and bicycle trips have risen 96 percent. Freiburg's success at "taming the automobile" is attributed to sharply restricting automobile use in the city; providing affordable, convenient and safe alternatives to auto use; and strictly regulating development to ensure a compact land-use pattern conducive to public transport, bicycling, and walking. Restricted auto use has been achieved by pedestrianization of the city center, area-wide traffic calming (city-wide speed limit of 30 kilometers (about 19 miles) per hour in residential areas) and more difficult, expensive parking. Transit improvements have focused on upgrading the light rail system, with buses used as feeders to the system. Land use was regulated by limiting the overall amount of land available to development and strictly zoning land for agriculture, forests, wildlife reserves, or undeveloped open space (Pucher and Clorer 1992).

Car Co-ops

Car cooperatives and neighborhood car rental agencies allow individuals to share access to a vehicle, without incurring the high costs associated with ownership. They are popular in Europe, where over 60 towns and cities have established car cooperatives since 1994 (Engwicht 1996). North American car co-ops exist in Montreal, Vancouver, Victoria, B.C., and Eugene, Oregon.

Council-run Car Club: In Scotland, the Edinburgh Council has approved a $13 million, 100-unit housing development in which residents will sign an agreement not to own a car but to use one from a "pool." Residents will pay about $320 to join a council-run car club that will maintain and insure a fleet of vehicles in an on-site garage. They will be able to reserve cars at any time of the day or night at an hour's notice and will pay mileage and rental charges for each journey (Arlidge 1997).

Traffic Calming on a commercial street

Street Trees\Plantings

Retain Onstreet Parking

Bus Bulges

Narrow Traffic Lanes

Bike Lanes

Curb Extensions

Christopher Small.

Road Pricing

There is a growing interest in road pricing strategies to check the trend in increased automobile use and its adverse environmental effects, especially in inner-city areas. The Singapore Area Licensing Scheme, a form of road pricing instituted in 1975, demonstrated that such schemes can be used successfully for reducing peak-hour traffic volumes, reducing single-occupant vehicle traffic, and encouraging buses and car pools.

Toll System: In February 1990, Oslo, Norway implemented a toll system. Oslo motorists are charged NKr 10 (U.S.$1.50) to pass through one of the 18 gantries set up around the central business district. Prepayment coupons costing NKr 180 (U.S.$27) for 20 trips or NKr 2,200 (U.S.$330) for an annual pass are also available. Coupons need to be displayed in the windshield. Prepayment lanes are enforced by a number plate video surveillance and a 1:20 spot check to deter sneak drivers. Some 100,000 people were reported to subscribe to the prepayment system in the first few months (*Public Innovation Abroad* 1990b).

Traffic circles work to slow traffic in residential neighborhoods. This Vancouver traffic circle was built by the city and planted by local residents

Traffic Calming

Traffic calming is used widely in Europe and Australia, and increasingly in North America. Traffic calming measures include installation of stop signs, speed bumps, and/or traffic circles to slow or calm traffic, allowing roads to better accommodate a range of different road users and activities.

Former West Germany's traffic calming schemes have multiplied into the thousands since they were started in the 1970s. Originally intended for residential areas, the technique is now spreading over whole cities. Traffic calming greatly improves the quality of life in neighborhoods where it is implemented, and so is gathering popularity in many countries, including Italy, Japan, Australia, Sweden, and Switzerland. Such restraints are so well-received in Denmark that local residents themselves are often willing to pay for the measure. In North America, Berkeley was one of the first communities to experiment with a slow-streets system. Many others are now experimenting as well.

Collision Decrease: A recent study for the Insurance Corporation of British Columbia reviewed 85 traffic-calming case studies from around the world and found that the decrease in collision frequency ranged from 18 percent to *100 percent*. Traffic calming is also cost-effective. In four

This formerly two-lane road was "calmed," and the excess road space converted into park space

detailed Vancouver-area cases, collision frequency was reduced from 18 percent to 60 percent, saving the insurance company from $50,000 to $300,000 per year in each case (Hamilton 1996).

Layout Change: For more than two decades Dutch cities like Delft, Groningen, and Maastricht have calmed traffic by changing the layout of the residential street, transforming it into a *woonerf*, or "living yard." In the *woonerf*, cars are forced to navigate slowly around carefully placed trees and other landscaping. Since motor traffic cannot monopolize the entire breadth of the street, much of the space becomes more open to walking, cycling, and children's play. Automobiles are free to enter the *woonerf*, but only as guests, while non-motorized traffic has priority. Experience with traffic calming has shown that it is most effective if widely implemented, so that motor traffic problems are not simply diverted to nearby streets. Traffic has been calmed on over 30 percent of residential roads in Maastricht.

Parking Measures

Ending the widespread employer practice of providing free or heavily subsidized parking to employees is a promising option for relieving both congestion and air pollution. By one estimate *free parking induces more travel than free gasoline would*. Parking pricing can be regressive, so it is important to investigate variations of pricing policies that minimize regressive impacts, or to develop complementary policies that mitigate those effects. According to Cameron (1991), "Studies of employer-paid parking indicate that middle- to upper-income groups are the principal recipients of these benefits. Even this is not a critical finding since the policy prescription for parking is simply to offer employees the cash equivalent of the parking space, which could be a progressive policy."

Transportation researchers estimate that residential parking requirements add more than $600 per year, or $50 per month, to the average cost of rental housing, regardless of whether or how much the residents need or use the parking facilities (Cameron 1991).

Reduction in Required Parking: Several cities have found that parking programs pay. Sacramento, California grants developers a five percent reduction in required parking for providing bicycle facilities, 15 percent for providing marked car/van-pool spaces, and 60 percent for purchasing transit passes for tenants of new offices.

Preferential Parking for Car-Pools: Portland, Oregon and Seattle, Washington lead in on-street preferential parking programs for car-pools. Among the incentives: poolers are allowed to park downtown all day at specific metered locations; are exempted from hourly parking limits and meter fees; and enjoy spaces closest to building entrances.

Increased Parking Rates: The Canadian federal government increased its parking rates for federal employees in Ottawa, resulting in: a 23 percent reduction in employees driving to work; a 16 percent increase in transit ridership among federal employees; and an increase in average vehicle occupancy from 1.33 to 1.41 passengers.

"In the US, each car consumes 4,000 square feet of parking space (including at home), which is almost three times the living area of the average family home" (Renner 1988).

HOV Pricing Strategies: Preferential high-occupancy vehicle (HOV) pricing strategies are also highly effective. Differential parking rates paid by the employer are applied, with two-person car-pools getting a 50-percent reduction, three-person car-pools 75 percent, and van-pools 100 percent. Montgomery County, Maryland has achieved over 75 percent use of HOV spaces. Seattle has achieved 95-percent HOV use in public spaces and 35 percent in private spaces (Totten 1989).

Area Wide Traffic Management

The aim of area wide traffic management is improving transportation efficiency by reducing over-reliance upon motorized vehicles within urban centers. Monheim (1986) describes this approach as "[reducing] car traffic in general by changes to other transport modes, i.e. change from car use to walking, bicycle and public transport, and by reducing many privileges and road space which in recent years have been given uniquely to the car." It focuses on the whole road network, the public transport system, land use, and all different transport modes. Scandinavia, the Netherlands, Italy, Switzerland, Japan, and Germany currently practice its principles (Monheim 1986).

Groningen: In 1992, the Dutch City of Groningen (with a population of 170,000), dug up its city-center highways and took a variety of steps to make the bicycle the main form of transport. As a consequence, business has improved, rents have increased, and the flow of people out of the city has reversed. Local businesses who once fought any restraint on the automobile are now calling for more (MacDuffee 1996).

Saarbrücken: The capital of former West Germany's Saarland, along the French border, has a population of about 200,000. Saarbrücken now has plans calling for the entire municipal area to be a 30-kilometer- (almost 19 miles-) per-hour zone, although a speed limit of 50 kilometers (31 miles) per hour will still apply on certain priority roads chosen according to their importance for traffic. The aim is to achieve the greatest possible restraint of traffic and mainly to reduce the number of accidents involving children, old people, and bicyclists in residential areas. It is anticipated that the 30-kilometer-per-hour speed limit will also stabilize traffic flow and thus result in a significant reduction of noise and exhausts in the residential areas (Leonhardt 1990).

North America: Although area wide traffic management has not been attempted in any North American cities, one recent study (Davidson 1997) identified 36 traffic management measures that were potentially applicable within Vancouver's downtown core. The study says this innovative planning strategy has exciting implications for North American city centers struggling to balance social, economic, and environmental imperatives.

Transport Innovation

Improved transportation efficiency hinges upon improved public transport. Substantial volumes of car traffic can potentially be transferred to bus and rail; yet a number of different strategies are needed, including service innovations, payment innovations, and rail system development.

Curitiba, Brazil: Rather than invest in an expensive new metro or light rail system, Curitiba decided to improve upon its bus system in conjunction with supportive land

"The demand for traffic control was recognized at least as early as the first century A.D., when congestion caused Julius Ceasar to ban wheeled traffic from Rome in the daytime" (Rajan 1996).

Bus bulges are a good way to speed up buses and improve the sidewalk environment. The curb is extended to meet the buses so they do not have to pull in and out to wait for traffic

From City of Vancouver (1996)

use planning (Keeler-Hemphill 1992). From a single bus line serving the entire city of 600,000 people in 1974, Curitiba's bus network has continually expanded to meet growing demand. The transportation system is hierarchical, with different buses playing different roles. Silver buses, for example, have their doors on the left side, only stop at every third stop, and drive with regular traffic on normal streets, while express buses are bright red and have doors on the right side. Passengers can get anywhere in the city with a single fare of about 55 cents. In 1991, Curitiba introduced tube stations — elevated glass bus stops where passengers pay their fare, enter through a turnstile, then board at bus level. This "surface metro" accommodates three times as many passengers per hour as before, saves bundles of time, and costs one-three-hundredth the price of an underground metro (Alley 1996).

Curitiba's public transportation system is used by more than 1.3 million passengers each day, nearly two-thirds of the population. Twenty-eight percent of express bus users previously traveled in their cars, which translates into savings of up to 25 percent of fuel consumption city-wide. Fuel consumption per head in Curitiba is a quarter less than the Brazilian average, even though car ownership per head is the highest in the country, reversing the normal rule that high ownership means high fuel consumption. Curitiba also has one of the lowest levels of ambient air pollution in Brazil (Rabinovitch 1992; Economist 1996).

Transit Marketing

Job Ticket: In Frankfurt, Germany, transit operators have signed contracts with municipal administrators and private firms to allow their respective commuters free access to public transportation. The city and the employers consider the subsidized tab as a job benefit. The city led the way by signing an agreement to reimburse the regional transit authority for the issue of job-ticket flash passes to all 26,000 municipal employees (*Public Innovation Abroad* 1991).

Environment Pass: Freiburg, Germany (with a population of 172,000) introduced a public transit environment pass in 1985, which has since been adopted by more than 30 German communities. Freiburg's city council authorized the transit authority to lower season pass fares from the equivalent of U.S.$34 to $22 a month to give people an incentive to switch from their cars to public transit to protect the environment. During the first year, ridership increased by as much as 23 percent; between 3,000 and 4,000 car owners switched permanently to the Freiburg streetcar system, and ticket revenues increased while expenditures remained constant. Revenues and ridership continued to increase in succeeding years, with more than 350,000 passes sold in 1988, about 100,000 more than in the first year. The upward trend continues. An agreement with the transit authority of neighboring Basel (Switzerland) allows mutual acceptance of their respective environment passes (*Public Innovation Abroad* 1990b).

Encouraging wheelers, walkers, and bus riders helps make a pleasant street environment
From: City of Vancouver (1996)

Transit Passes for Hotel Guests: German transit authorities in Hamburg and Frankfurt have negotiated flash transit passes for hotel guests. Guests of one chain are offered an unlimited two-day transit pass good for all public transit in the city when they check in. The subsidized arrangement, negotiated between the hotel chain and the local transit authority, aims to make it easy for out-of-town hotel guests to use the city's transit system and leave their cars in the hotel garage or at home (*Public Innovation Abroad* 1990a).

Free or Inexpensive Transit

Eliminating Fares: Experiments with eliminating system-wide fares in Trenton, New Jersey and Denver, Colorado in the late-1970s found that the costs of doing so were high relative to benefits. Based on experiments in Seattle, Portland, Syracuse, and Salt Lake City, free fare programs limited to the downtown core have generally had better results. Seattle has had the most success (Cervero 1990).

Non-Motorized Modes

Alternative Transportation Centre: The Alternative Transportation Centre is a grassroots initiative of Better Environmentally Sound Transportation, a Vancouver nonprofit organization. The Centre encourages responsible transportation in its region by: undertaking trip reduction plans for employers in order to enhance facilities, policies and programs that promote "greener" trips; developing a public resource library on urban transportation issues; undertaking yearly promotional campaigns to encourage use of alternative modes; providing personalized support to individual commuters who wish to break their auto addiction; raising public awareness of the convenience, health, and economic benefits of cycling; creating communication networks for cyclists and cycling organizations; advising city councils and other legislative bodies on transportation issues; and ensuring that alternatives to the private automobile are emphasized in municipal and provincial transport systems (Davidson 1996).

*Yellow Bike*s: Over 450 donated, one-speed yellow bikes were scattered around the City of Portland in 1995. A local business volunteered to paint them bright yellow and U-Haul distributes them across the city. If a tire goes flat, the rider calls a number on the bike, and it's repaired by at-risk kids at the Community Cycling Center. Tom O'Keefe of the United Community Action Network had dreamed about the idea for years, after reading about a similar program in Amsterdam. He started Portland's program after his own bike was stolen (Wilson 1996).

RESOURCES

Alt-Transp List is an Internet list to exchange information with 200 plus alternative transport professionals and activists. Members send and receive e-mail messages concerning transport related issues. To subscribe, e-mail *Majordomo@flora.org* with the body (not subject) of the message being: *subscribe alt-transp*, followed by your e-mail address. For more information, simply send the message: *help*.

Cities and Automobile Dependence: An International Sourcebook, by Peter Newman and Jeffrey Kenworthy (Gower Technical 1989), is based on extensive research. This landmark study examines urban form, transport and energy use in 32 cities in North America, Europe, Asia, and Australia.

The data cover approximately 100 parameters for 1960, 1970, and 1980, and include parking, car ownership and use, roads, congestion, public transport, modal split and energy consumption; city form is characterized by central, inner and outer area population and employment data. The study confirms that the shorter distances inherent in medium- and high-density urban areas correspond with much more walking and cycling. For example, in the West European cities in the study — with an average of some 85 people and jobs per hectare (2.47 acres) — more than 21 percent of workers walk or cycle to work. By contrast, in the study's U.S. and Australian cities, with about 20 people and jobs per hectare, only 5 percent of workers walk or cycle to their jobs.

Newman and Kenworthy have produced numerous smaller studies based upon more recent census and other data, which update the original work. They are affiliated with the Institute of Science and Technology Policy at Murdoch University in Western Australia.

Conservation Law Foundation offers an interactive web site focused on sustainable transportation, and includes downloadable resources, electronic discussions, and a library of related sites.

3 Jay Street
Boston, Massachusetts
USA 02108-1497
Tel: 617/742-2510
Fax: 617/523-8019
Web site: www.tlcnetwork.org/index.html

Environmental Defense Fund's National Transportation Program has an excellent resource site with many U.S. transportation case studies.

257 Park Avenue South
New York, New York
USA 10010
Tel: 800/684-3322
Web site: www.edf.org/

Institute of Science and Technology Policy was established in 1988 to help create a better understanding of the roles and effects of science and technology. Search for their materials in your library or through their web site.

Murdoch University
South Street
Murdoch, WA 6150
Australia
Tel: 61-8-9360-2913
Fax: 61-8-9360-6421
E-mail: istp@central.murdoch.edu.au
Web site: wwwistp.murdoch.edu.au:80/istp.html

Transportation: An International Journal Devoted to the Improvement of Transportation Planning and Practice: If your library doesn't have it, the journal is available in microform from:

UMI
800/521-0600 toll-free in U.S.
313/761-4700 collect from Alaska and Michigan
800/343-5299 toll-free from Canada
Individual articles are available from:
UMI Article Clearinghouse
300 North Zeeb Road
Ann Arbor, Michigan
USA 48108

U.S. Department of Transportation's Bureau of Transportation Statistics has a web site that links many U.S. transportation problems and solutions, such as the U.S. Surface Transportation Policy Project. The site's table of contents is a massive library of transportation-related statistics and reports.

400 7th Street, S.W.
Washington, D.C.
USA 20590
Tel: 202/366-1270
Fax: 202/366-3640
Web site: www.bts.gov/
For statistical information:
Tel: 800/853-1351
E-mail: statistics@bts.gov

Victoria Transport Policy Institute specializes in progressive transportation decision making theory and practice. Their goal is to develop practical tools for incorporating social and environmental values into transportation decision-making. These tools include documents available free for downloading, documents for sale, and transportation cost-analysis software. This Institute is an extremely useful resource to bring a sustainability perspective into a transportation debate.

1250 Rudlin Street
Victoria, B.C.
Canada V8V 3R7
Tel/Fax: 250/360-1560
E-mail: litman@islandnet.com
Web site: www.islandnet.com/~litman

REFERENCES

Adams, J. 1996. Presentation to Barriers and Roadblocks, OECD International Conference, Toward Sustainable Transportation, Vancouver, B.C., March.

Alley, T. 1996. "Curitiba: A Visit to an Ecological City." *Urban Ecologist* 4:18-19.

Arlidge, J.1997. "Green Homes for People Without Cars," *Guardian Weekly* 27(April): 30.

Bleviss, D.L. 1996. "Looking Down the Road." Panel presentation, OECD International Conference, Toward Sustainable Transportation, Vancouver, B.C., March.

Cameron, M. 1991. T*ransportation Efficiency: Tackling Southern California's Air Pollution and Congestion*. Boulder, Colo.: Environmental Defense Fund and Regional Institute of Southern California.

Cervero, R. 1990. "Transit Pricing Research: A Review and Synthesis." *Transportation* 17:117-39.

City of Vancouver. 1996. *City of Vancouver Transportation Plan: Newsletter Number 4*. Spring.

Davidson, G. 1996. The Alternative Transportation Centre: An Innovative Initiative to Reduce Reliance Upon the Single Occupancy Vehicle. Prepared for OECD International Conference, Toward Sustainable Transportation, Vancouver, B.C., March.

— — — . 1997. *Area Wide Traffic Management: A Strategy for Improving the Economic, Social and Environmental Health of Urban Centres*. Masters thesis, School of Resource and Environmental Management, Simon Fraser University.

Economist, The. 1996. "Taming the Beast: Living With the Car." 339 (7971) June.

Egan, D. 1995. "Calming Traffic, Exciting People." In *Beyond the Car: Essays on the Auto Culture*, S. Zielinski and G. Laird, eds. Toronto: Steel Rail Press.

Elsworth, S. 1995. "A Car Every Second: The Experience of Greenpeace in Britain." In *Beyond the Car: Essays on the Auto Culture*, S. Zielinski and G. Laird, eds. Toronto: Steel Rail Press.

Engwicht, D. 1993. *Reclaiming Our Cities and Towns: Better Living with Less Traffic*. Gabriola Island, B.C.: New Society Publishers.

Engwicht, D., 1996. Presentation at Vancouver City Hall, B.C., 13 May.

Gurstein, P. 1996. "Planning for Telework and Home-Based Employment: Reconsidering the Home/Work Separation." *Journal of Planning Education and Research* 15(3): 101-13.

Hamilton, G.D. 1996. Associates Consulting Ltd. *Safety Benefits of Traffic Calming*, E. Geddges et al. February.

Illich, I. 1974. *Energy and Equity*. New York: Harper and Row.

Kay, J.H. 1997. *Asphalt Nation: How the Automobile Took Over America and How We Can Take It Back*. Crown.

Keeler-Hemphill, D. 1992. "Curitiba: Brazil's Ecological City." *Environmental Planning Quarterly* 9(2) Spring:5-14.

Kenworthy, J.R., and F.B. Laube. 1996. "Automobile Dependence in Cities: An International Comparison of Urban Transport and Land Use Patterns with Implications for Sustainability." *Environmental Impact Assessment Review* 16: 279-308.

Komanoff, C. 1995. "Charting the True Costs of Driving." In *Beyond the Car: Essays on the Auto Culture*, S. Zielinski and G. Laird, eds. Toronto: Steel Rail Press.

Leman, C., P. Schiller and K. Pauly. 1994. *Re-Thinking High Occupancy Vehicle Facilities and the Public Interest*. Annapolis: The Chesapeake Bay Foundation.

Leonhardt, W. 1990. Integrated Urban and Transport Planning in Saarbrücken. Presented to the World Congress of Local Governments for a Sustainable Future, United Nations, New York, 7 September.

Lovins, A. 1996. Hypercars and Negatrips: The Next Transport Revolution. Presented to OECD International Conference, Toward Sustainable Transportation, Vancouver, B.C., March.

MacDuffee, M. 1996. "Urban Good Governance and Global Initiatives: Lessons From Habitat II." In *Urban Green Governance: The View From the UN Conference on Human Settlements*, M. M'Gonigle, ed. Victoria: University of Victoria Faculty of Law, Eco-Research Chair.

Monheim, H. 1986. "Area Wide Traffic Restraint: A Concept for Better Urban Transport." *Built Environment* 12:74-82.

Mumford, L. 1964. *The Highway and the City*. New York: New American Library.

Newman, P., and J. Kenworthy, 1989. *Cities and Automobile Dependence: An International Sourcebook*. Brookfield, Vt.: Gower Technical.

Newman, P. 1991. "Succesful Ageing, Transport, and Urban Design." Presented to Conference on Succesful Ageing, Canberra, Australia. November.

Public Innovation Abroad. 1990a. 14 (3) March.

— — — . 1990b. 14(6) June.

— — — . 1991. 15 (9) September.

Pucher, J., and S. Clorer. 1992. "Taming the Automobile in Germany." *Transportation Quarterly* 46(3): 383-95.

Rabinovitch, J. 1992. "Curitiba: Towards Sustainable Urban Development." *Environment and Urbanization* 4(2) October 1992. In Hardoy, J.E., and D. Satterthwaite. 1992. *Environmental Problems in Third World Cities: An Agenda for the Poor and the Planet.* London: International Institute for Environment and Development.

Rajan, S.C. 1996. *The Enigma of Automobility: Democratic Politics and Pollution Control.* Pittsburgh: University of Pittsburgh Press.

Renner, M. 1988. "Rethinking the Role of the Automobile." Worldwatch 84. Washington, D.C.: Worldwatch Institute.

Replogle, M. 1995. "What's Sustainable?" In *Beyond the Car: Essays on the Auto Culture*, S. Zielinski and G. Laird, eds. Toronto: Steel Rail Press.

Replogle, M. 1996. Overcoming Barriers to Market-Based Transportation Reform. Presented to OECD International Conference, Toward Sustainable Transportation, Vancouver, B.C., March.

Roberts, W. 1995. "Blazing Saddles and Appropriate Technology: The Bike Path to a Green Economy." In *Beyond the Car: Essays on the Auto Culture*, S. Zielinski and G. Laird, eds. Toronto: Steel Rail Press.

Totten, M. 1989. *Energywise Options for State and Local Governments: A Policy Compendium* draft. Washington, D.C.: National Center for Policy Alternatives.

Toronto City Cycling Committee. 1990. "Bike to the Future: A Vision for a Bicycle-Friendly Toronto." Toronto: City of Toronto Cycling Committee.

Tunali, O. 1996. "A Billion Cars: The Road Ahead." *WorldWatch* January: 24-35.

Vancouver Bikeway Network Group. 1991. The Bikeway Solution: A Proposal to Vancouver City Council. Vancouver: Vancouver Bikeway Network Group.

Wachs, M. 1989. "Transportation Demand Management: Policy Implications of Recent Behavioral Research." Los Angeles: University of California. P. 1.

Whitelegg, J. 1996. "The Information Society and Sustainable Development." *Journal of World Transport Policy and Practice* 2:4.

Wilson, P. 1996. "Changing Direction: Toward Sustainable Culture." *Northwest Report* 19 (January).

Zuckermann, W. 1991. *End of the Road: From World Car Crisis to Sustainable Transportation.* Post Mills, Vt.: Chelsea Green Publishing.

Land Use and Urban Form

L and use permeates virtually every aspect of sustainable communities. Many of the goals discussed in previous chapters depend in large measure upon how we organize our use of land and the form that use takes.

Conventional land-use practices spread our destinations, increase our need for space and travel, and bring a host of related problems. The cost of real estate in cities, for example, is often too high to accommodate green space, biological wastewater treatment facilities such as wetlands, or fields of photovoltaic (PV) panels. By integrating planning and design for multi-purpose use, these ideas can become affordable. For example, PVs on rooftops take up no extra space, nor do rooftop gardens. Wetlands can process sewage and provide wildlife habitat, recreation areas, and drainage for stormwater run-off. Parks can provide recreation and edible landscaping. "Whole-systems" or "multi-purpose" design and planning is critical to sustainable land use.

Sustainable land use can help invigorate communities, and provide considerable environmental, economic, social, and cultural benefits. Redeveloping and reusing existing buildings and land can also revitalize economies and communities that are falling into decay. Sustainable community planning can recognize and respond to the diversity of interests and desires in our communities by encouraging land uses that cater to a range of incomes, ages, physical abilities, and cultural backgrounds.

LAND USE AND TRANSPORTATION

Transportation and land use are inextricably related. To encourage people to use the transportation system more efficiently, we need to adopt land-use policies that reduce our needs for transportation and let us meet those needs in more energy-efficient ways.

Per capita gasoline consumption in U.S. and many Canadian cities is now more than four times that of European cities, and over 10 times greater than Asian cities such as Hong Kong, Tokyo, and Singapore. The biggest factor accounting for these differences in energy use appears to be not the size of cars or the price of gasoline, but the efficiency and compactness of land-use patterns. Cities with low "automobile dependence" are more centralized; have more intense land use (more people and jobs per unit area); are more oriented to non-auto modes (more public transit, foot traffic, and bicycle usage); place more restraints on high-speed traffic; and offer better public transit (Newman and Kenworthy 1989). These patterns can be seen within communities as well.

For example, within the San Francisco region, odometer readings taken during biennial auto emissions (smog check) inspections were used to calculate the annual mileages for five communities. The study found that doubling residential or population density reduces the annual auto mileage per capita or per household by 20 percent to 30 percent. These findings are consistent with studies in Toronto, Chicago, New York City, British cities, and major U.S. urbanized areas. Most striking were the differences between the San Francisco areas of Nob Hill (177 households per acre) and Danville-San Ramon (3.8 households per acre). Using the Hertz Corporation's estimates of auto ownership and operating costs per mile, the average Nob Hill area family annually spends nearly $14,000 less on autos, uses 66 percent less gasoline, and emits 14 kilograms (about 31 pounds) less hydrocarbons, 12 kilograms (about 26 pounds) less nitrogen oxides, and 98 kilograms (about 215 pounds) less carbon monoxide than the average Danville-San Ramon family (Holtzclaw 1991).

Through zoning and other techniques, land-use patterns and densities dictate travel volume, direction, and mode. In the U.S. and Canada, our dispersed land-use patterns are typified by the low density suburb. The problem with the low-density land-use pattern is not just its high energy use. This settlement pattern has a complimentary set of environmental and social problems that all stem from its dispersed land use:

- high per capita auto emissions (both smog and greenhouse gases are directly related to the amount of gasoline used);
- high per capita water use (e.g., for lawn irrigation);
- high land requirements in both the block size and the road system required to service it (road provision is much greater in low-density areas than in medium density areas);
- high stormwater pollution from the extra urbanized land (low-density areas can have double the stormwater pollution of medium density areas);
- high domestic heating energy due to the lack of a shared insulating effect when buildings are grouped (50 percent differences can be found);
- poor recycling rates due in part to the large cost involved in collection compared to a compact housing system (European cities have four to six times the recycling rates of North America.);
- high physical infrastructure costs (utilities, pipes, poles, roads, etc.); and
- high social infrastructure costs (cars are required for participation in social life) (Newman 1991b).

Costs for social infrastructure deserve more attention than they have received. When our communities require cars for participation in social life, who is marginalized and excluded? Clearly, it is the non-drivers. And who are the non-drivers? They are our children, our senior citizens, our physically challenged, and our very poor (who are predominantly women). Add up the numbers, and we may be talking about half the population of our communities (Engwicht 1993).

All of this suggests a new approach to transportation and land-use planning in

As our populations become increasingly concentrated into urban areas, they are simultaneously becoming less concentrated within those areas. In other words, "our cities and towns are not just growing in population, but at the same time they are spreading out and changing their structure into a looser, more widespread urban pattern" (Richardson 1991).

North America. In the absence of comprehensive planning, transportation has, almost by default, guided land use. Instead, land-use planning should guide transportation, and transportation should be designed to accommodate and support planned growth, inducing the needed changes in urban form (Cervero 1991; Replogle 1990).

DENSITY AND HOUSING

Denser land use could help solve many of the environmental, social, and aesthetic problems of sprawl, yet widespread misconceptions about increased density — even moderate density — often prevent communities from adopting compact land-use strategies. Contrary to popular belief, augmenting the density of development does not necessarily create a harsh physical environment. For example, Copenhagen and Vienna — two cities widely associated with

Why Los Angeles Still Has Smog

"It is no wonder that Los Angeles still has smog more than 30 years after the battle to reduce it first began — the battle has concentrated on making vehicles cleaner and more efficient, it has done nothing to make them less needed. The principle that is often forgotten here is the Jevons principle. The Jevons principle was first enunciated in 1865 when an assessment was made that improving U.K. coal-burning efficiency would save coal — Jevons predicted that it would in fact lead to greater coal use as the efficiencies would lead to more economic uses for coal. The same principle seems to apply to our present assessment of transport fuel use. The price mechanism and urban sprawl ensure that for every increase in technological efficiency there is a rapid increase in the use of vehicles" (Newman 1991a).

Housing Forms and Density

Low Density — Single Family Form
about 0.6 FAR

Low Density — Attached Form
0.6 FAR

Medium Density — Ground-Oriented
0.7 to 1.1 FAR

Comprehensive Townhouse Development
about 0.6 FAR

Medium Density — Apartment
1.2 FAR

High Density — Apartment
about 2.0 FAR

FAR = Floor Area Ratio = $\frac{\text{Floor Area}}{\text{Lot Area}}$. Therefore Maximum Floor Area = FAR x Lot Area urban charm and livability — are of moderate density (measured by the number of residents and jobs in the city, including its central business district and outer areas). Copenhagen has 19 people per acre and Vienna has 29 people per acre. By contrast, low-density cities such as Phoenix (five people per acre) often are dominated by unwelcoming, car-oriented commercial strips and vast expanses of concrete and asphalt. People often assume that low density ensures more green space and easier living, yet as Chapter 4: Greening the City shows, with appropriate planning and design, dense urban areas can lend themselves to greater vitality, more inviting spaces, and even higher use of trees and other plants (Lowe 1992).

Although municipal officials will attest that the numbers of household units per building or per hectare can be the subject of intense debate, those numbers are relatively unimportant in terms of human well-being. Instead, the most important indicator that links overcrowding to human stress and psychosis is the number of people per room. Although many people mistakenly equate density with overcrowding, there is a world of difference between high-density living in high-rise residential blocks with low numbers of people per room (such as New York City), and overcrowding in low-rise shanty town developments, with high numbers of people per room (such as Rio de Janiero or parts of Mexico City).

There are areas of high-density populations with low levels of social disorder (such as parts of Boston), while there are areas of low-density population with high levels of social disorder (such as parts of Los Angeles). This seems to indicate that the real issues at stake are more likely to be a combination of social and economic factors, such as low income, poor education, and social isolation. These complicating factors surrounding urban density should make us wary of falling for the implicit environmental determinism which is sometimes found in arguments both for and against high-density living (Haughton and Hunter 1994).

THE COSTS OF SPRAWL

The flight of employment and people to the suburbs has underscored concern about the costs of sprawl. Preservationists are realizing that if suburbs drain city life there will be no impetus to protect historic buildings. Environmentalists are realizing that sprawl destroys rural environments, and that air quality is deteriorating due to commuter traffic. Concerned citizens everywhere sense that abandoned city neighborhoods and faceless suburban developments reduce a vital sense of community.

It has long been an axiom that development enhances the local tax base. However, extensive research now suggests that the costs of sprawl may exceed the benefits of low-density development. The Real Estate Research Corporation (1974) conducted a massive study for the U.S. government, *The Costs of Sprawl*, which still stands as a classic. Three community types were analyzed: the "low-density sprawl" community (entirely single-family homes, 75 percent in traditional grid-pattern, typical of suburban development); the "combination mix" community (20 percent of each of five types of dwellings, half in planned unit developments, half in traditional subdivisions); and the "high-density planned" community (40 percent highrises, 30 percent walkups, 20 percent townhouses, and 10 percent clustered single family homes, all clustered together into contiguous neighborhoods). A major conclusion of the study was that sprawl is "the most expensive form of residential development in terms of economic costs, environmental costs, natural resource consumption, and many types of personal costs . . . This cost difference is particularly significant for that proportion of total costs which is likely to be borne by local governments."

A more recent Melbourne, Australia study suggests that it is cheaper for cities to pay developers to build near downtown cores than it is to pay for the costs of sprawl in terms of infrastructure development and remediating pollution from automobiles. Given its findings of lower road, sewer, and education costs, the study showed a net benefit of CDN$32,000 for every household created in downtown rather than suburban Melbourne. With three million residents spread over 2,500 square kilometers (965 square miles), Melbourne considered a property tax holiday, bargain prices on city land and density zoning inducements to lure developers downtown. According to the Chief Executive of Melbourne's Planning Authority, "The net savings would be (CDN) $130 million over 20 years for every 8,000 people who move downtown instead of the suburbs" (Neilson 1990; O'Brien 1990).

The effectiveness of compact urban development can be fully achieved only if governments remove the conflicting incentives posed by other (often national) policies such as artificially low gasoline prices. For example, fuel taxes that more accurately reflect the true environmental and social costs of private vehicle use — from the health costs of air pollution to the military costs of policing the Persian Gulf — would give an enormous boost to more efficient urban land use and raise revenue for investment in a broader range of transport options (Lowe 1992).

Despite the absence of supportive national policy frameworks, communities can do a great deal to create more energy-efficient travel patterns by concentrating activities in specific areas and developing a mix of land uses in those areas. Our objectives should be to create travel patterns that can be effectively served by more energy-efficient travel modes, such as public transit, bicycling, and walking; and to reduce the average length of daily automobile trips where other modes are not feasible.

Land Use Terms

- **Urban containment**: the physical and functional separation of urban and rural areas, and planning processes that aim for efficient forms of towns and cities with minimal impact on surrounding areas (Gayler 1990).
- **Densification**: increasing the numbers of housing units or commercial facilities built per acre of land, with the goals of increasing the efficiency of land use and reducing the overall impact of growth.
- **Urbanization**: creation of urban landscapes in formerly rural areas.
- **Urban areas**: characterized by human residential, commercial, and industrial structures and activities, and can include low-density suburban areas as well as urban cores where human activity is intense.
- **Compact cities**: urban areas that make efficient use of land for all purposes through densification and mixed land uses. Compact cities contrast with sprawl.
- **Sprawl**: an inefficient, extensive use of land for urban activities. The term suburban is often used to describe sprawling urban development (BCRTEE 1994).

CHANGING THE PATTERN OF GROWTH

Land-use planning rarely addresses long-term or life-cycle costs, so taxpayers often end up paying the hidden costs of development infrastructure (roads, sewage, etc.). Citizens in many communities see something wrong with this picture, but the solutions commonly proposed rarely speak to the underlying issues.

Although many communities have attempted to stop or slow growth, *the critical issue for most communities is the pattern of growth*, not the pace of growth. Communities that attempt to halt further development by prohibiting growth in their own jurisdictions merely shift development to neighboring areas where controls are looser, and more conducive to further sprawl. Moreover, future development presents an invaluable opportunity to remedy the status quo. If communities do not want to be frozen in their current automobile-dependent patterns, they need to exploit new growth to their advantage by filling in underused space to make their urban areas more compact (Lowe 1991b). One key to changing growth patterns is rethinking the property tax system.

Sustainable communities require that we go beyond the notion that land is a mere commodity. However, even in conventional economic terms, land is a peculiar commodity in that its supply cannot increase, no matter how high the price. As demand for land grows, the wealth of landowners tends to grow regardless of how well or badly they use the land. In his 1879 classic *Progress and Poverty*, Henry George proposed a solution to this dilemma: taxing away the value of land produced by anything other than private efforts. Such a land-value tax would keep private landowners from unfairly capturing the benefits of natural resources, urban locations, and public services. George also believed that this tax would force landowners either to put their land to its "highest and best" use themselves, or make it accessible to someone who would (Brown 1997).

Several economists have since called for differentiated treatment of land and buildings in property taxation. Whereas a higher tax on buildings encourages holding land unused or allowing buildings to deteriorate, a higher tax on land often encourages efficient use of the property. Since land is not produced, a tax on land is a cost of ownership, not a cost of production. By making land ownership more costly (less desirable), a tax on land results in *lower* land prices. Taxing land values helps makes many infrastructure investments (like roads and subways) self-financing (Rybeck 1996).

Local governments typically assess vacant properties at far less than their market value, effectively rewarding property owners for keeping their land idle. Communities can go a step further to tax vacant land more heavily than developed parcels. To avoid spurts of sprawled growth, however, it is critically important to combine these tax strategies with clearly defined growth frontiers, such as greenbelts and urban growth boundaries, that contain development within the existing urban area (Lowe 1992).

Since the higher land tax cannot be avoided or passed on to space users, land owners are motivated to generate income from which to pay the tax. The greatest economic imperative to develop land will exist where land values are highest, adjacent to

"One of the great mysteries of the American suburb is this: How, with such low-density development, have we produced such extraordinarily high traffic? How have we achieved the traffic of a metropolis and the culture of a cow town?" (Duany and Plater-Zyberk 1992)

existing infrastructure and amenities. At the same time, a reduction in the tax rate applied to buildings makes that development more profitable. Away from infrastructure where land values are low, taxes will be low and there will be less economic motivation for development. The result is more compact development that can be served by existing infrastructure, at lower costs to taxpayers and the environment. Compact development also enhances opportunities to walk, cycle, carpool, or use transit in lieu of single-occupant vehicles (Rybeck 1996).

Even a reduced version of this tax could meet all local needs by capturing much of the gain from rising land values. To put this land tax into local hands would free localities from depending on state/provincial and federal financial help and its accompanying control (Daly and Cobb 1989).

An example of New Urbanist design

NEW URBANISM

New Urbanism is the name given to an emerging set of planning principles designed to reinvigorate communities and provide a meaningful alternative to suburban sprawl. Variations on New Urbanism include "neo-traditional town planning," "pedestrian pockets," "transit-oriented developments," "complete communities" and LASTING communities — Livable, Affordable, Safe, Transit-Oriented, Inclusive, Neighborly, Growing.

New Urbanism has attracted considerable media attention, including a *Newsweek* cover story describing "15 Ways to Fix the Suburbs." The *Newsweek* list, in this order, is to give up big lawns, bring back the corner store, make the streets skinny, drop the cul-de-sac, draw [urban growth] boundaries, hide the garage, mix housing types, plant trees curbside, put new life into old malls, plan for mass transit, link work to home, make a town center, shrink parking, turn down the lights [use more smaller street lamps rather than fewer larger ones], and "think green" [don't pave the planet] (Adler 1995).

Although New Urbanism is often characterized as a new model for suburban development, re-urbanization of existing urban areas is one of its principal tenets. Indeed, most New Urbanist principles have been deduced from successful cities that are made up of several independent neighborhoods, or "urban villages."

Urban villages provide a lifestyle with minimal car dependence and the kind of densities that make rail highly viable. Evidence suggests that those cities that have tried to build urban villages have found them to be an extremely attractive lifestyle option. The characteristics of these urban villages are:

Greenfields and Brownfields

Pristine rural areas are called "greenfield" sites, while urban areas are referred to as "brownfield" sites because they often contain pollutants left behind by past uses. Developers prefer greenfield sites because there is no pollution to remove; because banks, familiar with cookie cutter suburban developments, are eager to lend money for them; and because zoning may not be in place and building permits are easy to obtain. To develop brownfield sites, developers must find their way through a maze of permitting agencies, clean up a plethora of pollutants, and persuade banks to lend money for what is often a more risky return (Low 1997).

• mixed land use, with commercial offices and shops on main spines, surrounded by residential;

• high density so that everything within the "village" is within walking and cycling distance;

• considerable landscaping including gardens on top of buildings and on balconies;

• a mixture of public and private housing with an emphasis on families and hence quite large internal home spaces;

• extensive provision for children in good view of dwellings;

• community facilities such as libraries, child care, senior centers, and in a few cases, small urban farms;

• pedestrian links with parking lots placed underground and traffic calming on any peripheral roads;

• public spaces with strong design features (water, street furniture, playgrounds, etc.); and

Land Use Zoning

NOT this: *Isolation of home from work and services by exclusive zoning*

THIS: *Proximity of home to work and services by mixed-use zoning*

Drawings by David Rousseau

WHY NOT:
• Excessive commuting requirements; increases automobile dependency
• Empty residential areas in daytime and commercial areas at night; encourages crime
• Decreases contact among people; does not build community or support services
• High commuting costs and traffic congestion

"All that is not specifically required is strictly forbidden."

HOW:
• Design neighborhood centers within walking distance
• Flexible, mixed use zoning encourages participation in the community
• Increased hours of occupancy supports local services
• Design for local and in-home employment

"All that is not considered grossly objectionable is permitted."

• a large degree of self-sufficiency for the community with rail links to the rest of the city (Newman 1991a,b,c).

New Urbanism is perhaps most succinctly described in the charter developed by the Congress for the New Urbanism, a group formed in 1992 comprising architects, urban designers, planners, and landscape architects from across North America. Their 1996 charter states that: neighborhoods should be diverse in use and population; communities should be designed for the pedestrian and transit as well as the car; cities and towns should be shaped by physically defined and universally accessible public spaces and community institutions; and urban places should be framed by architecture and landscape design that celebrate local history, climate, ecology, and building practice. In practice, New Urbanism means:

• designing communities with a connected and permeable public framework of streets and open spaces as the main structuring element of the community;

• facilitating easy movement through all parts of the community by foot, bicycle, public transit, and automobile, without favoring any particular mode;

Subdivision

NOT this: *Subdivision of entire parcels into individual lots*

THIS: *Cluster designs with commons*

WHY NOT:
• Lack of common space impairs community self-image
• Residents isolated behind fences and in automobiles do not meet or watch out for their neighbors
• Heavy emphasis on the private domain does not encourage participation
• Utilities are widely extended and services dispersed

"All residential land is either private or dedicated to the automobile."

HOW:
• Thoughtful public and semi-public space integrated with private lots
• Design for meeting places and good visual supervision
• Provide small neighborhood parks, community gardens and playgrounds
• Cluster designs allow compact utility networks and concentrated services

"A community must have commons."

• fostering community activity through ensuring that buildings enhance pedestrian comfort in the way that they relate to the public streets, and thereby providing an attractive, safe, and inviting public realm;

• accommodating and integrating a diverse and wide range of land uses, densities, and building types within each neighborhood to include the full range of activities found in any healthy community, and to facilitate the provision of public transit;

• integrating the natural environment into the new community; and

• creating universally accessible public open spaces and community institutions that provide a sense of place and act as landmarks of community identity (Gabor and Lewinberg 1997).

With increasing attention and publicity, New Urbanism has also earned its share of criticism. For example, the "neotraditional" new town of Seaside, Florida does not employ ecological design techniques (e.g., passive solar) and infrastructure (e.g., provisions for reducing water consumption, such as recycling grey water systems or open rainwater drainage swales) (Okamoto 1991). Seaside's design may reduce traffic con-

Housing Types

NOT this: *Limited housing types: single family detached*

THIS: *Many housing types*

WHY NOT:

• Poor range of affordability
• Leads to limited social and economic mix among residents; ghettoization
• Inappropriate to aging residents and community-minded people
• Has highest individual land requirements
• Financially unstable due to dependence on only one market sector

"Everyone wants to live in a suburban home and can afford it."

HOW:

• Provide apartment and townhouses as a more affordable option
• Design mixed single-family and multi-family neighborhoods for diversity and social enrichment; healthier communities
• Provide supported seniors housing, co-housing and other options
• Design for mini-lots and strata lots to conserve common land
• Better financial stability by serving several market sectors

"Many people prefer townhouses, apartments and collective housing, particularly at some stage of their life."

gestion but does not reduce automobile dependence; its Traditional Neighborhood Development Ordinance does not in itself create proximity or even balance between jobs and housing (MacBurnie 1991). The model is more suitable for a project under single ownership than for a typical community trying to work with several developers (Knack 1991). And although Traditional Neighborhood Developments may be "designed" to encourage a mix of housing types and a diversity of income levels, they offer no mechanism to ensure any stock — never mind an adequate, permanent stock — of affordable housing. Even architect-designer Andres Duany admits that Seaside has in practice become a resort community for the wealthy (Duany 1991).

For New Urbanist development to be sustainable, it must incorporate energy-efficient land-use planning. There are several policies that communities can use to promote energy-efficient land use, such as:

• encourage greater density through multiple unit residential developments;

• integrate work, residence and shopping in mixed-use development;

• encourage residential clustering;

• zone higher-density development along established transit routes;

• decentralize commercial and community services to reduce travel distances, creating self-contained communities with a better balance between employment and population;

• place controls on outlying shopping centers, strip development, and urban sprawl;

• encourage the infilling (development) of existing vacant land in built-up areas;

• ensure that major public facilities have provision for walking and bicycling access to transit; and

• encourage the development of high-quality walking and bicycling facilities, including development design guidelines to support transportation alternatives to private automobile use, such as provision of on-site lunchrooms, daycare facilities, automated bank teller machines and other facilities (Federation of Canadian Municipalities 1990).

Portland, Oregon provides an example of a larger city-region experimenting with land-use policies to control energy demand — in this case within the framework of a mandatory state planning goal requiring that land use be managed to conserve energy. One of the main objectives of the Portland Energy Conservation Demonstration Project, completed in 1977, was to examine the links between energy saving and urban form. An energy zone map, dividing the city into five zones based on relative energy

---

Location-Efficient Mortgages

"A minor modification of mortgage-lending rules written by independent banks and government-sponsored mortgage guarantors, such as the Federal National Mortgage Association (Fannie Mae), could help the affordability of urban housing. These homes are often more expensive than suburban housing because they are close to jobs and city amenities.

Households in urban neighborhoods can often shed a second or third car, however, saving an average of $300 a month for each. Mortgage rules should allow them to spend some of these savings on a more expensive home. Fannie Mae already has a similar program for energy-efficient houses. Buyers of certified energy-efficient houses are allowed to borrow more than buyers of other houses since the saved energy expenses allow higher mortgage payments. . . .

Location-efficient mortgages would help both buyers and existing owners since some of the increased borrowing power would be capitalized in higher property values. This would create an incentive for neighborhoods to improve their 'location efficiency' by recruiting shops, workplaces, and other development and by lobbying for better transit service" (Durning 1996).

efficiency, was produced to guide new development to energy efficient locations; and an energy conservation policy was adopted by city council after extensive public consultation in 1979. The project included commitments to develop land-use policies using density and location to reduce the need to travel, and to improve the efficiency of the transport system and reduce its consumption of non-renewable fuels. More specific objectives related to the location of new developments and encouragement of energy-efficient transport modes. These strategies were then incorporated into the city's draft comprehensive plan (Owens 1990; Kasowski 1991; Lowe 1991a).

One of the main obstacles to creating New Urbanist communities is the conventional development standards behind most zoning codes. Kunstler (1996), a proponent of New Urbanism, explains the down side of zoning as follows:

> What zoning produces is suburban sprawl, which must be understood as the product of a particular set of instructions. Its chief characteristics are the strict separation of human activities, mandatory driving to get from one activity to another, and huge supplies of free parking. After all, the basic idea of zoning is that every activity demands a separate zone of its own. For people to live around shopping would be harmful and indecent. Better not even to allow them within walking distance of it. They'll need their cars to haul all that stuff home anyway. While we're at it, let's separate the homes by income gradients. Don't let the $75,000-a-year families live near the $200,000-a-year families — they'll bring down property values — and for God's sake don't let a $25,000-a-year recent college graduate or a $19,000-a-year widowed grandmother on Social Security live near any of them. There goes the neighborhood! Now put all the workplaces in separate office "parks" or industrial "parks," and make sure nobody can walk to them either. As for public squares, parks and the like — forget it. We can't afford them, because we spent all our money paving the four-lane highways and collector roads and parking lots, and laying sewer and water lines out to the housing subdivisions, and hiring traffic cops to regulate the movement of people in their cars going back and forth among these segregated activities.

Like most tools, zoning can be used for different purposes. Although historically, zoning bylaws are an inflexible instrument written to create certainty and offer only one way of doing things, a new set of zoning bylaws is emerging that reflects new aspirations for community building. Zoning can be a critical tool for integrating land uses, intensification and housing diversity, and pedestrian-oriented streetscapes, all of which support New Urbanism and sustainable transportation. A few of the many zoning tools available to communities include:

- *Planned unit development*: gives developers incentives to meet pre-determined land-use goals;
- *Floating zoning*: permits special uses within a jurisdiction in accordance with development criteria;
- *Bonus or incentive zoning*: provides developers with bonuses and incentives to achieve increased development density;
- *Mixed-use zoning*: requires a wide array of types of development aimed at reducing distances between houses and jobs;
- *Land banking*: allows outright purchase of land by the public sector well in

advance of any development to ensure appropriate land use; and

• *Transit zoning districts*: targets development in areas with transit systems already in place (Gordon 1991).

Related tools include:

• *Transfer of development rights*: allows landowners to get development value from their land even if they choose not to develop it;

• *Conservation land trusts*: local, regional, or state/provincial organizations directly involved in protecting important land resources for the public benefit;

• *Location-efficient mortgages*: aids urban housing affordability;

• *Growth management ordinances*: controls one or more of the familiar components of land-use planning: the rate, location, type, density, amount, timing, and quality of development; and

• *Building permit allocation*: allocates housing permits on a merit system that awards points for recreational amenities, landscaping and open space, design quality, impact on the local infrastructure, and energy efficiency (Heyerdahl 1991; Land Trust Alliance n.d.; Abberger 1991; American Planning Association 1991b; Durning 1996).

Alternative Development Standards are helping many communities meet environmental concerns and social needs while reducing the spiraling costs of new infrastructure. Features of the Standards, often referred to as "traditional neighborhood design," include grid road systems and narrower road widths, smaller lots, use of curbs and sidewalks, and car access to houses from rear lanes (BCMMAH 1997).

SOCIAL BENEFITS OF COMPACT COMMUNITIES

Clustered, pedestrian-friendly, transit-oriented communities are a key to reducing automobile dependency. As discussed in the previous chapter, achieving sustainable transportation requires technological, economic, and social solutions. Technological solutions, however, invariably forget that if gains in efficiency of motor vehicles are merely used to travel more, we do not have sustainable transportation. Economic solutions are often politically unacceptable due to the physical layout of our cities; and those who suffer most from user-pay schemes are those who can afford it least.

Social solutions can penetrate to the ultimate problem of automobile dependence. New Urbanism focuses on changing priorities in physical planning to ensure non-auto infrastructure; changing land use patterns to minimize the need for travel; and changing lifestyle values so that greater emphasis is on the community rather than private or isolated values (Newman 1996).

Comparative studies of residential satisfaction in low-density versus higher-density equivalent communities show that the relative disadvantages of low-density communities for working women are increasing as the percentage of employed women rises. For women who can't afford a second car, or who have difficulty making child-care arrangements, or who have specialized employment needs, low-density communities are much less satisfactory.

One of the most frustrated population groups in low-density suburbia is adolescents. When young people are entering a stage in which they are seeking more and more independence from their parents, they find themselves in an environment where getting together with friends is made difficult by distance, paucity of public transport, separation of housing from shopping centers, and so on. One study found American suburban teenagers more often bored and engaging in vandalism than their counterparts in Sweden living at higher density with easy access to shops, clubs, public transport, and so on. Teenagers in clustered housing are more likely to find others of the same age living within walking distance and may have access to shared facilities or hanging-out places where they can spend time together, out of sight of home, yet not far away (Cooper Marcus and Sarkissian 1986).

Tools and Initiatives

New Urbanism

Auto-Free Development: In Scotland, the Edinburgh Council has approved a $13-million housing development where no one owns a car, trees replace pavement, water is recycled, and heating and lighting are free. A landscaped garden will surround more than 100 homes on the site of an old railway yard near the city center. There will be no roads, no parking spaces, and no garages. Residents will sign an agreement not to own a car but to use one from a "pool." Residents will pay about $320 to join a council-run car club that will maintain and insure a fleet of vehicles in an on-site garage. They will be able to reserve cars at any time of the day or night at an hour's notice and will pay mileage and rental charges for each journey. Heating will be free all year since steam from factories will be used to heat homes and water, while solar panels on the roof of each home will provide electricity for lighting. Household utility bills are expected to be up to 25 percent below the U.K. average. Grey water from sinks and baths will be filtered and purified in reed beds before being reused; rainwater will be collected to be used in bathrooms; and all household waste will be recycled (Arlidge 1997).

Farmland Preserved: The town of Pittsfield, New York purchased 486 hectares (1,200 acres) of farmland to preserve it from development by floating a $10-million bond issue. Town planners calculated that providing services and schools for subdivisions built on that farmland would cost each taxpayer an additional $200 per year indefinitely, while paying off the bond issue would cost only $67 per year for 20 years (Low 1997).

Affordable Rental Housing: Near Boston, the Dorchester Bay Economic Development Corporation built 500 units of affordable rental housing, 58 home-ownership units, and two large commercial buildings. Working with local residents and merchants, the Corporation created a walkable town center so that people can shop locally without having to go to malls. A 2-hectare (5-acre) industrial park is being developed to stimulate jobs for local residents. Not far away at Harbor Point, once a devastated public housing project, private developers combined forces with the tenants' existing task force to build mixed-income apartments, creating an integrated community of different incomes, ethnicity, and race (Low 1997).

Urban Villages

Recent Examples: Urban villages appear to be succeeding and they are now appearing such as Arabella Park, Zamilla Park and Germering in Munich, Der Seepark in Freiburg and Kista in Stockholm. These are nearly all private developments with very high popularity. Examples of urban village style developments in North America include False Creek in Vancouver, B.C., River Place in Portland, Oregon, and Mission Bay in San Francisco (Newman 1991a,b,c).

Energy-Efficient Land-Use Planning

Auto-Use Reduction: Partly as a result of Portland's energy-efficient land-use planning, the number of jobs in downtown Portland has increased by 30,000 since the 1970s, with only a scant increase in traffic; in addition, 40 percent of commuters to the downtown area use public transportation. The number of days per year on which carbon monoxide levels violated federal health standards has dropped from 100 to zero. By encouraging high-density development along transit routes and limiting urban sprawl, Portland is showing that at least some reductions in car use are possible (World Resources Institute et al. 1996).

Residential Intensification Programs

Residential intensification means the creation of new residential units or accommodation in existing buildings or on previously developed, serviced land, generally including: creation of rooming, boarding and lodging houses; creation of accessory apartments; conversion of non-residential structures to residential use; infill; and redevelopment.

Kingston, Ontario: The City of Kingston created a low-interest loan program in 1981 to encourage the conversion of vacant, obsolete second- and third-storey commercial space in the downtown area into residential units. The program, which provides financial assistance to property owners within the central business district, was funded by an initial allocation of $250,000 from city council to serve as a revolving fund for future loans. The program's advantages include: business benefits to downtown merchants; cost-effectiveness; increased assessments; downtown revitalization; and easing a tight rental apartment situation (Ontario Ministry of Municipal Affairs and Housing 1989; Kingston Planning Report 1987).

St. Catharines, Ontario: St. Catharines instituted a similar program in 1987, creating a $300,000 revolving fund to provide 8 percent conversion loans of up to $20,000 per dwelling unit (St. Catharines Planning Report 1987).

Toronto, Ontario: The Metropolitan Toronto Planning Department (1987) estimated that the conversion aspect alone of a residential intensification program could produce 39,000 new housing units, the equivalent of 11 years of rental housing production (both private and social units).

Jobs/Housing Balance

The jobs/housing balance is a useful developer's tool, although no rule of thumb or actual values are available. Basically, when jobs and housing are not in balance, transportation problems are the likely result. Land-use planners can look at the range of incomes and housing costs to determine how far people have to move away from their jobs to find housing they can afford. The farther they must move, the more congestion, energy use, and air-quality problems an area will have (Gordon 1991).

Redirecting Development: Southern California has seized on the concept of balancing jobs and housing as a means of reducing traffic congestion and automobile emissions. In 1989, the South Coast Air Quality Management District, together with the Southern California Association of Governments, unveiled a plan that combines traditional approaches to air pollution abatement with strategies to reduce emissions by redirecting residential and commercial development. The plan establishes subregional "commute-sheds" that are designated as either job-rich or job-poor. Planners estimate that by redirecting 9 percent of the new jobs from job-rich to job-poor areas, and 5 percent of the new housing in the other direction, the number of vehicle-miles traveled per day could be cut by 33.4 million, or 9 percent (American Planning Association 1991a).

Proximity Planning

Striking a balance between jobs and housing, as discussed above, is not enough unless the people who work in a given area have the option of also living in that same area. This requires policies to encourage access by proximity.

Clouds of Change: Vancouver's Clouds of Change program makes "access by proximity rather than access by transportation" a central focus of city planning (City of Vancouver 1990).

Land Stewardship Guidelines

Halton, Ontario: The Regional Municipality of Halton, Ontario has advanced land stewardship as the first guiding principle for land-use planning in Halton (Regional Municipality of Halton 1991): "In this regard, we submit that the ownership rights of land are not absolute and the best and highest use of land is not an unfailing principle as there are other balancing factors to be considered. This is not meant as a denial of property rights, but an affirmation of a social responsibility. . . . The extent to which an individual realizes the economic benefit of a land use change should be balanced by the community's desire in preserving the environment or certain land forms in the landscape."

New Forms of Land Ownership

In recent years, land trusts and limited equity cooperatives have experimented with distributing the costs and benefits of land development in much the same way as proposed by Henry George, but through new forms of land ownership rather than taxation.

Common Property: In Boston's Dudley Street Neighborhood Initiative, for example, the project made the land in an inner-city redevelopment area the common property of a nonprofit group, while allowing private ownership of homes and other buildings.

Social Increment: Similarly, Connecticut's Equity Trust dedicates the "social increment" in property values (for example, the portion of a home's sale price that is due to the increase in land values rather than housing construction costs) to social purposes, such as subsidizing the purchase price for future homeowners (Ingerson 1997).

Dual Property Tax System

Land Levy: Fifteen U.S. cities levy a higher charge on land than on buildings to spur the regeneration of their blighted land. When Pittsburgh introduced a sharply graded dual tax system in 1978, the number of vacant lot sales, new building permits, and new dwellings quickly increased. At the same time, demolitions declined (Lowe 1992).

Building Permit Allocation

Growth Management Ordinance: In Florida, Key West's 1986 growth management ordinance establishes the number of dwelling units that still can be constructed before the island is completely built out. Before the enactment of the ordinance, the city approved an average of 400-500 dwelling units annually. Under the ordinance, the city can allow either 7 percent of the total units permitted or 300 units per year. Housing permits are allocated on a merit system that awards points for recreational amenities, landscaping and open space, design quality, impact on the local infrastructure, and energy efficiency.

The ordinance also requires that at least 40 percent of all residential housing units must be constructed as affordable housing. Affordable apartments have annual rental rates less than 30 percent of the median household income in the city, while affordable sale units have a sale price that is less than three times the city's median household income.

Developers must enter into a development agreement with the city. Deed restrictions guarantee that the unit will remain affordable for a period of 5-20 years, depending on the project. In addition, the ordinance contains provisions for the waiver of impact fees on affordable units. Developers can obtain waiver credits by offering the units at prices below those established by the affordability threshold, and by ensuring that the project will remain affordable for at least five years. Usually, at least half of the impact fee is waived for affordable units (American Planning Association 1991b).

RESOURCES

Cyburbia (formerly the Planning and Architecture Internet Resource Centre) contains a comprehensive directory of thousands of Internet resources relevant to planning, architecture, urbanism, and other topics related to the built environment.

State University of New York at Buffalo

School of Architecture and Planning

139 Hayes Hall

Buffalo, New York

USA 14214

Tel: 716/829-3485

Web site: www.arch.buffalo.edu/pairc/

Land Trust Alliance is the U.S. national organization of land trusts. Founded in 1982, the Alliance provides specialized services, publications, information, and training for land trusts and other conservation organizations, and works for public policies that advance land conservation. Alliance publications include *Starting a Land Trust: A Guide to Forming a Land Conservation Organization* (Alexandria, Va.: Land Trust Alliance, 1990). For more information, contact:

1319 F Street, N.W., Suite 501

Washington, D.C.

USA 20004

Tel: 202/638-4725

Fax: 202/638-4730

Web site: www.lta.org/

Lincoln Institute of Land Policy is a nonprofit school that studies and teaches about land policy, including land economics and land taxation. Its major goals are integrating the theory and practice of land policy and understanding the forces that influence it. The Institute offers courses and workshops in various cities, has an impressive publications list, and publishes the bi-monthly newsletter, *LandLines*.

113 Brattle Street

Cambridge, Massachusetts

USA 02138-3400

Tel: 617/661-3016

Fax: 617/661-7235

E-mail: help@lincolninst.edu

Web site: www.lincolninst.edu/lincoln

REFERENCES

Abberger, W. 1991. "Growth Management Through Land Acquisition." In *Balanced Growth: A Planning Guide for Local Government*, J.M. DeGrove, ed. Washington, D.C.: International City Management Association.

Adler, J. 1995. "Bye-Bye, Suburban Dream: 15 Ways to Fix the Suburbs." *Newsweek* 15 May 15, pp. 40-53.

American Planning Association. 1991a. "Solving Traffic Woes by Balancing Jobs and Housing." In *Balanced Growth: A Planning Guide for Local Government*, J.M. DeGrove, ed. Washington, D.C.: International City Management Association.

— — — . 1991b. "Taming the Exclusionary Effects of Growth Controls." In *Balanced Growth: A Planning Guide for Local Government,* J.M. DeGrove, ed. Washington, D.C.: International City Management Association.

Arlidge, J. 1997. "Green Homes for People Without Cars." *Guardian Weekly* 27 April: 30.

British Columbia Ministry of Municipal Affairs and Housing (BCMMAH). 1997. *Taking Action.* Victoria, B.C.: BCMMAH.

British Columbia Round Table on the Environment and the Economy (BCRTEE). 1994. *State of Sustainability: Urban Sustainability and Containment.* Victoria, B.C.: Crown Publications.

Brown, H.J., ed. 1997. *Land Use and Taxation: Applying the Insights of Henry George* Cambridge, Mass.: Lincoln Institute of Land Policy.

Cervero, R. 1991. "Congestion Relief: The Land Use Alternative." *Journal of Planning Education and Research* 10(2): 119-29.

City of Vancouver. 1990. *Clouds of Change: Final Report of the City of Vancouver Task Force on Atmospheric Change.* Vancouver: City of Vancouver.

Cooper Marcus, C., and W. Sarkissian. 1986. *Housing as if People Mattered: Site Design Guidelines for Medium-Density Family Housing.* Berkeley: University of California Press.

Daly, H.E., and J.B. Cobb, Jr. 1989. *For the Common Good: Redirecting the Economy Toward Community, the Environment, and a Sustainable Future.* Boston: Beacon Press.

DeGrove, J.M., ed. 1991. *Balanced Growth: A Planning Guide for Local Government.* Washington, D.C.: International City Management Association.

Duany, A. 1991. Reinventing the Suburb. Presented to the Urban Development Institute, Pacific Region, Vancouver, B.C., 24 September.

Duany, A., and E. Plater-Zyberk. 1992. "The Second Coming of the Small Town." *Wilson Quarterly* (Winter). Reprinted in *Utne Reader* 1 (May/June): 97-100.

Durning, A.T. 1996. *The Car and The City.* Seattle: Northwest Environment Watch.

Engwicht, D. 1993. *Reclaiming Our Cities and Towns: Better Living With Less Traffic.* Gabriola Island, B.C.: New Society Publishers.

Federation of Canadian Municipalities. 1990. *A Guidebook on Transportation Energy Management.* Ottawa: Federation of Canadian Municipalities.

Gabor, A., and F. Lewinberg. 1997. "New Urbanism, New Zoning." *Plan Canada* 38(4): 12-17.

Gayler, H. 1990. "Changing Aspects of Urban Containment in Canada: The Niagara Case in the 1980s and Beyond." *Urban Geography* 11(4): 373-93.

Gordon, D. 1991. *Steering a New Course: Transportation, Energy, and the Environment.* Cambridge, Mass.: Union of Concerned Scientists.

Haughton, G., and C. Hunter. 1994. *Sustainable Cities.* Regional Policy and Development Series 7. London: Jessica Kingsley.

Heyerdahl, B. 1991. "TDRs: An Innovative Approach to Growth Management." In *Balanced Growth: A Planning Guide for Local Government,* J.M. DeGrove, ed. Washington, D.C.: International City Management Association.

Holtzclaw, J. 1991. Explaining Urban Density and Transit Impacts on Auto Use. Presented to State of California Energy Resources Conservation and Development Commission, Docket No. 89-CR-90, 15 January.

Ingerson, A.E. 1991. "Urban Land as Common Property." *LandLines* 9(2): 1-3.

Kasowski, K. 1991. "Oregon: Fifteen Years of Land-Use Planning." In *Balanced Growth: A Planning Guide for Local Government*, J.M. DeGrove, ed. Washington, D.C.: International City Management Association.

Kingston Planning Report. 1987. Item No. 213, File 60.73.70, 15 April.

Knack, R.E. 1991. "Tony Nelessen's Do-It-Yourself Neotraditionalism." *Planning* 57(12) December: 18-22.

Kunstler, J.H. 1996. "Home From Nowhere: How to Make Our Cities and Towns Livable." *Atlantic Monthly* 278 (3) September: 43-66.

Land Trust Alliance. n.d. Land Trusts. Washington, D.C.: Land Trust Alliance.

Low, S. 1997. "Using Suburban Amenities to Reshape, Revitalize Cities." *Boston Sunday Globe* 15 June, p. E3.

Lowe, M.D. 1991a. "Portland Bypasses Progress." *Worldwatch* 4(5) Sept./Oct.: 9, 30.

— — — . 1991b. "Shaping Cities: The Environmental and Human Dimensions." *Worldwatch* 105. Washington, D.C.: Worldwatch Institute.

— — — . 1992. "City Limits." *Worldwatch* 5(1) Jan./Feb.: 18-25.

MacBurnie, I. 1991. Reconsidering the Dream: Towards a Morphology for a Mixed Density Block Structure in Suburbia. Presented to Colloquium on Sustainable Housing and Urban Development, Institute of Urban Studies, University of Winnipeg, Manitoba, 16 November.

Metropolitan Toronto Planning Department Policy Development Division. 1987. "Housing Intensification." In *Metropolitan Plan Review Report No. 4*. Toronto: Planning Department

Neilson, L. 1990. Economic Perspective on Better Urban Space. Presented to Globe '90 Conference, Vancouver, B.C., 20 March.

Newman, P. 1991a. "Greenhouse, Oil and Cities." *Futures* May: 335-48.

— — — . 1991b. "Suffocate City." *Consuming Interest* June/July: 13-18.

— — — . 1991c. Urban Villages — Concept for the '90s. Presented to ECODESIGN Conference, RMIT, Melbourne, Australia, 18-20 October.

— — — . 1996. Reducing Automobile Dependence. Presented to OECD International Conference, Toward Sustainable Transportation, Vancouver, B.C., March.

Newman, P., and J. Kenworthy. 1989. *Cities and Automobile Dependence: An International Sourcebook*. Brookfield, Vt.: Gower Technical.

O'Brien, F. 1990. "Toward a Greener, Cleaner Planet and a New Environmental Perspective." *Canadian Building* May.

Okamoto, P. 1991. "The Neo-Traditionalists: Peter Calthorpe and Andres Duany/Elizabeth Plater-Zyberk." *Urban Ecologist* Fall.

Ontario Ministry of Municipal Affairs and Housing. 1989. "Land Use Planning for Housing." Toronto: Ministry of Government Services.

Owens, S.E. 1990. "Land Use Planning for Energy Efficiency." In *Energy, Land, and Public Policy*, J.B. Cullingworth, ed. New Brunswick, N.J.: Transaction Publishers. Pp. 53-98.

Real Estate Research Corporation. 1974. *The Costs of Sprawl*. Volume I: Detailed Cost Analysis. Washington, D.C.: U.S. Government Printing Office.

Regional Municipality of Halton (Ontario). 1991. Land Stewardship and Healthy Communities: A Vision for the 90's and Beyond. Official Plan Review Report B4 draft,

January.

Replogle, M. 1990. Sustainable Transportation Strategies for World Development. Presented to the World Congress of Local Governments for a Sustainable Future, United Nations, New York, 7 September.

Richardson, N. 1991. Sustainable Development and Land Use Planning. Presented to Association of Municipal Clerks and Treasurers of Ontario and Intergovernmental Committee on Urban and Regional Research Management Symposium, Implementing Sustainable Development in Municipalities, Hockley Valley, Ontario, 8-10 May.

Rybeck, R. 1996. Tax Reform Fights Sprawl. Prepared for OECD International Conference, Toward Sustainable Transportation, Vancouver, B.C., March.

St. Catharines Planning Report. 1987. Item No. 433, File 60.80.1. 22 July.

World Resources Institute, United Nations Environment Program, United Nations Development Program, World Bank. 1996. *World Resources 1996-97: The Urban Environment*. New York: Oxford University Press.

Housing and Community Development

Reducing the environmental impact of housing and urban development is critical for the survival of our planet, but improving livability and fostering community is imperative for the survival of humanity. Mobility and migration have splintered many communities that were long based on blood ties, cultural heritage and life within a narrow geographic region. Yet new challenges have arisen to connect people — to share common interests, share burdens, and develop healthy relationships with other members of the human community. In other words, "Community is a group of people who commit themselves for the long-term to their own, one another's and the group's well-being" (Shaffer and Anundsen 1993).

Despite myriad opportunities for social interaction, cities and towns are lonely places of isolation for many people. Community development requires good urban design to foster connection and neighborliness, and programs, policies, and initiatives to encourage healthy human interaction, including safety, respect, and social equity. Social equity means more than equal opportunity. It implies opportunities for adequate housing, healthcare, education, employment, and mobility. Homelessness alone strikes thousand of people in North America, and millions more live in abject poverty and subsistence housing.

Sustainable community development implies that we address not only the "hard" urban environmental issues such as transportation, land use, air quality, and energy conservation, but also the "soft" issues such as social and environmental justice.

MORE THAN A ROOF OVER OUR HEADS

Housing is a key factor influencing both environmental and social aspects of community development. Many, many people in North America live without adequate housing, or lack any form of permanent and secure shelter. In addition to these inequities, even those fortunate enough to have a home may live in a neighborhood lacking "a sense of place."

Affording a Home

A growing number of people cannot afford housing. Subsidized programs provide assistance to some, while others are leaving the city to find lower-cost housing in suburbs and small towns. Residents of low-cost housing are often stereotyped as jobless people who bring with them numerous social problems. While unemployment is a growing problem, many *employed* people don't earn enough to afford adequate housing. A survey of low-income residents of Contra Costa County, California, indicates most families who need affordable housing are simply hardworking people caught in the squeeze between rising housing costs and eroding wages. As real estate prices escalate and the cost of living continues to increase, many people working as secretaries, clerks, nurses aides, and truck drivers may not earn enough money to afford market-rate housing, and if they are supporting children or other family members, their financial stress magnifies.

A variety of strategies exist to finance affordable housing development and to support people seeking ways to lower housing costs. Community Development Corporations, credit unions, community development banks, and various other government and non-governmental agencies provide funding for construction, rents and mortgages, or in-kind support for affordable housing construction. (See also Chapter 12: Community Economic Development.) Unfortunately much of the affordable and lower-cost units built in the last few decades have failed to provide healthy, safe, and nurturing environments for residents. Single-mothers and the aged or infirm are groups whose needs are often neglected in housing design and planning. By "designing as if people mattered" (Cooper-Marcus 1986), architects, planners, and developers honor the needs of all people and seek to provide places where all can thrive.

Alternative housing development strategies, such as cooperatives and cohousing, are planned with the participation of future residents. This enables residents to influence design so that it represents their needs. The focus is on community in these and other forms of shared-living communities, but they also offer opportunities for lower costs. Shared space such as gardens and common areas enable people to live comfortably in more compact space, and sharing of cars, computers, laundry service, and childcare can reduce living expenses.

Cohousing is gaining popularity among people of varying incomes as the desire for greater community prompts increasing dissatisfaction with the design of conventional residential developments. As with other shared living communities, homes are clustered together; however unlike intentional communities, each family lives in a separate apartment or house. Residents share common areas and management of the

---

Social Sustainability

Social sustainability is another way of discussing social capital (see chapter 1). It requires social equity and responsible citizenship. Socially sustainable community members are able to:

• achieve and maintain personal health: physical, mental and psychological;

• feed themselves adequately;

• provide adequate and appropriate shelter for themselves;

• have opportunities for gainful and meaningful employment;

• improve their knowledge and understanding of the world around them;

• find opportunities to express creativity and enjoy recreation in ways that satisfy spiritual and psychological needs;

• express a sense of identity through heritage, art and culture;

• enjoy a sense of belonging;

• be assured of mutual social support from their community;

• enjoy freedom from discrimination and, for those who are physically challenged, move about a barrier-free community;

• enjoy freedom from fear, and security of person; and

• participate actively in civic affairs (BCRTEE 1993).

Municipal Initiatives to Promote Affordable Housing

Municipalities can plan for and promote affordable housing in many ways, including the following:

- *Development Approval Process*: Streamline the approval process and fast-track applications for rentals, special needs housing, and non-market housing.
- *Financing for New Developments*: Generate new funds for affordable housing projects through municipal initiatives.
- *Intensification of Existing Areas*: Re-zone to allow higher density housing in existing areas, e.g., secondary suites.
- *Intensification in New Areas*: Regulate zones to encourage compact forms of residential land use.
- *Land Use*: Lease or provide municipal land for affordable housing at lower than market rates.
- *Partnerships*: Collaborate with nonprofit or private organizations, churches, developers, etc.
- *Protect Existing Housing Stock*: Regulate existing housing stock to ensure it remains as affordable housing.
- *Technical Support and Housing Information*: Collect, maintain, and disseminate information regarding affordable housing in the community.
- *Zoning Regulations*: Develop creative zoning to promote affordable housing programs, e.g., mixed-land use or density bonuses (BCMHRC n.d.).

complex, and abide by agreed upon guidelines, but individuals choose how much they want to participate in community activities such as shared meals and social gatherings (McCamant and Durrett, 1988).

Creating a Community

To create a "sense of place" and foster connection among people, the physical characteristics of neighborhoods must draw people together and encourage an atmosphere of peace, security, and pride among residents of a community. In addition to thoughtful building design, clean streets, gardens and trees, and places to gather can create a village-like atmosphere even in inner-city neighborhoods. Ideally, closeness to other people is mirrored in a closeness to nature and integration of ecology into community living.

However, the physical design of housing and neighborhoods alone cannot create communities. Government policies and the actions and initiatives of local citizens are critical. Churches have often been the center of community, but in more recent times, people have also sought connection through involvement in neighborhood groups and activities, and participation in other non-government organizations such as environmental groups.

While responsible participation in governance is important, getting to know your neighbors is a simple first step. Getting involved and creating opportunities for inclusiveness are even bigger steps. True and rich community is a mix of young and old, rich and poor, men and women of varying ethnicity and abilities sharing their lives.

TOOLS AND INITIATIVES

Affordable Housing Programs

Housing Scholarship Program: Fremont, California's Housing Scholarship Program arranges for reduced rents for low-income family providers for a one-year period. In that time the provider agrees to complete job training and find work. Apartment owners participate by reducing rents during the period, and the city is encouraging housing developers to set aside units for this program in future developments financed with city assistance. So far, more than 90 percent of scholarship recipients have successfully completed job training (*Urban Ecologist* 1996).

Nonprofit Affordable Housing Organization: In the 1970s, the U.S. Department of Housing and Urban Development provided low-interest loans to encourage construction of affordable housing. Twenty years later, low-income people are losing their subsidized housing as building owners repay these loans and convert apartment buildings to market-rate rents. The Ecumenical Association of Housing is a nonprofit affordable housing organization in San Rafael, California raising financing to purchase many of these apartments before tenants face rent increases. In 1996, the Association used Housing and Urban Development grants and other financial sources to invest $95.1 million to acquire 831 units of affordable housing (Anders 1997).

Habitat for Humanity: This nonprofit organization has chapters across North America which raise funds (and in-kind contributions) to construct low-cost homes. Mimicking the Amish style of community barn-raising, volunteers work together to construct houses. Some Habitat chapters are building energy-efficient homes so that the new homeowners will not be saddled with high utility bills. Others are experimenting with strawbale or adobe environmentally sound construction materials.

Service-Enriched Housing

Beyond Shelter: In 1990, Beyond Shelter, a nonprofit affordable housing and social services provider, purchased and renovated a 41-apartment complex to provide service-enriched housing in Los Angeles, California. Residents help make decisions about appropriate services such as child care, employment, education, health, and recreation. A resident manager and a services coordinator work with the Tenant Management Committee to manage the building and common areas, and to plan monthly activities for tenants of all ages.

Self-Help Housing

Urban Homesteading: The Urban Homesteading Assistance Board in New York City began in 1973 by training tenants to own and manage their own buildings. The Board also promotes the conversion of city-owned buildings into limited equity co-ops in which the tenants together own the building and share responsibilities such as maintenance and book-keeping. The experience helps build skills, empower people, and reduce crime rates in and around these buildings.

Mutual Housing Associations

Mutual Housing Associations are private, nonprofit corporations created to develop, own, and manage affordable hous-

---

Small Steps to Create Neighborhoods

• Learn the names of your neighbors and local merchants. Share ideas and conversation with them.
• Send out postcards suggesting a babysitting or pet-sitting cooperative.
• Invite a few neighbors to dinner or a barbeque, and suggest a meal rotation (one household at a time cooking one day each month).
• Start a neighborhood newsletter or newspaper. This reinforces neighborhood identify.
• Ask the police department to help sponsor a block meeting to discuss safety. Plan a social time afterwards.
• Invite local architects and planners with vision to speak to your community group. Design is a key element in creating a feeling of community.
• Request some city land be made available for citizen planting of trees and community gardens (Shaffer and Anundsen 1993).

Family-focused community-building

Family-focused community-building is a model of community organizing in response to a lack of organizing efforts from more traditional models such as Community Development Corporations. The family-focused community-building model, as developed by the Community Organizing and Family Issues organization in Chicago, returns to the notion that community empowerment begins from within and is based on the following:

• Prospective leaders are recruited from low-income families, particularly women.
• Leadership training emphasizes continuities between family and community leadership.
• Visioning conversations are framed in terms of what will make the community a better place for families.
• Recognition of many different kinds and levels of leadership.
• Recognition that many of the conditions making communities unsafe and unhealthy are rooted in public policies beyond the local level.

Housing can be designed to accomodate greenery or to grow food by providing set-back terraces and deep flower boxes

ing. All residents are stockholders and therefore participate in decision-making. Housing Associations unite groups of buildings, such as limited equity co-ops and low- and middle-income dwellings, into larger associations. It is believed that larger associations will improve the delivery of housing services and assist in on-going development. Other benefits are providing resident training and professional property management, and pooling capital and leadership resources.

Financing through Bonds

Municipal Bonds: The City of Portland, Oregon is financing affordable housing development by borrowing against future taxes to set up municipal bonds.

In 1994, residents of San Antonio, Texas voted to approve a $41.6-million bond to be used to for urban rehabilitation and acquisition of land for city parks. The bond was marketed as a "quality-of-life investment" (*Urban Ecologist* 1995).

Linkage Programs and Partnerships

Linkage policies represent "a new social contract to build lasting bridges of economic opportunity between areas of the city experiencing rapid growth, and the people . . . who, historically, have not shared in the benefits of that growth" (Boston Redevelopment Authority 1988). Linkage programs collect a portion of the value created by investment in neighborhoods undergoing substantial development and direct that value to build affordable housing, provide job training, and fund social services in less fortunate neighborhoods. Linkage programs could also provide a means for financing investment in environmental protection and restoration. While these programs have operated for several years in U.S. cities such as Boston and San Francisco, they are also becoming more common in Canada.

Daycare Center: In December 1990, Vancouver, B.C. approved its first agreement with a commercial developer in which the capital costs of a daycare center were financed as a condition of rezoning.

Mixed-Use Complex: In an unusual partnership, Habitat for Humanity teamed up in 1996 with an Equity Housing Cooperative to construct a mixed-use complex in East Vancouver, B.C. A commercial partner is developing the street level shops, and 29 units of housing make up the second and third stories. Some of the units will be co-op owned, and others will be Habitat homes provided to low-income families. By helping construct the complex, people earn equity toward their new home.

Community Grants

Block Grants: In Embarrass, Minnesota, a Community Development Block Grant is funding conversion of a donated old log warehouse into a visitors' center with a replica of a Finnish smoke sauna inside. As well, grants funded a survey of log buildings to place some of them on the National Register of Historic Places, and supported a workshop on barn restoration. The community also gathered to build a community center, the Embarrass Timber Hall, using traditional log-house building techniques (Renew America 1997).

Community Land Trusts

Community Land Trusts have acquired or developed several thousand units of permanently affordable housing, and heritage buildings, and have provided land for shelters, health centers, farms and other community social and economic development needs. The land is owned by a nonprofit organization and protected by it for a specific use. (Institute for Community Economics 1982; Roseland 1992).

Governments have formed several kinds of partnerships with Community Land Trusts, such as allocating funds or city-owned lands to them. Municipal zoning has the power to negotiate commitments from developers to donate land for Trusts and to build affordable housing. Trusts also manage publicly owned lands, such as bike paths, conservation areas, and community gardens.

Burlington Community Land Trust: In 1987, the affordable housing shortage in northern Vermont inspired the creation of the Burlington Community Land Trust. The organization obtains land and places it within the Trust, thereby taking the land out of the speculative market and making the housing perpetually affordable. An eligible prospective homeowner buys a house and pays a monthly fee to lease the land the house is on. Upon future sale, the owner receives the equity paid on the mortgage, the value of any capital improvements, and 25 percent of the appreciation in market value. The Trust receives support from governments and the private sector (Roseland 1992).

Cooperative Housing Land Trust Foundation: In 1993, the Cooperative Housing Federation of B.C. formed the Cooperative Housing Land Trust Foundation to ensure access to affordable housing in B.C. The Foundation works with nonprofit housing co-ops to protect the existing stock of affordable housing. Nonprofit co-ops cannot distribute their assets to residents who buy into the co-ops, yet as agreements with government expire, tenants may lose their homes as prices jump to keep pace with market values. By joining the Foundation and transferring the asset value, the value is held in perpetuity by the land trust (B.C. Working Group 1995).

Shared-living Communities

Cohousing: Residents of the Doyle Street co-housing complex in Emeryville, California live in loft-style apartments in a converted brick warehouse. Adaptive reuse of an old building helped to revitalize an economically disadvantaged area; it also encouraged a sprawling community to embrace the neighborhood by, among other things, establishing a community garden nearby.

Cooperative Housing: Recognizing the need for safe, affordable housing options for single-mothers, the nonprofit Entres Nous Femmes Housing Society is helping build co-operative housing units in Vancouver, B.C. Primarily occupied by single-parent families, the townhouse-style complexes provide both a home and a community to many people who were previously isolated. Empowerment of the co-op's members is key. Residents sit on the board of directors and make decisions about maintenance and management of the facilities, which provides opportunities to learn management and organizational skills useful in the job market.

Urban Cooperative Block: In a suburb of Davis, California, residents formed an urban cooperative block called N Street Community by removing fences and sharing their lives. Residents of eleven houses merged their backyards to share paths, patios, fruit trees, compost bins, gardens, greenhouses, a chicken pen, and a clothes line. One house was converted into a common house, and the group pooled their resources to purchase two adjacent houses to enable rental tenants to join the community. Efforts toward sustainability include organically managing gardens, growing fruits and vegetables, and installing solar collectors. Neighbors share cars, compost, and reuse and recycle materials.

Community Revitalization Programs

Don't Move, Improve! Campaign: Faced with urban decay and an exodus from the South Bronx in New York, a community-group initiated an urban revitalization program addressing health, daycare, economic education, housing, environment, transportation, and capital development. The "Don't Move, Improve!" campaign has channeled $100 million of investment into the community, rehabilitated and constructed 25,000 units of affordable housing, implemented energy-efficiency retrofits in more than 8,000 units, and provided technical and financial assistance to 125 small businesses (Wheeler 1996).

Nuisance Alley Program: Residents convert debris-ridden alleys in Los Angeles, California into common gardens and recreational areas. Efforts by the Los Angeles Neighborhood Initiative to revitalize the city's streets also include funding and spearheading renovation of storefronts, tree planting, and other improvements in eight of the city's most rundown neighborhoods. Local residents and businesses recommend improvements, and funds come from a variety of federal, state, and private monies.

Mosaic Park: East Vancouver, B.C. has fewer parks per capita than any other neighborhood in the city. Modest funding from local grants and city support helped a group of citizens, including an architect and a landscape architect, come together to convert a vacant lot into a playground and park. With no vegetation or streams on the barren lot, the group found another way to create some connection with nature. A meandering stream was designed and built with mosaic tiles, assisted by a local artist who taught school children and community groups how to create ceramic tile mosaics. Large boulders (free byproducts of city excavation work) and logs were brought in for children to climb on, and locals planted trees. Mosaic park is the pride of the community who built it.

HEALTHY COMMUNITIES

A healthy community reflects the health of its citizens. A century ago, municipalities were instrumental in improving public health by preventing the spread of disease through slum clearance, community planning, water treatment, and the provision of certain health services. These initiatives were based on the view of health as the absence of disease, and disease prevention as the main challenge for local government. Yet health is influenced more by our physical and social environments than by interventions of the health care system.

Since the mid-1980s, a broader conception of public health has been adopted by municipal governments in Europe and North America. Although the name "healthy communities" implies a focus on medical care, the Ottawa Charter for Health Promotion (WHO et al. 1986) recognizes that "the fundamental conditions and resources for health are peace, shelter, education, food, income, a stable ecosystem, sustainable resources, social justice, and equity." Local governments play a big role in all these areas through their impact on public hygiene (waste disposal and water systems), food handling and other public health regulations, recreational facilities, education, transportation, economic development, and land-use planning.

The Healthy Communities approach is based on a worldwide Healthy Cities movement which now numbers over 1000 cities. Launched with the support of the World Health Organization, the movement had its genesis in Toronto at a 1984 health conference workshop called "Healthy Toronto 2000." The Healthy Communities approach is based on four main ideas:

• *Wide community participation*: People from all walks of life work together toward a healthier community.

• *Multi- or inter-sectoral involvement*: Residents join sectors of the community (such as business, labor, churches, service providers, planners, environmental groups) to form a common vision of a healthy community. Each finds ways to contribute toward this goal.

• *Local government commitment*: Each government department (such as parks and recreation, public works) focuses on the same vision of a healthy community and applies it in their jurisdiction.

• *Healthy public policy*: The key to promote health in its broadest sense is often changing legislation instead of providing more services (ORTEE 1995).

TOOLS AND INITIATIVES

Healthy Communities/Healthy City Programs

Healthy City Office: Since its establishment in 1989, Toronto's Healthy City Office has: initiated neighborhood study circles; celebrated community successes at the annual Neighborly Awards; coordinated development of a municipal strategy to reduce traffic and air pollution, and a bylaw to restrict unnecessary motor vehicle idling; completed the "State of the City" report, documenting key trends in the city and assessing conditions regarding the environment, economic life, housing, etc.; involved homeless people in planning and building housing; and facilitated formation of a Young People's Advisory Board to provide city government with input from a youth perspective (ORTEE 1995).

Environmental Justice

The environmental justice movement (also known as environmental equity) addresses the inequity particularly associated with hazardous-waste sites located in areas inhabited by racial minorities or the poor (Agyeman and Evans 1996). Environmental justice includes:

- *Procedural equity*: the "fairness" with which rules, regulations, and assessments are made and reinforced; unequal protection arises from unscientific, secretive, and non-democratic behaviors.
- *Social equity*: the way in which sociological factors such as race, ethnicity, class, culture, and political power influence environmental decision-making practices, so that certain groups seem to be systematically disadvantaged in terms of, for example, living in the most polluted neighborhoods (or countries).
- *Geographic equity*: the way in which the location of communities and their proximity to non-desirable land uses, such as toxic-waste incinerating plants, landfills, and sewage works, is not randomly configured, but located in the most environmentally disadvantaged areas (Bullard 1993).
- *Inter-generational equity*: refers to the environmental impact on future generations.
- *Inter-species equity*: concerns balancing human needs with ecosystem survival.

Environmental justice may be defined as the "sum" of the interactions of these dimensions of equity (Haughton 1996). In 1992, the Bush administration created the U.S. Office of Environmental Justice, and in 1994, President Clinton ordered every federal department and agency to "make achieving environmental justice part of its mission." By 1997, at least seven states had passed environmental-justice laws, and many more are considering them (*Economist* 1997).

Health and Wellness Programs

Health and Fitness Campaign: Obesity and heart disease require billions of dollars of money spent on medical care each year, and are leading causes of death in Canada and the U.S. With promotional support from the local newspaper, the City of Vancouver developed a huge annual health and fitness campaign that is linked to a charitable fund-raising event. From "couch potatoes" to athletes, the program is helping people join others in improving their health. The three-month program, which includes weekly walking/jogging training and lessons on nutrition and fitness training, culminates in a popular fitness fair and 10-kilometer (6.2-mile) run.

Anti-Smoking Bylaws

Smoking Ban: The Cities of Aspen, Colorado, and Vancouver, B.C. are heeding warnings about the hazards of cigarette smoke. In a effort to protect people from second-hand smoke, the cities banned cigarette smoking in restaurants and all public buildings.

Vending Machine Ban: In order to prevent school children from purchasing cigarettes, New York City Council's health committee unanimously passed a bill banning cigarette vending machines from laundromats, gas stations, apartment buildings, and some restaurants (*Los Angeles Daily News* 1990).

Safety Audits

Metro Action Committee: Informal groups of people get together and, using a safety audit checklist, evaluate lighting, access to emergency phones, overgrown shrubbery near bus shelters, and so on. Government authorities use the information to guide decisions about safety improvements within their jurisdiction. Safety audit programs are now being used in Hamilton, Ontario and on several university campuses (Hamilton Spectator 1991; Canadian Press 1991; *Urban Ecologist* 1995).

Community Police and Patrol

Community Police: In downtown Vancouver, B.C. community police centers are opening up in small store-front centers to help bring police closer to citizens. As they walk or bike throughout the neighborhood, police officers get to know local residents and inform "street people" about opportunities for assistance.

Volunteer Park Patrollers: In Vancouver, volunteer park patrollers rollerblade or bicycle around the 15-kilometer (9.3-mile) long seawall path in Stanley Park. In addition to enjoying comradery, the wheeling park patrollers ensure that the many cyclists, joggers, and rollerbladers are safely enjoying the spectacular public park.

Local Food Supplies

Organic Community Garden: Concerned about poor nutrition and health in their community, the Cariboo Health (B.C.) Unit partnered with the Salvation Army to start an organic community garden. Volunteers grow fruit and vegetables for low-income residents and garden space is also available for people who don't have land of their own.

Hydroponics at Prison: The Southeast Regional Correctional Center in Bridgewater, Massachusetts produces food for the prison and the community while training inmates for future employment. Prisoners use hydroponics to cultivate fish and vegetables in a prison greenhouse. The produce and fish are sold to the culinary arts program at the prison, to staff, to a high school, and a local health-food store (Zweig 1990; Levi 1991).

Community Kitchens

Community Kitchen: Support from the Health Department in Williams Lake, B.C. helps low-income residents gain food security. Each month members of the kitchen gather to plan healthy meals, and a part-time coordinator and a nutritionist lend support. Everyone shares duties for shopping and food preparation, and meals are divided up and taken home to share with families. The Salvation Army also helps by collecting grocery donations from local stores. The program helps build skills and confidence, while creating bonds in the community (B.C. Working Group 1995).

Lovin' Spoon Full: A volunteer group in Vancouver, B.C. called Lovin' Spoon Full delivers prepared meals to people debilitated by AIDS.

Environmental Justice Advocacy Programs

Environmental Benefits Program: Greenpoint-Williamsburg is one of the poorest and most highly industrialized areas in the New York City borough of Brooklyn. Many residents suffer from the risks and consequences of waste, pollution, and odors caused by nearly 1000 industrial firms. The Environmental Benefits Program, a partnership between the city and local citizens, integrated public participation into the process of remediating environmental problems. The state ordered establishment of a benefits fund made up of money collected for non-compliance of environmental regulations; the Citizens' Advisory Committee directs the funds to local environmental initiatives. An Environmental Watchperson contracts with community-based organizations to implement and administer initiatives (ICLEI 1995).

Labor/Community Watchdog: An environmental justice project of the Labor/Community Strategy Center in Los Angeles, California, Watchdog criticized the policies of the state's regulatory agency that oversees the reduction of smog levels. Watchdog pointed out that trip-reduction policies, such as increased parking fees, would be too costly for low-paid workers and would burden working mothers responsible for shuttling children to school and daycare. Instead, Watchdog proposed company-paid van pools and employee transit subsidies. These proposals (eventually accepted) shifted the burden of payment for pollution control to employers (Boyce 1995).

Neighborhood-Building

Family Reunion: Gerald Mason is a citizen concerned about the rift between the African American and the "white" population in Chattanooga, Tennessee. His perception is that "what's keeping blacks and whites from coming together as a community is our inability to be together socially" (Shaeffer and Anundsen 1993). Mason sent a letter to two or three hundred black and white acquaintances, inviting them to bring a member of the opposite race to Sunday brunch at a restaurant. More than a hundred people showed up, and so began the Chattanooga Family Reunion, which is now a monthly event. There's no agenda — blacks and whites just socialize and friendships are formed. As both races grow to understand each other, the community is flourishing.

Residents Plant Flowers: In an ad hoc organizing effort, residents of one East Vancouver, B.C. street gathered to plant flowers in their new traffic calming circle. Now their neighborhood is more attractive as well as safer.

Outdoor Volunteers: The small towns of the Roaring Fork Valley in Colorado rely heavily on volunteers for the many social events and social programs offered throughout the community. Roaring Fork Outdoor Volunteers helps to improve the quality of the environment and life in the valley. Outdoor Volunteers build and repair nature trails, plant trees, and help those in need. On designated volunteer days, locals get together to paint the exterior (or interior) of nursing homes or the homes of elderly or lower-income residents. The gatherings always include a big outdoor picnic, and sometimes live music and a camp-out.

Publicity

Act Locally Calendar: The Eco-City Network in Vancouver, B.C. publishes the "Act Locally" calendar. The calendar, which is distributed in hard copy and through the Internet, features free listings of community activities and initiatives for community improvement and urban revitalization.

Connecting to Other Communities

Mega-Cities Project: A network of professionals and institutions in the world's largest cities is committed to promoting urban innovations for the 21st century. Its focus is reducing poverty and environmental degradation, and encouraging popular participation. Mega-cities are cities with over 10 million inhabitants — by 2000 there will be 23 of them, including New York, Los Angeles, and Mexico City. The project gives particular attention to urban innovations that empower women.

Awards for Community Contributions

Canada Trust and VanCity: Two financial institutes in Vancouver, B.C. help to support and publicize recognition of citizens active in the community. Each year, Canada Trust awards scholarships to students for outstanding contributions to the community. VanCity Credit Union sponsors the Ethics In Action Awards, honoring organizations and individuals demonstrating exemplary programs or efforts toward social equity and environmental justice.

RESOURCES

Institute for Community Economics is a nonprofit corporation providing technical and financial assistance to community land trusts, limited-equity housing co-ops, community loan funds, and other grassroots organizations. The Institute also provides information and educational material to the general public, such as *The Community Land Trust Handbook* (Rodale Press 1982) and the quarterly journal, *Community Economics.*
57 School Street
Springfield, Massachusetts
USA 01105-1331
Tel: 413/746-8660

Labor/Community Strategy Center
The Wiltern Center
3780 Wiltshire Blvd., Suite 1200
Los Angeles, California
USA 90010
Tel: 213/387-2800
Fax: 213/387-3500

Office of Environmental Justice
Environmental Protection Agency
401 M Street, S.W.
Washington, D.C.
USA 20460
Tel: 202/564-2515
Toll-free: 800/962-6215
Fax: 202/501-0740
E-mail: environmental-justice-epa@epamail.epa.gov
Web site: www.es.epa.gov/oeca/oej.html

Toronto Healthy City Office
20 Dundas Street, Suite 1036
P.O. Box 22
Toronto, Ontario
Canada M5G 2C2
Tel: 416/392-0099
Fax: 416/392-0089

REFERENCES

Agyeman, J., and B. Evans. 1996. "Black on Green: Race, Ethnicity and the Environment." In *Environmental Planning and Sustainability*, S. Buckingham-Hatfield, and B. Evans, eds. Chichester, U.K.: John Wiley and Sons.

Anders, C. 1997. "Housing Association Preserves Low-Cost Apartments." *San Francisco Examiner and Chronical*, 6 April, pp. E1, E3.

B.C. Working Group on Community Economic Development. 1995. *Sharing Our Stories.* September.

Boston Redevelopment Authority. 1988. *Linkage* (Winter).

Boyce, J.K. 1995. "LA Watchdog Group Challenges Traditional Solutions to Environmental Problems." *Alternatives* 21(1) Jan./Feb.: 15.

British Columbia Ministry of Housing, Recreation, and Consumers (BCMHRC). n.d. *Affordable Housing and Local Government: Building Strong Communities.* Victoria: BCMHRC.

British Columbia Round Table on the Environment and the Economy (BCRTEE). 1993. *Strategic Directions for Community Sustainability.* Victoria, B.C.: Crown Publications.

Bullard, R., ed. 1993. *Confronting Environmental Racism: Voices from the Grassroots.* Boston: South End Press.

Canadian Press. 1991. "Melbourne Looks to Toronto for Ways to Makes Streets Safe." Vancouver Sun, 26 October, p. C9.

Cooper-Marcus, C. 1986. "Design as if People Mattered." In *Sustainable Cities*, Sim Van der Ryn, Peter Calthorpe, eds. San Francisco: Sierra Club Books.

Economist, The. 1997. "In Their Back Yard: Race and the Environment." 343(8017) May: 31.

Hamilton Spectator. 1991. "Hamilton Women's Group Plans to Take Safety Audit of City." Reprinted in Vancouver Sun, 18 September, p. A4.

Haughton, G. 1996. Spheres of Influence and Sustainable Urban Development. Presented to the Annual Conference of the Association of America Geographers, Charlotte, North Carolina, April.

International Council for Local Environmental Initiatives (ICLEI). 1995. *The Role of Local Authorities in Sustainable Development: 14 Case Studies on the Local Agenda 21 Process.* Nairobi: UN Centre for Human Settlements.

Institute for Community Economics. 1982. The Community Land Trust Handbook. Emmaus, Pa.: Rodale Press.

Levi, C. 1991. "Growing Fish Salad: An Experiment in Integrated Aquaculture." *Nor'Easter* Spring: 14-17.

Los Angeles Daily News. 1990. "L.A. City Council to Vote on Total Restaurant Smoking Ban." Reprinted in *Vancouver Sun*, 16 October, p. A5.

McCamant, K. and C. Durrett. 1988. *Cohousing: A Contemporary Approach to Housing Ourselves.* Berkeley: Habitat Press.

Ontario Round Table on the Environment and the Economy (ORTEE). 1995. *Sustainable Communities Resource Package.* Toronto: ORTEE.

Renew America. 1997. *Success Stories.* 1400 16th Street, N.W., Suite 710, Washington, D.C. <solstice.crest.org/environment/renew_america/>.

Roseland, M. 1992. "Linking Affordable Housing and Environmental Protection: The Community Land Trust as a Sustainable Urban Development Institution." *Canadian Journal of Urban Research* 1(2): 162-80..

Shaffer, C., and K. Anundsen. 1993. *Creating Community Anywhere*. G.P. Putnam's Sons Publishers.

Urban Ecologist. 1995 "Ecological Rebuilding: U.S." 1.

— — — . 1995. "Making Cities Safer: METRAC's Safety Audit." 1.

— — — . 1996. "Fremont's Housing Scholarships." 3.

Wheeler, S. 1996. "Best Practices in Urban Development." *Urban Ecologist* 3.

World Health Organization (WHO), Health and Welfare Canada, and Canadian Public Health Association. 1986. "Ottawa Charter for Health Promotion." *Canadian Journal of Public Health* 77:425-27.

Zweig, R. 1990. "Development of an Integrated Aquaculture System at the Southeast Correctional Center in Bridgewater, Massachusetts." Cambridge, Mass.: MIT Sea Grant Program.

COMMUNITY ECONOMIC DEVELOPMENT

The social and natural capital of many communities is controlled by outside interests. In recent years, the inadequacies of conventional economic development have been manifested in disparity in distribution of economic benefits, under-employment, and "downsizing" as companies automate or require more work from less employees. But what is the alternative?

DEVELOPMENT REDEFINED

Sustainable community economic development (CED) is a feasible, community-based alternative to the economy we are familiar with — an economy focused on growth rather than development, on global trade and currency rather than people and ecosystems. By placing greater emphasis on sustainability, including social equity and environmental responsibility, citizens and their governments choose economic development that provides opportunities for people of different incomes and skills, promotes a better quality of life, *and* protects the environment.

Sustainable CED borrows from the principles and practices of both "green business" development and CED. The Community Economic Development Centre at Simon Fraser University defines CED as "a process by which communities can initiate and generate their own solutions to their common economic problems and thereby build long-term community capacity and foster the integration of economic, social, and environmental objectives." CED calls for citizens to help shape their local economies by influencing the type of business, industry, and employment opportunities in their own backyards. "Green business" refers to economic activities that avoid harm to the environment, or help protect the ecosystem in some way. By merging the goals and principles of CED and green business, it is possible to move toward sustainable communities.

Many communities pursuing CED focus on social and economic goals, neglecting the environmental agenda, but this is starting to change. The main goal of most CED initiatives is individual and community self-reliance through collaborative action, capacity building, and returning control of business enterprises, capital, labor, and other resources from the global marketplace to communities. It targets job creation and poverty alleviation, and uses economic activity to help improve the quality of life for citizens; it recognizes the value of non-monetary transactions, such as bartering, and non-material transactions such as child- or elder-care offered by friends and neighbors. Development of local, small businesses has been a common goal of many CED initiatives, along with job training and provision of affordable housing.

Local Self-Reliance

Local self-reliance does not mean isolation. It means diversification of local economies to support local needs, encourage cohesiveness, reduce waste and enable more sustainable trade practices with other communities. Local self-reliance strives to strengthen connections between producers and consumers, whether local farmers, clothing manufacturers, furniture builders or travel agents. One way to enhance the self-reliance of a community is to identify the imports and, where possible, substitute local products, in order to invest in the local economy. As communities organize to find substitutes for imports, people become more aware of the social and environmental impacts of economic activities, and the benefits of supporting their local economy through wise investment in local goods and services. Local self-reliance fosters greater responsibility because the costs and benefits of decisions are directly borne by the community in which they are made.

The goal of a self-reliant community is to enhance local wealth by developing the community's existing resource base. Every community has some resources — physical, human, social — which can be harnessed for creating local wealth. The four basic tools communities can use to generate local wealth are:

1. Making more with less — maximizing use of existing resources.
2. Making money go round — circulating dollars within a community.
3. Making things ourselves — import replacement.
4. Making something new — creating a new product (Nozick 1992)

Community Development Organizations

CED may be driven by social entrepreneurs in the community, and municipal governments can help by structuring social services and support systems to enable self-reliance rather than creating dependency (Bruyn 1987). Chambers of Commerce

CED Principles

In 1991, a group of individuals and community organizations formed to promote community economic development in British Columbia. Over 30 provincial groups endorsed their "Statement of CED Principles," condensed below:

- *Equity*: equitable access to community decision-making processes and resources.
- *Participation*: of all members of the community in planning and decision-making.
- *Community Building*: CED seeks to build a sense of community.
- *Cooperation and Collaboration*: because many problems can't be solved in isolation, CED encourages connections within and between communities.
- *Self-reliance and Community Control*: building on local strength, creativity, and resources to decrease dependency on economic interests outside the community.
- *Integration*: of social, cultural, and ecological dimensions of community well-being.
- *Interdependence*: local community exists within the context of a larger complex web of relationships.
- *Living within Ecological Limits*: CED encourages processes and initiatives that respect ecological limits and helps to sustain, regenerate, and nurture both the community and the Earth.
- *Capacity Building*: self-reliance requires skills development and other supportive structures and institutions.
- *Diversity*: CED encourages diverse economic activities appropriate to each community.
- *Appropriate Indicators*: CED monitors and evaluates progress according to its goals (B.C. Working Group 1995).

promote local business and services, but other kinds of community organizations can help to support and sustain economic development as well.

Community development corporations offer a range of financial and other services for CED, but they are only one source of financing. Other community financing institutions or financing programs provide a variety of means for access to capital for CED. This is especially critical in areas experiencing disinvestment or shortages of conventional sources of investment capital for business and economic development.

Financing Community Economic Development

Financing and support for community development and new business development projects can come from government agencies, foundations, corporations, venture capital, educational institutes (providing research or training), religious investors, and a variety of financing sources organized specifically to support community-based projects:

- *Local Development Corporations*: certified small business administration lenders providing funds for job creation and retention in small and medium-sized businesses.
- *Community Development Corporations*: may provide loans, function as real-estate developers, or invest in local businesses or community development organizations.
- *Downtown Development Authorities*: nonprofits created by local governments to support downtown businesses. They organize special events, marketing campaigns and finance downtown improvements.
- *Credit Unions*: cooperative, nonprofit corporations created by and for people affiliated by a common bond, for the purpose of promoting thrift among their members and of loaning funds to their members at reasonable interest rates.
- *Community Development Credit Unions*: a specific type of credit union, serving low-to moderate-income communities and individuals. The Union's goal is community economic empowerment, and they typically provide financial services (such as loans) to people who need them, but cannot get them readily from banks.
- *Community Loan Funds*: a not-for-profit corporation, or a program within a not-for-profit corporation, that accepts loans from individuals and institutions and uses this capital to make loans for community development projects. Community Loan Funds usually target community-based organizations that are unable to get loans from conventional sources, offering the financial support as well as technical assistance in developing sound financial plans.
- *Revolving Loan Funds*: funds created specifically to provide alternative financing to small businesses and non-profit organizations. Often administered by community development corporations or other nonprofits, funding may be in the form of loans provided at lower rates than conventional lenders, supporting business start-up, expansion, job creation, or affordable housing.
- *Micro-Enterprise Loan Programs*: a few financial intermediaries are serving clients who require very small loans for entrepreneurial initiatives. The programs are a

"Whether CED . . . is practised in hinterland resource towns, urban ghettos, obsolescent manufacturing cities, or Native communities reserves, the general objective is the same: to take some measure of control of the local economy back from the markets and the state. Within this common objective, CED practice is variously oriented to controlling the local economy for narrow ends (increasing the capacity of a community to make money), for broader purposes (e.g., to increase economic stability and control of resources) or to serve fundamental goals of economic justice. That is to say, CED varies according to whether 'economic,' 'development,' or 'community' is emphasized" (Boothroyd 1991).

way to help low-income people get access to capital for entrepreneurial initiatives. Borrowers may not have any collateral so they are too risky, or the amount is too small, to be acceptable for conventional loan programs. Programs are usually organized as lending circles wherein borrowers receive guidance and support from others who have successfully repaid a micro-loan in the past.

• *Community Land Trusts and Housing Trusts*: strategies to finance affordable housing. (See Chapter 11: Housing and Community Development.)

• *Trust Funds*: permanent endowments, dedicated to the investment of capital assets in housing or other community economic development activities. Endowments may be capitalized by one-time contributions, or by annually renewable revenue sources.

• *Linkage Programs*: provide funds for affordable housing, job development, and daycare. Linkage works by taking a portion of the value created by investment in areas undergoing substantial development, and directing that value to build affordable housing, provide job training, and fund social services in less fortunate neighborhoods.

• *Reinvestment Policies*: The Community Reinvestment Act requires that U.S. depository institutions, such as banks and many insurance companies which extract capital from communities in the form of deposits, have an obligation to reinvest significant portions of their assets in those communities. Community economic stability is largely dependent on the availability of investment capital (Kinsley 1996).

The Deli Dollar, from Great Barrington, MA, helped to finance the move of a favorite deli to an alternative location, the finance raised by its customers who purchased food ahead of time with these locally-made notes

TOOLS AND INITIATIVES

Bartering and Local Currencies

Bartering systems and local currencies are becoming increasingly popular in North America. Bartering provides access to goods and services for people who may not otherwise have cash available for transactions, thereby strengthening local economies. Local currencies encourage investment and re-investment in local business and discourage the flow of dollars outside the community.

Ithaca Currency: "In Ithaca We Trust" are the community-minded words printed on the local currency used in Ithaca, New York. More than 3,500 local businesses and entrepreneurs in Ithaca accept "Ithaca Hours" which entitle the bearer to goods or services at participating businesses. About 2,000 people have bartered some $2 million in commerce since the alternative currency first appeared in 1991 (Spayde 1997).

Shuswap Barter Club: Founder Erik Hansen believes the Shuswap Barter Club in Salmon Arm, B.C. is a tool for community-building and self-empowerment. The system fosters a climate of optimism and cooperation as members attend Barter Potlucks to make club decisions and exchange ideas. Members come from all walks of life including children, professionals, home-based entrepreneurs, and unemployed and retired people (B.C. Working Group 1995).

Local Exchange Trading System: The LETSystem is a local exchange trading system that originated in Courtenay, B.C. in 1983. Adopted by hundreds of communities around the world, it uses a computerized accounting system to record transactions instead of alternative paper currency. Each account holder purchases goods and services by transferring credits from their account to a seller. A negative balance does not indicate debt, but a commitment to do work or exchanges goods within the community. LETS uses a dollar as the unit of exchange, so accounting is easy and taxes can be paid accordingly.

"Buy Local" Policy

Examining Purchasing Policy: A study done by students and faculty of Hendrix College in Fox, Arkansas found that the college purchased most of its food from out-of-town suppliers. Realizing most of the food could be supplied locally, the college changed its purchasing policy in 1987, and area farmers adapted to the needs of the college (Kinsley 1996).

"Fair Trade" Programs

While CED places an emphasis on improving local self-reliance, it also recognizes interdependency with other towns and regions. In North America there are more than 200 local and national organizations working to promote fair trade by supporting and promoting economic exchange (import or export) with groups that produce goods in an equitable manner.

Overseas Partners: The CED Resource Society of Vancouver teamed up with two larger nonprofits to provide fair trade opportunities for worker co-ops, artisans and small entrepreneurs from lesser developed countries, such as in Pakistan, Nicaragua, and Guatemala. OXFAM and CUSO (Canadian University Students Overseas) identify appropriate trade partners and help bring the imports to Vancouver, B.C. where clothing, jewelry, coffee, and carvings are available in a local shop (staffed mostly by volunteers). Products are also available via mail order, and the shop accepts LETS dollars.

Cooperative Enterprises

Evangeline: The Evangeline region of Prince Edward Island is home to a network of cooperatives that emphasizes decentralization and community control. Despite being a small community, the co-ops have helped residents of Evangeline control their own economy, succeeding where externally-driven development failed (Wilkinson and Quarter 1996).

Skills Training and Small Business Development

Van Buren County Hospital: The Board of Directors and staff of Van Buren County Hospital in Iowa began an extensive community planning process in 1990. The goal was to find diverse and creative ways to provide quality medical care and contribute to community health. Instead of buying expensive medical technologies, they helped improve community health by creating economic opportunities for the county's high number of single mothers, unemployed people, and low-income residents. With local and state funding, they started a daycare center, computer training program, and job linkage services using hospital facilities and computer equipment. In a vocational training program, they used the hospital kitchen to start up a bakery which now operates at an outside location. By using hospital facilities, the costs of these programs and business start-ups were lower. The hospital generated revenues, local people gained career training and job opportunities, and Van Buren county gained much needed community services.

Community Development Corporations and Foundations

New Dawn Enterprises: Founded in 1976, New Dawn Enterprises in Cape Breton, Nova Scotia is Canada's oldest community development corporation. From modest beginnings, it has grown to encompass nine companies that pursue a range of real estate and health care related enterprises. Today New Dawn employs more than 100 people and has over $20 million in assets with a $4-million annual operating budget. It operates much like a business in its pursuit of viable economic activities, but the focus of the outcome is not return on equity but benefits to the community. New Dawn creates jobs, affordable housing, and care for the elderly, to name a few social benefits.

Greyston Foundation: For more than 12 years, Greyston Foundation in Yonkers, New York has worked to create jobs and housing opportunities for homeless people. Greyston built a bakery that now sells $3.5 million a year in cakes and brownies to Ben and Jerry's ice cream shops. The bakery employs 45 formerly homeless or ex-convict workers. Greyston also renovates burnt-out buildings, and started a daycare center, job training program, and life skills classes to help people move from welfare to work.

ENVIRONMENTAL RESPONSIBILITY

Community economic development is not just about business creation; it's about creating self-sustaining communities. Citizens who protect their natural resource base and preserve their environment from deterioration contribute to more sustainable economies. Growing public awareness, fear, and intolerance of the pollution and ecological devastation associated with conventional business and industrial growth has prompted some communities to move toward sustainable economic development. Some communities (and businesses within them) are recognizing it is possible, and even advantageous, to support a thriving economy while preserving the quality of the environment in our communities.

Green Business is Good Business

Despite often being viewed as an economic burden, environmental stewardship, pollution control, and resource efficiency offer significant economic opportunities. For businesses, environmental responsibility can mean lower operating costs associated with waste reduction, energy-efficiency, water conservation and reduced pollution, assured regulatory compliance, enhanced public image, and perhaps even new market

"The fortunes of local economies, communities, and ecosystems go hand in hand" (Northwest Report 1996).

opportunities. For communities that attract and support environmentally responsible business, the rewards include less burden on local infrastructure (waste disposal, sewage, electric and water utilities, etc.), protection of the ecosystem, and opportunities for jobs and tax revenues without compromising the quality of life for local citizens.

Often short-term economic gains in tax revenues and job creation are accompanied by erosion in the long-term quality of life of the community. Many people believe the choice to be jobs *or* the environment, yet green businesses and certain policies and initiatives can create more employment opportunities than conventional economic development (Renner 1991). Mandatory container reuse and recycling policies, energy-efficiency and enhanced public transportation programs have stimulated thousands of new business and employment opportunities in North America. Policy changes sometimes cause dislocations in jobs, but special job training programs and new forms of social safety nets can help people in transition from unsustainable forms of employment (Rees 1995; Roseland 1997). Pollution control and other environmental policies and regulations may also serve as economic stimulators. For example, prior to the passage of local government regulations on ozone-depleting compounds, there were few manufacturers and few models available of CFC "vampire" units — machines that remove freon from refrigerators and air conditioners to enable the freon to be recycled. Since local governments started passing CFC regulations in 1989, more manufacturers have begun producing the vampire units, making available a variety of models at lower, competitive prices. (Skinner 1990).

Many green business and economic development initiatives are market driven. Companies recognize the bounty of opportunities to sell greener products and services, or a more ecologically responsible image, to the growing market of environmentally aware customers. Other businesses identify financial savings or benefits associated with environmental improvements to their operations. Local governments can play a role by supporting, encouraging, or even demanding improvement in the environmental performance of businesses in their communities. Municipal or local governments can also implement policies and strategies to attract and support new ecologically responsible businesses and economic activities in their community.

In addition to lobbying governments for legislation and policies that promote ecologically sound economic development, citizens (and governments) can encourage environmentally responsible corporate behavior by exercising consumer power. By choosing to purchase greener products or goods that are produced by more responsible companies, citizens can influence business decisions and direction. Banks and other financial intermediaries can also get involved by supporting green business development, offering preferred interest rates, and applying environmental standards as criteria for loans. Community policies can also encourage more sustainable business development.

"A more sustainable economy promises great environmental and economic benefits, though the transition will not be without pain. It will produce many losers, particularly among extractive and heavy industries. But the evidence is strong that the winners will outnumber the losers: more jobs will be created in energy efficiency, recycling, and public transportation than will be lost in the oil and coal industries, car manufacturing, and waste disposal. In fact, automation is a much more important cause of job loss than environmental protection is. And while extractive industries tend to be geographically concentrated, jobs arising out of energy conservation, renewables, and recycling are likely to be more evenly spread" (Renner 1991).

Local Government Policies, Programs and Regulations

Energy Conservation Program: The Fox River sock company in Osage, Iowa was one of the beneficiaries of the town's energy conservation program that began in 1974 and continues today. In 1984, Fox River was a struggling medium-size textile manufacturer, when an energy audit revealed opportunities to reduce energy costs per unit output by 29 percent. Since implementing the energy-efficiency initiatives, Fox River company is not only thriving, but has expanded production by about 300 percent and almost tripled its workforce. Fox River is not the only beneficiary of the city's programs; the 3,600 residents of Osage, Iowa use 25 percent less electricity than the state average, and the city estimates energy savings amount to more than $1 million per year in savings to residents, local government, and local businesses. The savings, which amount to more than $200 per year for homeowners (and more for most businesses) translate into enhanced economic activity because energy conservation has an economic multiplier of $2.32 (meaning that every $1 spent conserving energy generates $2.32 in local economic activity). The economic multipliers associated with consuming, rather than conserving, energy are far lower (Renew America 1997; Hubbard and Fong 1995).

Energy-Efficiency Program: In the early 1980s, the City of San Jose, California began an energy-efficiency program that reduced home, business, and agency energy utility bills by a total of $5.5 million annually. The city predicts its programs will produce a county-wide $33 million increase in wages and salaries, with a net gain of 1,753 jobs over a 10-year period (Hubbard and Fong 1995).

A city plan called for municipal government investment ($645,000) for technical assistance educational campaigns to show consumers how to save energy, and energy reduction in government buildings and transportation. Economic benefits were projected to spur nearly $20 million in private spending in San Jose, while the program paid for itself in two-and-a-half years (Flavin and Lenssen 1991). (See Chapter 7: Energy Efficiency and Renewables for more discussion of tools and initiatives.)

Mandated Recycling Rate: Compared with incineration and landfilling, recycling offers more long-term employment and is a cheaper alternative due to its lower capital requirements. In New York City, the cost of building an incinerator (about $500 million) is three times that of recycling facilities that can handle the same amount of trash (Renner 1991). Boosting the city's mandated recycling rate from 18 percent to 25 percent in 1994 created jobs in collection and sorting, and stimulated remanufacturing business activity.

Defining Green Business

There are myriad ways to improve the environmental performance of industry and commerce:

- Employ "end of the pipe" strategies to reduce waste and pollution.
- Employ "front of the pipe" strategies to avoid waste, pollution, and environmentally harmful materials and processes.
- Conserve water, optimize energy efficiency, and/or use renewable energies such as wind power.
- Employ strategies to protect or enhance the environment, preserve biodiversity, and protect the ecosystem.
- Target environmental issues for business activities. "Environmental businesses" help to improve environmental quality (e.g., soils remediation business).

Business and NGO Programs and Policies

Benefits from Environmental Protection: Under U.S. environmental regulations, a 3M manufacturing facility in Chicago earns pollution credits by exceeding its target for reducing air emissions. The company can sell these credits, but because it has a policy not to profit from environmental protection (apparently unique among U.S. corporations as of this writing), it donates the credits to the State of Illinois and to a community foundation run by the Center for Neighborhood Technology. The community foundation, in turn, sells the credits and uses the millions of dollars realized by them for local sustainability initiatives, including environmental literacy programs, energy conservation, and local job creation. Truly a win-win trade, 3M gains community recognition and tax write-offs, while creating a new capacity to transfer wealth to local citizens (Johnson Foundation 1997).

Good Neighbor Agreements: The Good Neighbor Project trains community activists to engage in negotiations with corporations to establish Good Neighbor Agreements that address the community's needs and concerns, especially related to pollution control. The Project worked with the West County Toxics Coalition and several community groups concerned about pollution from a Chevron oil refinery in Richmond, California. The groups negotiated with Chevron to convince the multinational corporation to upgrade and improve pollution controls, and spend $100,000 to restore native vegetation, provide skilled job training to 100 local residents, contribute $2 million to a local health center, and contribute $5 million in philanthropic support to the predominantly poor African-American neighborhood.

Green Maps and Directories

Green Maps: New York City's *Green Apple Map* is among the dozens of maps produced all over the world to provide a tool for residents and visitors seeking green businesses and environmentally sound tourist opportunities. Copenhagen's *Wonderful Ecopenhagen* map (in English and Danish) includes explanations as to why certain businesses green, and definitions for environmental terms such as "organic."

Green Business Directory: With funding from local foundations, an entrepreneur published a green business directory for Vancouver, B.C. In addition to addresses of companies providing environmentally sound products or services, the directory included clip-out coupons for discounts, and the text explained the environmental benefits of recycled paper, washable diapers, and other such products.

Local Currencies

Prairie Bucks: In 1988, the local Energy Commission in Lester Prairie, Minnesota (with a population of 1,229) developed an innovative way to invest state energy grant money for long-term local development: the "Prairie Buck." Residents and businesses who signed up for an energy audit received 15 Prairie Bucks, good for the purchase of a compact fluorescent lamp at local hardware stores. Instead of flowing out to distant energy suppliers, local dollars stay in town and bolster the local economy. To encourage carpooling to nearby towns, Lester Prairie began offering "Rideshare Bucks" according to the number of passengers in the car and the number of gallons required for their commute (Rocky Mountain Institute 1991).

Government Funding for Green Business and Jobs

Environ: Peter's Community Development Corporation and the City of St. Peter (Minnesota) helped finance business start-up and construction of a manufacturing plant for Phenix Biocomposites. The company's product is an environmentally-friendly biocomposite material made of recycled newsprint fibers mixed with soy flour. The new product, "Environ," keep 50 people busy manufacturing materials suitable for furniture, cabinetry, flooring, and other products.

SunLine: In Thousand Palms, California, the suburban bus company SunLine joined forces with a local gas company to purchase and operate 40 alternative-fuel buses. Financing came from federal, state, and county grants, and a local guarantee was issued. SunLine converted its fleet of cars and trucks to compressed natural gas, and Southern California Gas utility also got involved, constructing a compressed natural gas fueling station. A local college created the first U.S. training facility for maintaining alternative-fuel vehicles, and SunLine's switch to alternative fuel vehicles created at least 28 jobs while saving the company thousands of dollars in fuel costs (Makower 1995).

Funding Energy Efficiency and Recycling

All over North America, electric utilities, municipal, state/provincial, and federal government programs have helped businesses and industry improve energy performance of buildings and manufacturing operations, conserve water, and reduce waste and pollution. Rebates, tax breaks or grants to "green" their operations provide the push needed and close the "payback gap."

Post Office Retrofit: The Reno (Nevada) Main Post Office received federal government funds to finance an energy-efficiency retrofit. The goal was to reduce operating costs by saving energy, yet the $300,000 retrofit yielded unexpected dividends in worker productivity. The energy-efficient lighting and better acoustics improved working conditions so much that in 1986, Reno's mail sorters became the most productive sorters in the western U.S., and operators of the mail sorting machines achieved the lowest error rate. In addition to savings in energy costs of about $22,400, the Post Office yielded productivity gains worth $400,000 to $500,000 per year (Browning and Romm 1995).

Economic Network: St. Paul, Minnesota's "Home-Grown Economy" project experimented with a number of attempts to establish closed-loop, self-sustaining economic networks. Rubber tires, for example, are ordinarily a disposal nuisance. St. Paul learned that tires can be recycled by freezing them in liquid nitrogen, pulverizing them, and using them as a filler for repairing potholes, another nuisance for which the city is responsible. The recycling costs were $1 per tire; the disposal costs were $3.25 per tire (Meehan 1987).

Financial Institution Support

Shore Trust: Ecotrust, a Portland-based conservation organization partnered with Shorebank Corporation, the oldest community development banking institute in the U.S., to support conservation-based economic development in the Pacific Northwest. The bank holding company, "Shore Trust, the First Environmental Bancorporation," offers financing, technical assistance, marketing, and brokering services for entrepreneurs and business to support local innovation and help individual businesses develop sound ways to manage their land and resources. Their long-term goal is "to create a remarkably different economy, one that can restore and protect the environment, while bringing forth innovation, prosperity, meaningful work, and true security" (Von Hagen and Kellog 1996).

Revolving Loan: The Cascadia Revolving Loan Fund in Seattle, Washington is a private nonprofit organization providing loans to low-income borrowers (often women- or minority-owned businesses) for business start-ups. Private investors provide money for loans and receive a market-rate return on their investment. In 10 years of operation, the Fund has lost less than 1 percent of money lent, and 90 percent of the businesses supported are still in operation. In a newer program to promote environmentally responsible business, the Fund lends money for implementation of pollution-control measures or equipment. Loans to five drycleaning shops in the area enabled these businesses to purchase closed-loop drycleaning machines. Because the machines reduce the use of chemicals and water, operating costs for both supply and disposal, as well as environmental impact, are reduced.

Technical Support and Education

Stay in the Black Guide: The Boulder Energy Conservation Center, sponsored by the Colorado Small Business Development Centers, Chamber of Commerce and others produced the guide, *Stay in the Black by Being Green*. The book covers energy, waste, water, and transportation issues, as well as support for businesses going green.

Seminars for Green Grocers: Spurred by the popularity of their own environmental initiatives, the environmental manager of Larry's Markets (a Seattle area grocery store chain) conducts seminars and offers guidance to other area stores trying to become "green grocers."

U.S. Department of Energy Support: A business park in Soldiers Grove, Wisconsin is heated by solar energy, thanks to the Department of Energy's Argonne National Lab. In 1978, Argonne was doing research on solar thermal energy, so they offered the service to the business park and continued to study the solar energy in use. Argonne has also assisted groups in Chicago in designing affordable housing. In Chattanooga, Tennessee, Oak Ridge National Labs is helping an electric-bus manufacturer to design improvements for city buses.

Job Training

Casa Verde Builders: In Austin, Texas, Casa Verde Builders helps high school dropouts (17- to 25-year-old men and women) learn carpentry and construction skills while completing course work to earn a high school diploma and certificate of mastery. Participants earn a salary for spending 40-hours per week doing studies and working in crews building environmentally responsible housing. They learn sustainable construction techniques by building affordable housing that is sold to low-income families. A private lender and federal funding provide financing for home purchases and mortgages, and proceeds from the sale of these houses is returned to Casa Verde to build more houses.

Big City Forest: Bronx 2000 Local Development Corporation in New York City is a community-based development organization dedicated to affordable housing, community-based enterprise, economic development, and environmentalism. They have established two for-profit, community-based national recycling companies and a reclaimed wood products manufacturing facility. Their Big City Forest program uses discarded wooden shipping pallets to make furniture, flooring, and fiberboard, which helps local business save money by avoiding disposal costs for pallets. In less than five years, Big City Forest diverted over 5,500 tons of wood from waste disposal, reused about 113,314 cubic meters (4 million board feet) of lumber, and trained 180 workers in carpentry and other skills.

A farmer's market in the city

Community Forestry, Fisheries, and Agriculture

Community Supported Agriculture: In hundreds of North American towns and cities, Community Supported Agriculture is gaining popularity as a way for urbanites to supply themselves with fresh vegetables while supporting small local organic farms. Urban families or individuals pay yearly fees for shares that entitle them to weekly shipments of locally grown fruits and vegetables. Purchasers share the risks of farming with farmers — they may receive less of one vegetable than expected, but more of another. In addition to supporting sustainable agriculture, city folk gain connection with local farmers and the bioregion. (See Chapter 4: Greening the City for more discussion.)

Menominee Forest: A community forest is "a tree-dominated ecosystem managed for multiple community values and benefits to the community" (Duinker et al. 1994). Managed by the community, this type of forestry lends itself to more sustainable practices that preserve the resource base and provide long-term sustainable employment in forestry and related activities. In 1890, the Menominee Tribe obtained authorization for commercial logging in Wisconsin. The Tribe pioneered sustained yield management including selection harvest methods that balanced annual growth with timber production. The Tribe lost control of the land for a time, but when they regained reservation privileges, they continued their sound forestry practices. Sawmill profits have funded social services, such as medical programs, education, and law enforcement activities (Bernard and Young 1996).

Adding Value to Forestry

"To explore the potential of community-based, value-added manufacturing, a single cedar tree was cut and a variety of products were manufactured by a group of Slocan Valley, British Columbia, residents in their spare time. Products were made from all parts of the tree, even those that would have otherwise become wood waste, such as bark, branches, leaves, top and stump. The result was over 50 different items (over 275 value-added wood objects, including drums, baskets, coasters, and games), amounting to a potential sale value of $4,052 for the local economy. Even without accounting for the avoided disposal impacts and associated costs, valley volunteers generated 80 times the amount of revenue to the local economy than the timber company would have using the same tree" (Martineau 1997).

Natural Balance Forestry Cooperative: The for-profit worker cooperative, Natural Balance Forestry Cooperative, is establishing criteria for sustainable forest management in western Washington State. The Cooperative seeks small- and large-scale forest owners to help develop forest management plans that produce economic yields while protecting the long-term survival and health of the forest ecosystem.

Fishing Quotas: The current system of fisheries management separates conservation responsibilities from fishing rights, pits individual fishers against one another, and promotes short-term individual profit over community cooperation and shared responsibility for resource management. A proposed alternative is to establish community quotas whereby fishing rights are allocated to communities, and distributed in turn to local fishers, just as timber-cutting rights are distributed in community forests. By providing the opportunity for long-term economic benefits to a community, quotas may foster community stewardship of resources.

Alliances and Partnerships

Green Business Alliance: Architects, publishers, booksellers, builders, consultants, educators, nonprofits, retailers, and wholesalers in the San Francisco Bay area committed to a sustainable economy formed the Green Business Alliance. Among their goals, they aim to foster an understanding by the business community of the importance of sustainable business practice and develop networks of businesses where the public can be assured that the companies are attempting to follow sustainable practices. They conduct forums and seminars for education and to discuss challenges of green business.

Inner-City Recycling Plant: With a goal of setting a new standard for community participation and environmentally sound paper manufacturing, an environmental organization, a community group, and a private development company teamed up to create jobs and save trees. The National Resource Defence Council and Banana Kelly are working with Affordable Housing Development Corporation to construct an inner-city recycling plant where tons of waste paper will be remanufactured into newsprint for the *Wall Street Journal* and *New York Times* (Harris 1995). A chlorine-free de-inking process will reduce pollution, and use of reclaimed water from a nearby municipal sewage treatment facility will conserve the city's water resources. The urban location is an economic advantage as transportation costs for raw materials (waste paper) and finished products will be significantly lower than for mills (typically located near forests far away from cities). The plant is expected to create 300 jobs, and financing includes $5 million earmarked for funding local community projects.

Technology Transfer: Bethel New Life, a community development corporation in

Chicago partnered with the U.S. Department of Energy's Argonne National Laboratories to create a technology transfer program designed to support environmentally-sound job creation programs and community development initiatives. Projects include training of local residents in environmental analysis and clean-up of abandoned industrial facilities. The initiative provides job opportunities and training in site restoration. As hazardous sites in the community are cleaned up and refurbished they are made available for new tenancy (Renew America 1997).

Environmental Business Clusters and Incubators

Environmental Business Cluster: The Thousand Oaks Environmental Business Cluster is the first business park in California that caters specifically to start-up companies with products, technologies, or services that are environmentally

A community garden within the city

responsible. The nonprofit public-private initiative, sponsored by local government and large established corporations provides 15 companies in the Cluster with below-market rental rates, furnishings, and management services. The emerging environmental technologies and service companies share offices equipment and services, such as photocopiers, conference rooms, and kitchens to minimize costs. Companies support each other's business activities and seek synergies. Sponsoring organizations are encouraged to engage in technology transfer and licensing agreement opportunities with the smaller firms. The maximum period for a business to stay is two years, and acceptance into the Cluster is based on potential economic impact on the community, such as job creation and sales tax revenue, as well as business potential and evaluation of the management team.

Greenmarkets: New York City's Council on the Environment, a citizens' organization based in the mayor's office, initiated a system of Greenmarkets in 1976. Operating at 10 sites year-round and 20 in summertime, Greenmarkets aim to preserve farmland and help struggling upstate farmers, while making fresh fruits and vegetables available in city neighborhoods. The markets offer many New Yorkers their only chance to get local produce without journeying to the suburbs (Lowe 1991).

Eco-Industrial Parks

Eco-Industrial Parks are a burgeoning sustainable business concept in North America. Businesses in these parks are interdependent because one business' byproduct or waste is the feedstock or energy source for other businesses. Collaboration in redesigning the industrial food chain enables industries to achieve higher standards of environmental performance while improving operating efficiencies and profit margins as well. Planning is underway for Eco-Industrial Parks in several North American cities such as Baltimore, Maryland; Burlington, Vermont; Brownsville, Texas; and in Nova Scotia.

Building an Environmental Economy in Berkeley, California

Berkeley has come to be known as the "green valley" (in comparison to the nearby "silicon valley") because of its policies and programs promoting sustainable economic development. Recognizing economic development opportunities associated with protecting the environment and supporting the emerging environmental business sector, city council, the Community Development Department, local citizens, and consultants worked together to develop strategies for building an "environmental economy." The following are some of the strategies proposed or adopted by the city:

• policies, guidelines, zoning bylaws to attract and retain green businesses;
• regulatory streamlining;
• innovative financing opportunities;
• technical assistance and support;
• public/private partnerships (government or universities with private businesses) for research, financing and business development;
• environmental business incubator and value adding networks (flexible networks) to help small businesses team up (virtually or physically) for research, development, operations, or marketing of products and services;
• environmental business directory;
• export trade shows, eco-fairs and conferences;
• media strategies to attract and promote the green valley; and
• programs, committees, and task forces to develop and support the above initiatives (Friend 1993; Skinner 1997).

Burlington, Vermont: Developers in Burlington, Vermont are planning an eco-industrial park that will use excess heat from a municipal power plant to grow food and flowers in a greenhouse, and provide heat and energy for other park businesses. The University of Vermont helped form the nonprofit Partnership of Environmental Technologies and Science to encourage Vermont universities to partner with private and public sectors on projects such as this one. A federal community development block grant through the City of Burlington provided the funds for a feasibility study on the park.

Chattanooga, Tennessee: In the 1960s, Chattanooga, Tennessee had one of the worst air pollution problems in the U.S. Today it is one of the few cities to meet the federal Environmental Protection Agency's clean air standards. A program to make Chattanooga a model of sustainability is the reason for the improvements and the driver behind four eco-industrial parks under development in the city. Parks are planned at a 2,834-hectare (7,000-acre) army munitions facility being converted to civilian use, on a brownfield site of an abandoned manufacturing facility, and at two other sites.

RETHINKING ECONOMIC DEVELOPMENT

Just as sustainability has prompted a shift in our transportation and energy planning away from the traditional focus on increasing supply to a focus on managing demand, so too can the emphasis of economic development shift from growth (increase in supply of products and services) to sustainable economic development, or economic demand management (EDM). EDM should seek to satisfy our economic needs without requiring endless growth. The outdoor goods chain store, Patagonia, defied conventional marketing practices a few years ago when they claimed they didn't intend to keep expanding and their hope was that people would buy less, but buy quality (of course, they felt their product represented that quality). Individuals perceive that growth is synonymous with success and very often that is measured by gross income. Yet economic demand management redefines values to acknowledge contributions, such as unpaid work, that enhance the community and indirectly help strengthen the economy.

Calculating the true cost of work will enable people to better evaluate economic costs and benefits. Unemployment and job security threaten many Canadians and Americans in the 1990s, and yet those who are employed work longer hours than people in past decades. This is taking its toll on individuals and their families. Many households spend a significant portion of their income on transportation costs to and from work, childcare services, and take-out meals because parents are too tired to cook. What is the financial cost to support this work-oriented lifestyle, and what is the cost to quality of life? In a 1991 survey conducted by *Time* magazine and CNN, 61 percent of the respondents agreed that "earning a living today requires so much effort that it's difficult to find time to enjoy life" (Elgin 1996). The true cost of economic growth cannot be measured by new cars, big houses, and the latest computer games.

The Living Wall Garden project in Vancouver, B.C.

In a commodity-intensive economy, people are compelled to seek full-time employment and an increasing income, but some people are making a shift. By re-evaluating their needs and wants and realizing that their true demands are for comfort, security, health, and happiness, some people are finding alternative ways to satisfy these demands.

TOOLS AND INITIATIVES

Voluntary Simplicity: Programs such as Voluntary Simplicity, named after the book by Duane Elgin (1993), provide the rationale and framework for people seeking a return to the simple life. People are making choices that reduce their costs and give them time to enjoy their families, friends, and the world around them. Voluntary Simplicity calls for living in a way that is "outwardly more simple and inwardly more rich." By living a more conserving lifestyle, people are moving toward sustainability and reducing dependence on financial and material affluence for their quality of life (Elgin 1993; Burch 1996).

Buy Nothing Day: November 29 is "Buy Nothing Day," thanks to the Media Foundation, publisher of *Adbusters* magazine. The purpose is to demonstrate the power of consumers so that business responds to consumer demands for greater corporate environmental and social responsibility. The impact of non-consumption — even for a day — would reduce waste and output of pollution by staggering amounts. Imagine what a conserver society could achieve!

RESOURCES

Centre for Community Enterprise is a nonprofit organization committed to building the capacity of community-controlled organizations to generate durable social and economic benefits. Their journal is must reading: *Making Waves: Canada's Community Economic Development Quarterly.*

"There is no getting around the fact that material consumption is at the heart of the sustainability crisis" (Rees 1995).

S-142, C-14, 9777 Somers Road
Port Alberni, B.C.
Canada V9Y 7L5
Tel: 250/723-1139
Fax: 250723-3730
E-mail: ccelewis@port.island.net
Web site: www.island.net/~ccelewis/index.html

Community Economic Development Centre at Simon Fraser University provides research, advisory and training programs in British Columbia and around the world (through distance education courses and a web site).
Simon Fraser University
Burnaby, B.C.
Canada V5A 1S6
Tel: 604/291-5850
Fax: 604/291-5473
E-mail: cedc@sfu.ca
Web site: www.sfu.ca/cedc

Ecotrust/Ecotrust Canada are private, nonprofit organizations developing creative and innovative approaches to conservation-based development in the coastal rainforests of British Columbia, Washington and Alaska. They work to help communities "get rich slow."
Ecotrust Canada
420-1122 Mainland Street
Vancouver, B.C.
Canada V6B 5L1
Tel: 604/682-4141
Fax: 604/682-1944
E-mail: info@ecotrustcan.org
Web site: www.ecotrust.org/etcan.htm

Ecotrust
1200 N.W. Naito Parkway, Suite 470
Portland, Oregon
USA 97209-2800
Tel: 503/227-6225
Fax: 503/222-1517
E-mail: info@ecotrust.org
Web site: www.ecotrust.org/

Green Map Systems
Modern World Design
P.O. Box 249
New York, New York
USA 10002
Tel: 212/674-1631
Fax: 212/674-6206
E-mail: web@greenmap.com
Web site: www.greenmap.com

Institute for Community Economics is a national nonprofit organization providing technical assistance and financing to community land trusts and organizations committed to affordable housing, land preservation, and green economic development. Their journal, *Community Economics*, is a source of inspiration.
57 School Street
Springfield, Massachusetts
USA 01105-1331
Tel: 413/746-8660
Fax: 413/746-8862

International Journal of Ecoforestry is devoted to the practices, science, and philosophy of ecologically responsible forest use, and is an important forum for community forestry.
Ecoforestry Institute Society
P.O. Box 5783, Station B
Victoria, B.C.
Canada V8R 6S8
E-mail: ies@islandnet.com

Landsman Community Services Ltd. offers information on LETS.
1600 Embledon Crescent
Courtney, B.C.
Canada V9N 6N3
Tel: 250/338-0213
E-mail: lcs@mars.ark.com
Web site: www.u-net.com/gmlets

REFERENCES

British Columbia Working Group on CED. 1995. *Sharing Our Stories*.

Bernard, T, and J. Young. 1996. *The Ecology of Hope: Communities Collaborate for Sustainability*. Gabriola Island, B.C.: New Society Publishers.

Boothroyd, P. 1991. *Community Economic Development: An Introduction for Planners*. Vancouver: UBC Centre for Human Settlements.

Browning, W.D. and J. Romm. 1995. *Greening Business and the Bottom Line*. Rocky Mountain Institute.

Bruyn, S.T. 1987. "Beyond the Market and the State." In *Beyond the Market and the State: New Directions in Community Development*, S.T. Bruyn and J. Meehan, eds. Philadelphia: Temple University Press.

Burch, M. 1996. *Simplicity: Notes, Stories and Exercises for Developing Unimaginable Wealth*. Gabriola Island, B.C.: New Society Publishers.

Duinker, P. et al. "Community Forests in Canada: An Overview." *The Forestry Chronicle* 70(6).

Elgin, D. 1993. *Voluntary Simplicity*. New York: William Morrow.

Flavin, C., and N. Lenssen. 1991. "Designing a Sustainable Energy System." In *State of the World 1991: A Worldwatch Institute Report on Progress Toward a Sustainable Society*. New York/London: W.W. Norton and Company. Pp. 21-38.

Friend, G., and Associates. 1993. *Building an Environmental Economy*. Berkeley, Calif.

Harris, L. 1995. "Banana Kelly's Toughest Fight." *The New Yorker*, 24 July.

Hubbard, A, and C. Fong. 1995. *Community Energy Workbook*. Rocky Mountain Institute.

Johnson Foundation. 1997. "Tradable Assets for Sustainable Communities." *Wingspread Journal* 19(2).

Kinsley, M. 1996. *Economic Renewal Guide: A Collaborative Processing for Sustainable Development*. Rocky Mountain Institute.

Lowe, M.D. 1991. "Shaping Cities: The Environmental and Human Dimensions." *Worldwatch* 105. Washington D.C.: Worldwatch Institute.

Makower, J. 1995. *Good, Green Jobs: How Business is Putting the Environment to Work for California*. California: California Department of Conservation.

Martineau, S., and M. Martineau. 1997. "Slocan Valley Residents Ask for Community-Based Forestry." *International Journal of Ecoforestry* 12(3): 267-70.

Meehan, J. 1987. "Working Toward Local Self-Reliance." In *Beyond the Market and the State: New Directions in Community Development*, S.T. Bruyn and J. Meehan, eds. Philadelphia: Temple University Press.

Northwest Report. 1996. "Special Issue on Sustainable Development and Culture." 19 (January).

Nozick, M. 1992. *No Place Like Home: Building Sustainable Communities*. Ottawa: Canadian Council on Social Development.

Rees, W.E. 1995. "More Jobs, Less Damage: A Framework for Sustainability, Growth and Employment." *Alternatives* 21:4:24-30.

Renew America. 1997. *Success Stories*. 1400 16th Street, N.W., Suite 710, Washington, D.C. <solstice.crest.org/environment/renew_america/>.

Renner, M. 1991. "Jobs in a Sustainable Economy." *Worldwatch* 104. Washington, D.C.: Worldwatch Institute.

Rocky Mountain Institute. 1991. *Newsletter* VII(1) Spring.

Roseland, M. 1997. *Eco-City Dimensions: Healthy Communities, Healthy Planet*. Gabriola Island, B.C.: New Society Publishers.

Skinner, N. 1990. "Ecocity Legislation." In *Report of the First International Ecological City Conference*. Berkeley, Calif.: Urban Ecology.

— — — . 1997. "Economic Development as a Path to Sustainability: The Berkeley Experience." In *Eco-City Dimensions: Healthy Communities, Healthy Planet*, M. Roseland, ed. Gabriola Island, B.C.: New Society Publishers.

Spayde, J. 1997. "Our Kind of Town (Ithaca, NY)." *Utne Reader* May/June.

Wilkinson, P., and J. Quarter. 1996. *Building a Community-Controlled Economy: The Evangeline Cooperative Experience*. Toronto: University of Toronto Press.

Von Hagen, B., and E. Kellogg. 1996. "Entrepreneurs and Ecosystems." *Northwest Report*, Northwest Area Foundation (January): 10-15.

PART 3

MOBILIZING CITIZENS AND THEIR GOVERNMENTS

Applying the concept of sustainable development in North American communities requires unprecendented and simultaneous emphasis on the efficient use of urban space, minimizing consumption of essential natural capital, multiplying social capital, and mobilizing citizens and their governments toward these ends. Part 3 focuses on mobilizing citizens and their governments toward sustainable communities.

CHAPTER 13

GOVERNING SUSTAINABLE COMMUNITIES

Governance and government are not the same. *Government* is about "doing" things, and delivering services, whereas *governance* is "leading" society, convincing its various interest groups to embrace common goals and strategies (Osborne and Gaebler 1993).

This chapter is about governing sustainable communities, and explores both governance and government in this context. In particular, it focuses on public participation, decision-making, the role of local government, and planning for action.

PUBLIC PARTICIPATION

In the last several years there has been an enormous shift toward the "politics of inclusion." These new politics are here to stay, not only because they are demanded, but also because they ensure results that better fulfil the broad public interest than decisions that are shaped by the lobbying of powerful and vocal interests. For some categories of decisions that affect a broad spectrum of interests, a fair hearing is no longer sufficient to achieve a lasting and equitable result. Direct participation in the decision-making process is necessary (Owen 1994).

The traditional approach to public demand for greater participation has been described as "decide, educate, announce, defend," otherwise known as DEAD. Collaborative processes are an alternative which can lead to better communication and understanding. Quite different perspectives can find common ground and agree to recommendations regarding particularly difficult issues. This does not necessarily mean that everyone comes to full agreement, but rather that there is no substantial disagreement; participants can live with the outcome.

Democratic decision-making, where decision-making power is shared in reality if not in name, has been effective in some contexts and some regions. Community development corporations in the Maritimes, community land trusts in the United States, and the Mondragon system of industrial cooperatives in the Basque region of Spain are all examples of the potential of democratic decision-making.

Shared Decision-Making

The primary rationale for enhanced stakeholder participation in community planning and governance is based on the democratic maxim that those affected by a decision should participate directly in the decision-making process. Within the broader framework of representative democracy, participatory democracy provides a system of checks and balances against the limitations of a purely representative system (Duffy, Roseland and Gunton 1996).

The benefits of participatory democratic structures have far-reaching implications for community planning. So-called "consultation" of stakeholders is no longer adequate (Arnstein 1969). Stakeholders often demand genuinely cooperative decision-making, if not outright control over decision-making. In response, formal recognition has been provided at some levels of government through legislation legitimizing public participation initiatives. Policy statements supporting stakeholder participation are inadequate, however, if they are not backed by sufficient resources, staff, and commitment to implement meaningful participation. Truly meaningful participation requires that all concerned and affected stakeholders are provided the information and resources they require to influence and contribute to the decision-making process, and that planning and decision-making processes must be designed and implemented to foster comprehensive stakeholder participation. The issues of who participates, when they participate and how they participate are critical to achieving fairness, efficiency, and stability in decision-making.

The essential difference between conventional and collaborative, or "shared decision-making," is the level of true collaboration and involvement of those not traditionally involved in decision-making (Crowfoot and Wondolleck 1990). Specifically, shared decision-making involves planning *with* stakeholders rather than *for* stakeholders. Shared decision-making processes depend on the explicit recognition that all stakeholder values and interests are legitimate.

Consensus Decision-Making

Consensus is a process for making group decisions without voting. Agreement is reached through a process of gathering information and viewpoints, discussion, persuasion, a combination of synthesis of proposals and/or the development of totally new ones. Consensus does not necessarily mean unanimity. Rather, the goal of the consensus process is to reach a decision with which everyone can agree. Consensus at its best relies upon persuasion rather than pressure for reaching group unity.

The consensus method is most useful for groups whose members value their association highly. Consensus decision-making sometimes requires a great deal of patience. It is necessary to listen carefully to opposing viewpoints to reach the best decision. In spite of this drawback, the consensus method has the following advantages over a voting method (Beer and Stief 1997; Coover et al. 1977; Kaner et al. 1996): it produces more intelligent decisions, by incorporating the best thinking of everyone; it keeps people from getting into adversary attitudes where individual egos are tied to

"The processes that occur in our [societies] are not arcane, capable of being understood only by experts. They can be understood by almost anybody. Many ordinary people already understand this; they simply have not considered that by understanding these ordinary arrangements of cause and effect, we can also direct them, if we want to"
(Jacobs 1961).

The President's Council on Sustainable Development recommended that all levels of government, especially local government, should identify barriers to greater citizen involvement in decision-making — such as lack of child care or transportation — and develop strategies to overcome them. Employers should give employees flexibility and incentives to increase the time they and their families can devote to community activities
(PCSD 1996).

a proposal that will win or lose; it increases the likelihood of new and better ideas being thought up; everyone has a stake in implementing a decision, because all have participated in its formation (participants have more energy for working in groups with which they are fully in agreement); and it lessens significantly the possibility that a minority will feel that an unacceptable decision has been imposed on them.

Canada's National Round Table on the Environment and the Economy, in conjunction with several provincial and local Round Tables, has articulated some of the guiding principles that characterize consensus processes:

- *Purpose Driven*: People need a reason to participate in the process.
- *Inclusive*: All parties with a significant interest in the issue should be involved in the consensus process.
- *Voluntary*: The parties who are affected or interested participate voluntarily.
- *Self-Designed*: The parties design the consensus process.
- *Flexible*: Flexibility should be designed into the process.
- *Fair*: All parties must have equal access to relevant information and the opportunity to participate effectively throughout the process.
- *Respectful of Diverse Interests*: Acceptance of the diverse values, interests, and knowledge of the parties involved in the consensus process is essential.
- *Accountable*: The parties are accountable both to their constituencies and to the process that they have agreed to establish.
- *Time Limited*: Realistic deadlines are necessary throughout the process.
- *Implemented*: Commitment to implementation and effective monitoring are essential parts of any agreement (NRTEE 1993) .

Alternative Dispute Resolution

Consensus is also used in the context of conflict management. Alternative dispute resolution is a form of shared decision-making. Two key strategies are negotiation and mediation. These processes are "alternative" in the sense that they are outside the conventional judicial, litigious route of problem-solving. Conventional legal channels are often criticized for being excessively costly and slow in resolving disputes (and therefore favoring those with time and money), for contributing to a climate of uncertainty in decision-making, and for emphasizing win/lose over win/win solutions. In response, interest in alternative dispute resolution has grown significantly.

Interest in consensus-based dispute resolution strategies is also increasing. In the context of dispute resolution, consensus generally refers to a situation in which all parties agree to a decision. This outcome may have been arrived at by one party being persuaded by arguments of another, or by both parties finding a new common goal (Minnery 1985). Reaching a consensus may involve bargaining, negotiation, consultation, facilitation, fact-finding and/or mediation in order to resolve conflicts. In contrast to a decision resulting from a vote or made unilaterally by a decision-making authority, a consensus process is qualitatively different in that each participant has an effective veto. This veto "levels the playing field" and provides each stakeholder with equal authority in reaching the decision. The power of consensus as a dispute resolution tool lies in its ability to protect the minority or single party from the "tyranny of the majority" (Cormick 1989).

THE ROLE OF LOCAL GOVERNMENT

All of us play many roles in our society, such as worker, employer, parent, child, consumer, student, teacher, and so on, and all of these roles are important for moving toward sustainable communities. However, it is primarily in our role as citizens (and to a lesser extent, as consumers) that we can create sustainable communities and a sustainable economy. It is through participating in the governance of our communities that we can take the necessary measures to create a sustainable society. Sustainability will be adopted through active pressure on governments (for example, from citizen organizations and voluntary environmental groups) and through the power of the electoral system. Individual actions and lifestyle choices, such as recycling or bicycle commuting, are important personal contributions, but sustainability requires a *collective* shift in individual actions and political choices, which governments can only gain the authority to call for if people have voted for sustainability (Jacobs 1993). Democracy is fundamental to sustainability.

Local government provides one of the best ways to demonstrate the necessity, the desirability, and the practicality of moving toward sustainable communities. Although local governments are not the only agencies charged with community planning and development, they are locally elected, representative, and accountable bodies responsible for community decision-making. This makes them critical players in the movement toward sustainable communities. In the words of Peterborough, Ontario Mayor Sylvia Sutherland (1991):

> We in local government are closest to our communities. We are closest to the people who must participate in a very direct and active way if the transition to sustainability is to have any hope of success. We are uniquely situated to assist in the evolution of new social values and practices. We can encourage cooperation between the sectors of the community with a stake in the environment and in development and sustainability. We can act as a catalyst for local action beyond the boundaries of our own jurisdiction.

Local governments are also important actors in their local economies. They build and maintain infrastructure that is essential for economic activity, and set standards, regulations, taxes, and fees that determine the parameters for economic development. Local governments procure large numbers of services and products and can influence markets for goods and services. Like private enterprises, local governments serve as public enterprises to produce "products" that are sold on the market. These products include environmental services (e.g., water, waste management, and land-use control), economic services (e.g., transportation infrastructure), and social services (e.g., health and education) (ICLEI 1996). Burlington, Ontario Alderman Jim Ryan (1992) notes that:

> [Sustainable development] requires that communities protect and enhance the environment upon which their future depends by changing the way they make deci-

"We ask our citizens to change their behavior, to leave their sacred cars at home, to pay a higher price for the future, and moreover, to vote for us. This is a real challenge for the leadership in our democracy. But in a sustainable city that thinks globally, the future of our planet has to be more important than the outcome of the next election" (Amsterdam Mayor E. Van Thijn 1991).

sions and by developing an ecological framework for planning sustainable communities. Translating the concept of sustainable development into action at the municipal level will require far-reaching institutional changes, changes in thinking, decision making, policy and process. . . .

Sustainable development is a global imperative with an urban focus, because that is where the greatest growth is occurring and where the majority of our global and regional environmental problems originate. It calls for a fundamental change in the way we plan and manage our urban centers. Municipal officials as stewards of local communities have a vital role to play in effecting the necessary change.

There are a variety of ways that local governments can respond to sustainable development and global environmental concerns. For example, Gilbert (1991) characterized eight styles of local government response with respect to potential climate change and global warming (table 1).

"Governments are formed to preserve and protect the general good. Protecting the environment, safeguarding human health and preserving the national habitat should be an integral part of every government's environmental responsibilities. Local governments, in their own operations and in their regulation and monitoring of actions by others, should be model environmental citizens" *(New York City Environmental Charter 1990).*

Table 1: Local Government Styles of Response Regarding Global Warming

Style	*Examples*
1. Flout the law.	Use illegally polluting vehicles.
2. Merely obey the law.	Do no more, or less, than is required.
3. Set a good example within the administration	Intra-office recycling; use natural gas vehicles.
4. Advocate within jurisdiction.	Encourage reduction, reuse, and recycling; promote transit and district heating.
5. Legislate within jurisdiction.	Ban certain materials at landfill sites; local restrictions on automobile use.
6. Advocate outside jurisdiction.	Push for tighter automobile pollution standards; promote inter-city rail.
7. Seek new legislative authority.	Tax automobile ownership; ban sale of items made with CFCs.
8. Legislate outside jurisdiction.	Ban sale of items made with CFCs; ban use of many kinds of packaging.

Local governments also operate under the considerable constraints of most public agencies: limited resources, jurisdiction, imagination, courage, time, and so on. For local governments to fulfill their potential in moving toward sustainable communities, they need citizen organizations as community partners.

Citizen organizations provide many innovative programs and concepts, and furnish whole new paradigms for problem definition, because they are able to tap and organize information laterally. They can network across borders as well as across corporate and government boundaries, enabling rapid syntheses of overlooked and new information into fresh approaches and paradigms. Today, the most creative, energetic forces addressing the planetary problems of poverty, social inequity, pollution, resource depletion, violence, and war are grassroots citizens' movements. Hazel Henderson calls this "grassroots globalism" — pragmatic, local solutions that keep the planet in mind. These approaches "bubble up" rather than "trickle down," and they are often innovative, stressing positive action and role models (Henderson 1996).

A good example of grassroots globalism is the overwhelming interest and participation of all kinds of organizations in the UN global conferences organized in the 1990s. This is not accidental, but rather the "tip of the iceberg" in a wide social process affecting all the continents: the emergence of organized civil society (ICPQL 1996).

Civil society groups vary in the causes they stand for and in their goals. Some are structured, capable of action with a sense of continuity; others are more "prophetic" in nature, likely to act intensively in a more episodic way. Still others endure changes from outside or within, intervening with forms of action that are permanent or else change during the entity's lifetime. Once empowered, citizens are quite capable of turning to those forms of organized action allowing them to apply pressure where they themselves are affected. The multiplicity of these forms of action, their cross-fertilization and their potential for confrontation create an enormous vitality within the social fabric (ICPQL 1996).

Leadership by Example

Local government is an influential employer and consumer in most communities. A key step toward making our communities sustainable is leadership by example, particularly "greening" city hall. We need to insist that our local officials lead by example. As described throughout this book, a variety of tools are available for this purpose. Every community member has a legitimate interest in knowing what measures their local government is, could, or should be taking to make their community more sustainable.

Unfortunately, energy-efficient light bulbs and reusable china in the city hall cafeteria will not in themselves achieve sustainable development or slow global climate change. These kind of well-intentioned initiatives are but small steps toward creating sustainable communities.

Environmental Administration

Another key step toward sustainable communities is conceptual and organizational. One of the greatest obstacles to sustainability is the reductionist administrative mindset that subdivides problems and prevents the left hand of government from understanding what the right hand is doing. For example, despite considerable trumpeting of environmental protection programs (which are sometimes themselves endangered species), most sober analyses of public budgets and spending estimates conclude that governments spend billions of dollars more on programs and policies that *create* pollution and *encourage* environmental degradation. Such bureaucratic schizophrenia is perpetrated at all levels of government as well as throughout academia.

Sustainable communities cannot be achieved through the kind of fragmented and

"The terms non-governmental organization (NGO) and non-profit don't explain what these organizations do or stand for, only what they are not. A new acronym has been coined to describe those organizations and activities sometimes referred to as civil society or the social economy. CSO stands for civil society organization. From this perspective many governments and corporations are NCOs, or non-civil organizations"
(Henderson 1996).

bureaucratized administration that characterizes senior government. At the community level, such issues as transportation, land use, economic development, public health, environmental protection, and housing affordability cannot be successfully managed as separate problems by separate agencies using separate strategies.

Conventional wisdom considers the environment as an administrative problem, to be solved by better management — understood as cutting the environment into bite-size pieces. This approach seems increasingly unable to deal effectively, sensitively, and comprehensively with environmental complexities.

Rather than the environment as an administrative problem, it would appear that administration is itself an environmental problem. One alternative to conventional municipal administration is an emerging form of what has been called "environmental administration." It can be characterized as non-compartmentalized, open, decentralized, anti-technocratic, and flexible (Paehlke and Torgerson 1990). Environmental administration provides a holistic way of addressing both "environmental" issues and a whole range of community issues. Some examples of this approach are discussed below.

It will take a great effort over a long time to turn the system of local government into a paragon of environmental administration, though try we must. In these transition decades, however, an effective and popular way to implement sustainable community development is urgently required.

Beyond Local Government

A third key step toward sustainable communities is improving the context for sustainable community planning and governance. This requires looking beyond the local level toward regional, state/provincial, and federal policies and programs. These programs encourage, enable, and empower those communities that have already started to plan local initiatives for a sustainable future, and require the rest to begin.

PLANNING FOR ACTION

We can only develop community sustainability if we plan for it. A citizen's group planning process for community sustainability can be organized in six steps (ORTEE 1995). First, develop a widely shared *vision* of the type of community the group would like to work towards. Second, *develop plans* on how to achieve this vision. This involves several sub-steps, including formulating a clear mission statement, analyzing the strengths and weakness of the group and the community, and assessing the many opportunities and obstacles that may be encountered. Then realistic goals and objectives can be set, and an action plan outlining specific tasks and activities should be developed. Third, *get city hall onside.* Fourth, d*evelop the resources* necessary to implement the plans. Fifth, prepare a strategy for *communicating* ideas and activities to the community. Sixth, be sure to *evaluate* your efforts regularly (see chapter 14). This will help you to assess the degree to which your actions are helping the group move toward its stated goal, identify and keep track of successes, and communicate your successes to the community.

Getting City Hall Onside

One of the barriers encountered by many community groups intent on promoting sustainability in their community is the reluctance of city hall to be part of the quest and process. Yet the understanding and cooperation of both elected officials and professional staff are essential to making progress along the path to sustainability, for they must support the changes that must occur for things to be done differently. Here's some "how-to" advice obtained from both politicians and professional staff (ORTEE 1995):

1. Crucial to being taken seriously by city hall is having truly broad, multi-sectoral community representation at your "sustainability" table from the outset.

2. Obtain up-to-date information about the community that will provide you with a baseline picture of current community management.

3. Educate yourselves about the civic process. Administration is part of the town or city corporation. Council acts like a board of directors. Knowing how ideas get considered and subsequently translated into policy and programs can be very helpful when trying to promote new ideas. Understand the budget process as well.

4. When you feel you have an idea of the state of affairs in your community, develop a vision of where you want to go. But don't try to do too much at once. Choose one, two or three key issues to focus on. Avoid trying to sell the big sustainable picture at the outset. Action will not result from sustainability principles or ideals on their own. The approach should always be proposed on a smaller scale, in practical and "doable" terms.

5. Build allies for your initiative:
• Look for allies within the community at large. Develop constituencies of support. Politicians and staff respect such support.

• Approach the bureaucracy before the politicians. Research the work already underway by municipal departments. Look for allies on staff who can speak in support of your initiative. Explain the initiative to them in practical terms. See if it is possible to build on municipal initiatives that are in the planning stages. Could a pilot program be developed? Sell specific targets which can later be used as a springboard to larger programs.

• In terms of city council, look for a possible political champion for your initiative. Consider who on council has the ability to communicate the need for change in a non-intimidating manner. Work with these councillors to bring them onside. Demonstrate the extent of community support you have for the initiative.

6. Don't go to city council until you have everything lined up, including:
• a committed steering group made up of individuals from the community who command some respect and represent key sectors;
• baseline facts and figures that are pertinent to your initiative;
• goals and objectives that fit with any stated municipal priorities;
• allies and champions on council and in the municipal departments;
• sound community support for the initiative; and
• a sound proposal for financing the sustainability measures being recommended.

7. When change is underway, develop a set of indicators that will show/measure progress being made. People must see and feel the results of the initiative. Tie the indicators into community goals where possible.

Community Visioning

Most communities that have created sustainable development plans have used some form of community involvement process. For example, Racine, Wisconsin (with a population of 85,000) developed the following principles in order to assure that its "visioning" process is productive and open:

"We believe the community visioning process must:

• Be equitable and just, so that *all* residents become fully engaged in it.

• Generate resident and organization ideas throughout the process that reflect the overall demographics of the community.

• Provide multiple ways for ideas and suggestions to be brought forward and for residents to become engaged.

• Be simple, understandable, positive, open, transparent, trustworthy, and flexible in order to generate widespread community buy-in and ownership.

• Nurture a culture of full participation and commitment of community residents *and* organizations in the development and implementation of the vision.

• Appeal to the self-interest of individuals and organizations by showing them how their individual lives as well as the life of the community will be better as a result.

• Recognize that youth need to be a driving force in the development of a community vision and its implementation.

• Run on as short a timetable as possible in recognition of the community's pent-up desire to begin working on solutions.

• Put the visioning process in the context of the overall community effort. This will demonstrate that visioning is only the *first* step in an ongoing movement towards a sustainable community.

• Encourage the community to become a learning community — one in which learning leads to continuous improvement" (Johnson Foundation 1997).

Co-Management

The term co-management has been used in a broad sense to designate a wide array of arrangements for shared decision-making between government resource management agencies and community-based parties. Co-management has now been widely recognized as contributing to solutions in the problematic management of "common property" or common pool resources such as fish, water, wildlife, forests and rangelands.

Co-management arrangements typically involve participatory decision-making by one or more government agencies working cooperatively with one or more community-based groups and involving one or more management functions. As long as there is significant overlap in management objectives (for example, sustainable harvest rates) and some commitment to joint problem-solving, it is not necessary for all of the community-based groups or parties to have the same level of power, rights, or management authority. Planning is more successfully implemented when all affected parties have a voice in decisions (Pinkerton 1996).

Examples of co-management include an agreement between the treaty tribes of western Washington State and the Washington Department of Fisheries, which share management authority over salmon, and do important aspects of joint harvest planning; the Gwaii Haanas Agreement for a national protected area in western Canada; and the Wendaban Stewardship Authority agreement for the Temagami area of Ontario (Duffy, Roseland, and Gunton 1996).

Local Round Tables

The aim of a local round table is to be a fully representative body, comprising many interests, seeking consensus on ways to achieve sustainability, and providing advice on local developments. These goals are met through a variety of methods and initiatives. To achieve multi-sectoral representation, for example, local round table members come from a wide variety of community sectors in order to build consensus and promote sustainability in the region. Membership seeks to achieve geographic representation, a mix of knowledge and skills, gender balance, and ethnocultural variety.

Local round tables provide advice and comments on local governments activities by conducting research, offering critiques, recommending new policies, plans and initiatives and monitoring reports and data. Another crucial element of their activities is educating the public about environmental and economic issues through speakers, special events and publications. These activities, in combination with networking with local action groups, assist in ensuring community input and involvement in local sustainability issues (ORTEE 1995).

Neighborhood Councils

At the community level, shared decision-making can take various forms. Neighborhood councils are an example of a participatory planning approach for community development (Clague 1993).

Neighborhood councils may be an informal association of neighbors or may be registered as a nonprofit society and charity; they also may be established by and officially connected to city hall. Generally they operate with nominal funds, although they may receive grant money for special projects or a small operating grant from the municipality.

Neighborhood councils are structured to have representation from each block in the neighborhood and/or other local organizations. They elect an executive, which is small enough that all members can meet regularly, to provide coordination and support to activities. The executive may also have the assistance of a social planner from the municipality or planning council.

Neighborhood councils foster information and communication on neighborhood issues/activities and on city activities that affect the neighborhood. They bring people together for planning and problem-solving on local interests, including advocacy to city hall. They facilitate good inter-group and inter-family relations in the neighborhood, and can address all issues of local concern, whether they concern social, educational, economic, land, environmental, or cultural dimensions of the community. Neighborhood councils also propose and act on projects and activities that strengthen community life.

Participation in neighborhood councils provides an opportunity for people to build their skills in democratic participation. Neighborhood councils offer an openness of agenda and flexibility, and maximum impact for minimum financial resources. They also can provide valuable sounding boards for municipal politicians on issues.

The limitations of neighborhood councils are that they require a core of very dedicated volunteers prepared to invest large amounts of personal time in their neighborhood for work that is not always appreciated. They also risk being dominated by a single issue group, or group that is not representative of the neighborhood. As well, they may require assistance in developing the skills for democratic community participation and decision-making.

Despite their limitations, neighborhood councils are very successful at promoting leadership, responsibility, and collaboration among community members. Seattle's neighborhood associations get deeply involved in economic development and neighborhood revitalization projects. Neighborhood associations initiated Education Summit, which resulted in a package for a levy seeking $65 million for the city to establish family support centers, health clinics, etc. The levy won overwhelming support.

Portland's 89 neighborhood associations represent all areas of Portland and participate in local government decision-making on virtually every aspect of civic business. They are consulted by the city and provide a neighborhood voice in areas ranging from input on proposed zoning and development changes, to priority setting on infrastructure improvements, to policing and crime protection strategy development.

Goal-Oriented Planning

Sustainable community planning works best in the context of a supportive regional, provincial or state planning framework. The key is goal-oriented planning — that is, planning *for* sustainable community development. Governance systems in some regions have been relatively successful in planning and managing for a healthy environment.

Supportive national planning programs exist in France, Norway, Finland, and Holland. In North America, provincial or state legislation can require each town's land use to be compatible with specified regional interests, but leave the actual planning process up to the local community. In Canada, British Columbia enacted growth strategies legislation in the mid-1990s. In the U.S., such legislation has given new force to urban planning in eight states: Florida, Georgia, Maine, Massachusetts, New Jersey, Oregon, Rhode Island, and Vermont. All cities and counties in these states are required to plan their own development according to stipulated goals, such as energy conservation, protection of open space, and provision of affordable housing. These statewide planning requirements not only enhance regional cooperation, but they also give cities the backing they need to apply a comprehensive, long-term vision to their land-use planning (Lowe 1992).

Sustainable Community Planning

Citizen organizations and local governments all over North America are engaging in sustainable community planning processes. Some notable initiatives are those of Chattanooga and the San Francisco Bay Area in the U.S,. Ottawa, Hamilton-Wentworth, and Greater Toronto in Canada, and Curitiba in Brazil.

"Neighbourhood organizations improve quality of community life. They keep the streets clean, fight crime, tutor children, organize recreation programs, plant community gardens, build housing, and more. They are by nature geographically based, volunteer driven, problem solving, empowering, multi-purpose and flexible" (Dobson 1995).

In 1969, Chattanooga, Tennessee was the most polluted city in the U.S. In 1990 it was recognized as the country's best turn-around story. How did it happen? In 1984, the entire community was invited to envision what they wanted their community to be like by 2000. The shared vision of sustainable community development that emerged put affordable housing, public education, transportation alternatives, better urban design, parks and greenways and neighborhood vitality at the top of the community's agenda. Energetic collaboration of government agencies, manufacturers and citizens resulted in successful initiatives to clean up the air and revitalize a city in decline. Several eco-industrial parks were established to rebuild the city's economic base, proving that economic development and environmental stewardship can be achieved together. Most importantly, all participants determined to set in motion a comprehensive, interrelated and strategic process for sustainable community development (Bernard and Young 1996; Gilbert et al. 1996).

Urban Ecology organized a five-year participatory process to develop their *Blueprint for A Sustainable Bay Area.* It is based on providing residents with new choices for a prosperous life; protecting, restoring and integrating nature into people's lives; working toward social, economic and environmental justice; promoting development and transportation alternatives that connect the region; encouraging resource conservation and reuse; designing with respect for local and historical uniqueness; and enabling residents to nurture a strong sense of place, community and responsibility (Urban Ecology 1996). The report's 95 recommendations reflect the range of tools and initiatives in this book.

The Health, Family, and Environment Committee of the San Francisco Board of Supervisors, with the support of the Mayor, unanimously endorsed in 1997 a Sustainability Plan that would guide decisions of all city commissions and departments. Air quality, solid waste, biodiversity, and food and agriculture are among the 10 major topics of the 150-page plan. The plan's transportation suggestions include creating 10 auto-free zones over the next four years, increasing the city parking tax, raising gasoline taxes and bridge tolls, and introducing "congestion pricing" charges for driving at rush hour. Critics such as right-wing radio talk-show host Rush Limbaugh and the conservative magazine *National Review* have called it "eco-totalitarianism." San Francisco joins Santa Monica, California and Chattanooga as American cities with extensive environmental plans (*GreenClips* 1997; Langton 1997).

Ottawa, Ontario's 1992 Official Plan, developed through an elaborate public consultation process with solid community support, is based on the concept of sustainable urban development. The city's commitment to sustainable development is manifested in the Mission Statement, Guiding Principles, and the Vision for Ottawa found at the beginning of the Plan. Specific policies contained in the Plan are designed to reflect this commitment. For example, the housing policies promote affordable housing, infilling and intensification, which reflect the guiding principles of adequate shelter, and conservation and enhancement of the resource base. The transportation policies encourage increased use of public transportation, cycling, and walking, which reflect the guiding principle of increasing non-automobile transportation. In addition, the plan outlines the city's environmental impact assessment process, which is designed to address the cumulative impact of everyday practices and development projects on the environment (ORTEE 1995).

The Sustainable Community Initiative is an ongoing collaborative process in which the Hamilton-Wentworth regional government, 75 kilometers (46.5 miles) west of Toronto, is working with thousands of citizens to turn a jointly-developed community vision into a reality. Since Vision 2020 was formally adopted in 1993, the regional government has devised an implementation strategy outlining the major policy shifts needed to achieve the vision, along with over 400 recommendations for specific action and a unique approach for monitoring progress. Twenty-eight sustainability indicators are compiled into the Annual Report Card, which is the basis of an Annual Sustainable Community Day and forum to assess progress in relation to the goals of Vision 2020. The Sustainable Community Initiative has already had a profound impact on the way the local government operates and is leading toward significant improvements to the local environment, including development of a bicycle commuter network, creation of habitat corridors for wildlife protection, and a home-energy and waste-auditing program (ICLEI 1995).

In 1988, a Royal Commission on the Future of the Toronto Waterfront was created to examine matters related to the use, enjoyment and development of the area. By the mid-1980s, the Toronto waterfront had become an embarrassment. Pollution had closed the beaches; expressways and condominium towers blocked public access; contaminated and abandoned industrial lands degraded the harbor area; and rehabilitation efforts were frustrated by jurisdictional squabbling among federal, provincial, regional, and municipal authorities. The Commission, headed by former Toronto Mayor David Crombie, initiated broad public discussion of waterfront issues and quickly saw that the conventional, fragmented, waterfront-specific approach would not work, so they expanded its scope from the waterfront to the watershed. This larger area, which the Commission called the Greater Toronto bioregion, is home to four million people as well as innumerable other creatures in complex social as well as ecological relations. Before the Crombie Commission, the notion of bioregional or ecosystem planning was little known outside professional and citizen planning circles, and did not seem likely to play a major role in guiding practical efforts to reunite economy, community, and ecology. Now it is a real possibility that has begun to be tested in practice (Gibson et al. 1997).

Curitiba, Brazil has received international acclaim as a city that works for its integrated transportation and land-use planning, and for its waste management programs. Both are good examples of sustainable community planning. But how did Curitiba manage to become a positive example for cities in both developed and developing countries? In part, the city's success can be attributed to strong leadership — city officials focused on developing simple, flexible, and affordable solutions that could be realized at the local level and adapted to changing conditions. In addition, "the government promoted a strong sense of public participation. Officials were encouraged to look at problems, talk to the people, discuss the main issues, and only then reach for the pen" (Rabinovitch 1996).

Cities are now banding together under the auspices of various regional associations and partnerships concerning approaches and solutions to common urban problems. The CO_2 Reduction Program is a partnership coordinated by the International Council for Local Environmental Initiatives (ICLEI). More than 100 local governments from 27 countries have joined an International Cities for Climate Protection Campaign. Participants pledge to meet and exceed the requirements of the Framework Convention on Climate Change by reducing carbon dioxide emissions by up to 20 percent by 2005. As part of this initiative, ICLEI worked with 14 cities to develop comprehensive local action plans to reduce carbon dioxide emissions (Brugmann 1996).

Jonas Rabinovitch, a long-time advisor to Curitiba Mayor Jaime Lerner, believes the lesson to be learned from Curitiba is that creativity can substitute for financial resources. Any city, rich or poor, can draw on the skills of its residents to tackle urban environmental problems (Rabinovitch 1996). All these examples confirm the importance, discussed in chapter 1, of multiplying social capital as a key to moving toward sustainable communities.

REFERENCES

Arnstein, S.R. 1969. "A Ladder of Citizen Participation." *Journal of American Institute of Planners* July: 216-24.

Beer, J, and E. Stief. 1997. *The Mediator's Handbook*. Gabriola Island, B.C.: New Society Publishers.

Bernard, T., and J. Young. 1996. *The Ecology of Hope: Communities Collaborate for Sustainability*. Gabriola Island, B.C.: New Society Publishers.

Brugmann, J. 1996. "Cities Take Action: Local Environmental Initiatives." In *World Resources 1996-97: The Urban Environment*, World Resources Institute, United Nations Environment Program, United Nations Development Program, World Bank. New York: Oxford University Press.

Clague, M.. 1993. *A Citizen's Guide to Community Social Planning*. Vancouver: Social Planning and Research Council of B.C.

Coover, V., et al. 1977. *Resource Manual for a Living Revolution*. Philadelphia: New Society Publishers.

Cormick, G. 1989. "Strategic Issues in Structuring Multi-party Public Policy Negotiations." *Negotiation Journal* 5(2): 125-32.

Crowfoot, J. E., and J. M. Wondolleck. 1990. *Environmental Disputes: Community Involvement in Conflict Resolution*. Washington, D.C./Covelo, Calif.: Island Press.

Dobson, C., ed. 1995. *The Citizen's Handbook: A Guide to Building Community in Vancouver*. Vancouver: Vancouver Citizen's Committee.

Duffy, D., M. Roseland, and T. I. Gunton. 1996. "A Preliminary Assessment of Shared Decision-Making in Land Use and Natural Resource Planning." *Environments: A Journal of Interdisciplinary Studies* 23(2): 1-16.

Gibson, R.B., D.H.M. Alexander, and R. Tomalty. 1997. "Putting Cities in Their Place: Ecosystem-Based Planning for Canadian Urban Regions." In *Eco-City Dimensions: Healthy Communities, Healthy Planet*, M. Roseland, ed. Gabriola Island, B.C.: New

Society Publishers.

Gilbert, R. 1991. *Cities and Global Warming*. Toronto: Canadian Urban Institute.

Gilbert, R., D. Stevenson, H. Giradet, and R. Stren. 1996. *Making Cities Work: The Role of Local Authorities in the Urban Environment*. London: Earthscan.

GreenClips. 1997. 76, 16 July. <GreenClips@aol.com>.

Henderson, H. 1996. *Building a Win-Win World: Life Beyond Global Economic Warfare*. San Francisco: Berrett-Koehler Publishers.

Independent Commission on Population and Quality of Life (ICPQL). 1996. *Caring for the Future*. New York: Oxford University Press.

International Council for Local Environmental Initiatives (ICLEI). 1995. *The Role of Local Authorities in Sustainable Development: 14 Case Studies on the Local Agenda 21 Process*. Nairobi: U.N. Centre for Human Settlements.

International Council for Local Environmental Initiatives (ICLEI), International Development Research Centre (IDRC), and United Nations Environment Program. 1996. *The Local Agenda 21 Planning Guide*. Toronto: ICLEI and Ottawa: IDRC.

Jacobs, J. 1961. *The Death and Life of Great American Cities*. New York: Vintage Books.

Jacobs, M. 1993. *The Green Economy: Environment, Sustainable Development and the Politics of the Future*. Vancouver: University of British Columbia Press.

Johnson Foundation. 1997. "Visioning Principles." *Wingspread Journal* 19(2).

Kaner, S., et al. 1996. *The Facilitator's Guide to Participatory Decision-Making*. Gabriola Island, B.C.: New Society Publishers.

Langton, J. 1997. "City's Plan to Kill Stray Cats Raises a Howl." *Vancouver Sun*, 11 August, p. A8.

Lowe, M.D. 1992. "City Limits." *Worldwatch* 5(1) Jan./Feb.: 18-25.

New York City. 1990. *The Environmental Charter for New York City*. New York: City of New York, Office of the Comptroller.

Minnery, J. R. 1985. *Conflict Management in Urban Planning*. Brookfield, Vt.: Gower Publishing.

National Round Table on the Environment and the Economy (NRTEE). 1993. *Building Consensus for a Sustainable Future: Guiding Principles*. Ottawa: NRTEE.

Ontario Round Table on the Environment and the Economy (ORTEE). 1995. *Sustainable Communities Resource Package*. Toronto: ORTEE.

Osborne, D., and T. Gaebler. 1993. *Reinventing Government*. New York: Plume.

Owen, S. 1994. "Introduction." *From Conflict to Consensus: Shared Decision-making in British Columbia*. M. Roseland, ed. Burnaby, B.C.: Simon Fraser University, School of Resource and Environmental management.

Paehlke, R., and D. Torgerson, eds. 1990. *Managing Leviathan: Environmental Politics and the Administrative State*. Peterborough: Broad View Press.

Pinkerton, E. 1996. "The Contribution of Watershed-Based Multi-Party Co-Management Agreements to Dispute Resolution: The Skeena Watershed Committee." *Environments* 23(2): 51-68.

President's Council on Sustainable Development (PCSD). 1996. *Sustainable America: A New Consensus for Prosperity, Opportunity, and a Healthy Environment for the Future*. Washington, D.C.: U.S. Government Printing.

Rabinovitch, J. 1996. "Integrated Transportation and Land Use Planning Channel Curitiba's Growth." In *World Resources* 1996-97: *The Urban Environment*, World Resources Institute, United Nations Environment Program, United Nations Development Program, World Bank. New York: Oxford University Press.

Ryan, J. 1992. "Sustainable Development: An Agenda for Change for Municipalities." *Municipal World* 102(3): 3-6.

Sutherland, S. 1991. Remarks to Association of Municipal Clerks and Treasurers of Ontario (AMCTO) and Intergovernmental Committee on Urban and Regional Research (ICURR) Management Symposium, "Implementing Sustainable Development in Municipalities." Hockley Valley, Ontario. May.

Urban Ecology. 1996. *Blueprint for A Sustainable Bay Area*. Oakland, Calif.: Urban Ecology.

Van Thijn, E. 1991. Mayor of Amsterdam, Remarks to World Cities and Their Environment Congress of Municipal Leaders, Toronto, 25-28 August.

TOOLS FOR COMMUNITY SUSTAINABILITY

M oving toward sustainable communities is a long-term goal, so it is important that the incremental steps we take in the short-term are leading us in the right direction. This chapter surveys some of the many tools available to citizens and their governments for managing community sustainability, and then discusses one of these tools, sustainability indicators, in more detail.

The tools described below (adapted from ICLEI et al. 1996 and Levett 1997, unless otherwise indicated) are organized into two categories: planning tools and assessment tools. Community planning and assessment tools can sometimes be conducted by citizen groups with little training, whereas technical planning and assessment tools more often require the involvement of trained staff or consultants. The latter may not lend themselves readily to public participation, but citizens can participate more effectively in decision-making if they know about many of the tools available to their communities.

PLANNING

Community Tools

Several community planning tools are useful for awareness building, problem diagnosis, and dialogue and participation in decision-making. These tools can be used from the pre-planning through to the evaluation stages of the planning process. Relatively familiar or self-explanatory tools include brainstorming, community meetings, field trips, media campaigns, open houses, public hearings, public meetings, role playing, vision building, and workshops. Popular education and search conferences are less well known.

Popular Education: The tools of theater, sculpturing, puppet shows, and storytelling have developed in communities where development practitioners and educators have worked. Popular techniques engage the community in the identification and critical analysis of issues, information gathering related to these issues, and problemsolving and decision-making methods. Popular education can enhance people's capacity to participate in decisions and actions affecting their lives.

Search Conferences: These are two- to three-day strategic community planning conferences designed to engage stakeholders in planning and managing the future. A search conference entails building consensus on a vision of the future as a basis for planning within and among all sectors. Future possibilities and trends rather than current problems or risks are the focus of subsequent action planning. The elements of a search conference include a review of past and current trends, an analysis of external and internal forces, the creation of a future vision, and development of an action plan.

Technical Tools

The following technical planning tools are used to establish environmental carrying-capacity limits and human impacts on them, and to guide policy.

Ecological Footprint Analysis: This tool estimates the land area required by any human activity, both directly — the land occupied by buildings or infrastructure — and indirectly — including the land needed to grow crops and assimilate pollutants. The ecological footprint may offer a meaningful single measure of all global ecological impacts of human activities, at household, municipal, national, or global levels. The degree to which the footprint of human activities exceeds the total productive area is a measure of unsustainability (Wackernagel and Rees 1996).

Environmental Space: The maximum sustainable rates of human use of key resources (energy, selected non-renewable resources, land, wood) are estimated, and then the resources are divided evenly among the world's population to give each individual's entitlement. The extent to which any country (or household) exceeds this is a measure of unsustainability. The calculations support calls for a ten-fold "dematerialization" of Western lifestyles.

Community-based State-of-the-Environment Reporting: The intention is to develop broad perceptions of ecosystems and our relationships with them, and to identify ecological approaches to planning and designing urban areas, on which residents and governments can ponder and act. As with all state-of-the-environment reporting, the question of appropriate indicators presents a major challenge, especially at the local government level. Ideally, state-of-the-environment indicators should be key measures that most represent the state of the environment and that collectively provide a comprehensive profile of environmental quality, natural resource assets, and agents of environmental change.

Sustainability Reporting: This is state-of-the-environment reporting broadened to include quality of life as well as aspects of sustainability; it is focused on information needed to guide decisions and action.

Environmental Budgeting: Local carrying capacities are used to set budgets for the maximum amount of environmental impact permissible in the municipal area. For example, the water extraction budget would be based on replenishment rates. The municipality works with all environmental consumers to keep impacts within budget.

More consumption of water by households, for example, would have to be offset by less consumption by industry, or by more recovery/treatment of wastewater.

ASSESSMENT

Community Tools

Assessment tools are used for figuring out where we're at, and for monitoring and evaluating where we're going. Some familiar or self-explanatory community assessment tools include risk assessment, focus groups, periodic monitoring reports, ranking, and surveys. Some less familiar assessment tools are described below.

Community Case Studies: These are collective descriptions and analyses of the community and its problems, documented in a local language or medium (e.g., drawing, storytelling, role playing, audio-visual). They can be used to promote awareness and discussion among community members, and to gather baseline information for assessment.

Community Environmental Assessment: Stakeholders can be involved in gathering information and analyzing the environmental and social impacts of proposed activities to predict their positive and negative effects. Designed for group observation and value judgment, the importance of any impact is determined by the community and given numerical value, such as environmental and social scores. Although not useful in themselves, these scores can be used to facilitate priority setting and to identify indicators for monitoring and evaluation.

Community Interviews: Interviews are a form of surveying in which all members of a community are invited to a meeting to answer specific pre-set questions. Discussion is restricted because the meeting size is large, so this tool is not useful for consensus-building; but it gathers preliminary information on community perspectives or solicits feedback on proposed strategies and actions.

Force Field Analysis: This is a facilitated and structured exercise in which participants identify specific hindering and facilitating forces affecting the functioning of any situation, assess the relative strength of each force, and plan alternative actions to overcome or promote these forces. It is useful for achieving a shared understanding of opportunities and constraints that can influence a desired goal, which helps participants determine effective strategies and priorities.

Geographic Information Systems: GIS is a computer-based data system for the storage, easy retrieval, manipulation, transformation, comparison, and graphic display of data. Intensive (and perhaps expensive) data gathering is often required, but once established, GIS can provide a user-friendly source of information that can be manipulated by non-experts as well as experts. In some communities, GIS systems have been used by community "watch-dogs" to monitor local environmental situations.

Community-Based Mapping: Mapping involves residents in the pictorial construction of information about their community. During a mapping exercise, maps are constructed from local knowledge and observation, and provide an excellent starting point for discussion about community-based issue identification, analysis, and problem-solving.

Oral History: This is a participatory technique for information sharing during the analysis of local issues. Historical accounts can be compared with present information to generate an analysis of underlying trends and structural problems in a community, and can be used to inform residents about the history of changes and development in their community.

Service Issues Mapping: This facilitated group brainstorming and analysis technique helps stakeholders "map" the diverse issues that must be considered in order to address a single priority issue. This exercise helps people see the systemic nature of local problems by highlighting complex sets of relationships among issues and by identifying different stakeholders who need to be involved in problem-solving.

SWOT Analysis: Strengths, Weaknesses, Opportunities, and Threats (SWOT) Analysis is a strategic planning tool that aids in the formulation of attainable long-range goals, action programs, and policies. Strengths and weaknesses refer to internal factors in the community, such as resources or declining budgets. Opportunities and threats refer to outside influences that could benefit or damage the community.

Technical Tools

Environmental Impact Assessment and Social Impact Assessment: These comprehensive tools integrate environmental and social considerations into project planning, development, and implementation. To be effective, assessment must be a decision-making tool. The application of an effective assessment process ensures that potential environmental and social effects are identified and mitigative measures put in place to minimize or eliminate these impacts. Effective assessment requires that the environmental and social implications of a proposal be considered prior to taking or making irrevocable decisions and as early in the planning process as possible. The assessment of a proposal should include the concerns of the public with regard to both environmental and social evaluation (City of Ottawa 1990).

Sustainability Appraisal: Appraisal of activities, projects, programs, plans and/or policies applies social and economic sustainability criteria as well as environmental ones, and considers their integration and reconciliation.

Environmental Audit: Such an audit is based on an assessment of the environmental impacts of a government's policies and practices. In some cases these will be known or easily identifiable, while in others, it will be possible only to indicate the likely consequences. The policy review should encompass all activities of the government, and all departments and arms of its service. It should not be restricted to official or approved policy, because much local government practice has evolved through tradition, or results from informal decisions of staff.

Environmental Action Planning and Management: This tool is a variation of an environmental audit; it involves setting environmental objectives, implementing environmental improvement actions, and monitoring and reporting on their effectiveness — in other words, applying familiar "management by objectives" to environmental effects.

Eco-Management and Audit System: Another variation of an environmental audit, an eco-management and audit system is a formal management systems standard for environmental "management by objectives." Originally designed for the manufacturing industry, it has been adopted for municipal use in the U.K. A proposed update is "sustainability management and audit system," which includes social and economic aspects of sustainability, and strengthens involvement of stakeholders in setting criteria and assessing performance, according to social audit principles.

Social Auditing: Just as financial accounting measures financial performance, social auditing measures social performance by better understanding its relation to the goals and key stakeholders of an organization. Social auditing is increasingly popular with large private institutions such as Ben and Jerry's Ice Cream, The Body Shop International, and VanCity Savings Credit Union. It can also be applied to smaller businesses, community enterprises, cooperatives, non-governmental organizations and public bodies (Pearce et al. 1997).

Sustainability Indicators: This effective tool for communities and governments to evaluate their progress toward sustainability is discussed below.

TOOLS IN ACTION

In June, 1992, the United Nations Conference on Environment and Development established Agenda 21, a sustainable development action plan for the 21st century. That plan includes a proposal made by the International Council for Local Environmental Initiatives (ICLEI) to support local governments in the development of their own Local Agenda 21s. ICLEI's Local Agenda 21 Initiative (ICLEI 1993) provides a common vehicle for local governments to strengthen local environmental planning. From 1992 to 1996, approximately 1,200 local governments in 33 countries established Local Agenda 21 campaigns (Brugmann 1996).

A Local Agenda 21 campaign can be any participatory, local effort to establish a comprehensive action strategy for sustainable development in that local jurisdiction or area. All local governments are urged to complete their campaigns and strategies and to report their results to both the United Nations Commission on Sustainable Development and to ICLEI. The proposed planning framework is based on the following four elements:

• *Community consultation processes*, such as round tables, to achieve input and participation from every sector;

• *Sustainable development auditing*, to provide sound information about current conditions;

• *Setting sustainable development targets*, both near and long-term, for quality of life, environmental quality, resource consumption, and human development; and

"The indicators a society chooses to report to itself about itself are surprisingly powerful. They reflect collective values and inform collective decisions. A nation that keeps a watchful eye on its salmon runs or the safety of its streets makes different choices than does a nation that is only paying attention to its GNP. The idea of citizens choosing their own indicators is something new under the sun — something intensely democratic" (Meadows 1972)

• *Development and use of indicators*, to inform the community about the impact of its programs and investments upon the sustainable development of the community.

Sustainability Indicators

Why are sustainability indicators important? According to Osborne and Gaebler (1993), what gets measured tends to get done. If you don't measure results, you can't tell success from failure. If you can't recognize success, you can't reward it. And if you can't recognize failure, you can't learn from it.

The steps involved in developing sustainability indicators are: clarify goals — the aim of the evaluation and the type of desired outcome; determine who will lead the process; invite participation — the process of evaluation may be as valuable as the eventual application of the indicators themselves; decide how to choose indicators; collect data by which to measure the indicators; report on the indicators; and update and revise the indicators. (For details on these steps and related issues, see Azar et al. 1996; Brugmann 1997; Forss et al. 1994; Kline 1997; Maclaren 1996; McLemore and Neumann 1987; Papineau 1996; Parker 1995; Schön and Rein 1994; Schwandt 1997; Waddell 1995.)

The following initiatives are a small sample of ongoing and emerging projects to design and use sustainability indicators. They represent the spectrum of aims for which sustainability indicators can be used — from the Sustainable Seattle Project, with a focus primarily on community education and empowerment, to the Oregon Benchmarks project, with a greater focus on providing feedback to government agencies.

Sustainable Seattle Project

The Sustainable Seattle Project began in 1992 with a meeting of 150 citizens. During this gathering, 99 indicators were proposed and 40 key indicators were selected; the first 20 of these indicators were assessed in 1993, and in 1995, the remaining 20 were assessed. Indicators ranged from total water consumption, per capita waste generation, and recycling rates to volunteering in schools and household incomes. The Sustainable Seattle Project plans to update and improve their indicators on an annual basis.

The people behind the Sustainable Seattle Project believe that "measuring progress is not the same as making it." The project promotes action by encouraging Seattle-area citizens to:
- employ local media to spread indicator results and analysis;
- use the political process to promote change in public policy;
- broaden the information base used for economic decision-making;
- use indicators in schools for education and as a basis for additional research;
- form a basis for linking local nonprofit and volunteer groups; and
- question personal lifestyle choices.

Willapa Bay Indicators

In southwest Washington State, the Willapa Bay Indicators Project is evaluating the

Goals, Targets, and Indicators

In 1994, the Santa Monica Task Force on the Environment developed a Sustainable City Program in partnership with the City of Santa Monica Environmental Programs Division. Each of the program's policy areas has clear goals reflecting the city's current and future programs. Specific targets were established for each goal, and an indicator was established for each target, as in the example below (ICLEI et al. 1996):

Policy Area: Community and Economic Development

Goals
- Encourage the development of compact, mixed-use, pedestrian-oriented projects.
- Promote the growth of local businesses that provide employment opportunities for Santa Monica residents.
- Facilitate education programs that enrich the lives of all members of the community.

Targets
- Provide 750 additional affordable housing units.
- Create three new community gardens.
- Establish partnership with local schools to create and complement a Sustainable Schools program.
- Increase total public open space by 15 acres.

Indicators:	1990 (Actual)	1993 (Actual)	2000 (Target)
Deed-restricted affordable housing units	1,172 units	1,313 units	1,922 units
Community gardens	2 gardens	2 gardens	5 gardens
Creation of a Sustainable Schools program	n/a	n/a	implemented
Public open space	164 acres	164.8 acres	180 acres

environmental, social, and economic sustainability of a rural watershed. The Willapa indicators explicitly tie the health of the environment to the vitality of the local economy and community. Environmental indicators are divided into three categories: water resource quality, land-use/vegetation patterns, and species populations. Economic indicators are included under the categories of productivity, opportunity, diversity, and equity. Finally, community measures fall under life-long learning, health, citizenship, and stewardship.

The Willapa Project links with other community groups and organizations. A joint effort by the Willapa Alliance and Ecotrust, the *Willapa Indicators for a Sustainable Community* report is intended to promote discussion of sustainability issues in the local communities. Published as a companion volume to the indicators report is *The Directory of Organizations and Services in Pacific County, Including Key Government*

Officials. And among other projects, the Alliance formed the Willapa Science Group, a group of local and regional scientists and educators who encourage scientific research that is meaningful to local people.

Hamilton-Wentworth's Sustainable Community Indicators Project

In Ontario, Hamilton-Wentworth's Sustainable Community Indicators Project arose out of the regional municipality's Vision 2020 initiative. This vision of a sustainable future was developed by a citizens' Task Force on Sustainable Development appointed by the regional council; over 400 individuals and 50 community groups took part in the visioning process (Maclaren 1996). The Indicators Project measured progress toward the goals outlined in the Vision 2020 document, and drew on participation of the community throughout the process. While the final set of indicators are intended for decision-makers, the prime goal was developing a set of indicators which were understandable and useful to local citizens.

Oregon Benchmarks Program

The Oregon Benchmarks process resulted from the State of Oregon's strategic plan, *Oregon Shines*. A multi-stakeholder organization supporting the plan, the Oregon Progress Board, presented a reporting framework to the state legislature after extensive consultation, and the benchmarks process was officially adopted in 1991.

The framework for reporting consists of 269 indicators. Rather than simply present indicators to measure and report trends, however, the Oregon process defines targets, known as benchmarks. The benchmarks cover a diverse range of issues around sustainability, including categories such as children and families, education and work force, health and health care, clean natural environment, equal opportunity and social harmony, and economic prosperity. The Board publishes a report card every two years to report on progress toward the stated targets.

While the Oregon Benchmarks program has drawn on public consultation and aims to inform the public, its main strength is its ability to promote action and accountability in the state government. Rational and clear sustainability goals have formed the basis for strategic planning throughout government agencies. The legislature even passed several bills directing agencies to work toward benchmarks. On a smaller scale, the Oregon Benchmarks are being applied by municipal governments and community organizations, and several cities and counties are adopting strategies to complement the state program.

The Need for National Indicators

It is too early to judge the impact of local and regional projects on community sustainability over the long-term, but they seem to be helping communities move in the right

---

Redefining Wealth

"In September 1995 the World Bank introduced a preliminary new index of national wealth which includes natural capital (environmental resources), produced assets (factories, infrastructure, financial assets — what is usually measured by the GNP), human resources (educated, healthy, productive people) and social capital (families, communities, institutions). Moreover, the World Bank acknowledges that 'produced assets' account for only some 20% of national wealth, while natural capital accounts for another 20% and human resources and social capital between them account for the remaining 60%. From this perspective the wealthiest nation in the world is Australia (with 70% of its wealth based on its land and natural resources) followed by Canada (also rich in natural resources) in second place. Luxembourg, Sweden, Japan and Sweden (3rd-6th place) owe their wealth mainly to human capital, as does the USA which ranks 12th on this scale" (Henderson 1996).

direction. Many researchers have also recognized the importance of developing sustainability indicators at the national scale. Currently, much national policy is driven by trends in GNP, which only considers narrow economic measures of a country's well-being; sustainability, including trends in natural and social capital, is not considered. Effective indicators of national sustainability would provide important information for citizens and governments supporting initiatives at the local and regional level.

RESOURCES

Community Indicators Network (CINet) is an initiative of Redefining Progress with the goal of linking existing and emerging indicator projects, and facilitating the development of more initiatives. The main products being developed by CINet include the *Community Indicators Handbook*, the CINet web site, and an e-mail discussion group, RP-CINET, for the exchange of information. These products promise to be a significant contribution to providing accessible and relevant information to groups interested in sustainability indicators.

One Kearny Street, 4th Floor
San Francisco, California
USA 94108
Tel: 415/781-1191 (ext. 312)
E-mail: besleme@rprogress.org

Guide to Sustainable Community Indicators by M. Hart (Ipswich, Mass.: QLF/Atlantic Center for the Environment, 1995) is a useful guidebook describing the entire process of developing and implementing sustainability indicators at the community level. The guide includes sample indicators, list of projects, and references. The author has also developed an excellent web site.

Web site: www.subjectmatters.com/indicators

Healthy Cities Indicators and Annual Awards
Healthcare Forum of San Francisco
425 Market Street, 16th Floor
San Francisco, California
Tel: 415/356-4300
Fax: 415/356-9300

Hamilton-Wentworth's *Sustainable Community Indicators Project* is available from:

Regional Environment Department
Regional Municipality of Hamilton-Wentworth
35 King Street East
Hamilton, Ontario
Canada L8N 4A9
Tel: 905/546-2153
Fax: 905/546-4365
Web site: www.hamilton-went.on.ca/vis2020

Life in Jacksonville: Quality Indicators for Progress is available from:
Jacksonville Community Council
2434 Atlantic Boulevard
Jacksonville, Florida
USA 32207
Tel: 904/396-3052
Fax: 904/398-1469

New Economics Foundation is a leading organization in the field of social auditing. The Foundation has contributed both to the development of a practical methodology and its increasingly widespread use through a combination of research and publications, training, and direct social auditing activities. The Foundation aims to promote social responsibility in the corporate, not-for-profit, and public sectors. Publications include *Social Auditing for Small Organizations*, and *Building Corporate Accountability.*
1st Floor Vine Court
112-116 Whitechapel Road
London, U.K. E1 1JE
Tel: +44-0-171-377-5696
Fax: +44-0-171-377-5720
E-mail: neweconomics@gn.apc.org
Web site: sosig.ac.uk/NewEconomics/newecon.htm

Office of Sustainable Ecosystems and Communities is working on products of interest to communities and citizens interested in sustainability evaluation, including an electronic database and annotated bibliography of community-level indicators handbooks, reports, and studies.
U.S. Environmental Protection Agency
401 M Street, S.W.
Washington, D.C.
USA 20460
Tel: 202/260-6380
Web site: www.epa.gov/ecocommunity/

Oregon Benchmarks reports are available from the Oregon Progress Board.
775 Summer Street, N.E.
Salem, Oregon
USA 97310
Tel: 503/986-0039
E-mail: Progress.Board@state.or.us
Web site: www.econ.state.or.us/opb/index/htm

Sustainable Seattle report is available from:
Sustainable Seattle
c/o Metrocentre YMCA
909 4th Avenue

Seattle, Washington
USA 98104
Tel: 206/382-5013
E-mail: sustnble@scn.org
Web site: www.scn.org/sustainable/

Willapa Indicators for a Sustainable Community report is available on its web site.

Willapa Alliance
P.O. Box 278
Smith Bend, Washington
USA 98586
Tel: 360/875-5195
Fax: 360/875-5198
E-mail: alliance@willapabay.org
Web site: www.willapabay.org/~alliance/wisc/wisc.htm#exec

REFERENCES

Azar, C., J. Holmberg, and K. Lindgren. 1996. "Socio-ecological Indicators for Sustainability." *Ecological Economics* 18:89-112.

Brugmann, J. 1996. "Cities Take Action: Local Environmental Initiatives." In *World Resources 1996-97: The Urban Environment*, World Resources Institute, United Nations Environment Program, United Nations Development Program, World Bank. New York: Oxford University Press.

— — — . 1997. "Is There a Method in Our Measurement? The Use of Indicators in Local Sustainable Development Planning." *Local Environment* 2(1): 59-72.

City of Ottawa. 1990. Urban Environmental Conservation Strategy: Framework Document, discussion paper. Ottawa: City of Ottawa, Department of Engineering and Public Works.

Forss, K., B.Cracknell, and K. Samset. 1994. "Can Evaluation Help an Organization to Learn?" *Evaluation Review* 18(5): 574-91.

Henderson, H. 1996. *Building a Win-Win World: Life Beyond Global Economic Warfare*. San Francisco: Berrett-Koehler Publishers.

International Council for Local Environmental Initiatives (ICLEI). 1993. "The Local Agenda 21 Initiative: ICLEI Guidelines for Local and National Local Agenda 21 Campaigns." Toronto: ICLEI.

International Council for Local Environmental Initiatives (ICLEI), International Development Research Centre (IDRC), and United Nations Environment Program. 1996. *The Local Agenda 21 Planning Guide*. Toronto: ICLEI and Ottawa: IDRC.

Kline, E. 1997. "Sustainable Community Indicators." In *Eco-City Dimensions: Healthy Communities, Healthy Planet*, M. Roseland, ed. Gabriola Island, B.C.: New Society Publishers.

Levett, R. 1997. "Tools, Techniques and Processes for Municipal Environmental Management." *Local Environment* 2(2): 189-202.

Maclaren, V.W. 1996. "Developing Indicators of Urban Sustainability: A Focus on the Canadian Experience." Toronto: Intergovernmental Committee on Urban and Regional

Research Press.

McLemore, J.R., and J.E. Neumann. 1987. "The Inherently Political Nature of Program Evaluators and Evaluation Research." *Evaluation and Program Planning* 10:83-93.

Meadows, D.H., et al. 1972. *The Limits to Growth* . New York: Signet.

Osborne, D., and T. Gaebler. 1993. *Reinventing Government* . New York: Plume.

Papineau, D. 1996. "Participatory Evaluation in a Community Organization: Fostering Stakeholder Empowerment and Utilization." *Evaluation and Program Planning* 19(1): 79-93.

Parker, P. 1995. "From Sustainable Development Objectives to Indicators of Progress: Options for New Zealand Communities." *New Zealand Geographer* 51(2): 50-57.

Pearce, J., P. Raynard, and S. Zadek. 1997. *Social Auditing for Small Organisations: A Workbook for Trainers and Practitioners.* London: New Economics Foundation.

Schön, D.A., and M. Rein. 1994. *Frame Reflection: Toward the Resolution of Intractable Policy Controversies.* New York: Basic Books.

Schwandt, T.A. 1997. "Evaluation as Practical Hermeneutics." *Program Evaluation* 3(1): 69-83.

Wackernagel, M., and W.E. Rees. 1996. *Our Ecological Footprint: Reducing Human Impact on the Earth* . Gabriola Island, B.C.: New Society Publishers.

Waddell, S. 1995. "Lessons from the Healthy Cities Movement for Social Indicator Development." *Social Indicators Research* 34: 213-35.

LESSONS AND CHALLENGES

After all the eager promises made by presidents and prime ministers at the Rio de Janeiro Earth Summit in 1992, it was only too clear that few of those promises were kept by the follow-up Earth Summit+5 in 1997. For example, despite commitments signed at the Rio Climate Convention in 1992 to stabilize greenhouse gas emissions at 1990 levels by 2000, U.S. emissions will probably have risen by 13 percent by 2000, while Canadian emissions are forecast to rise 18 percent by 2010.

The same kinds of promises are routinely broken closer to home, too. The road to sustainable development is paved with failed efforts to incorporate the environment into everyday municipal decision-making. Insincere politics may be partly to blame, but there is no doubt that even with the best intentions, these kinds of commitments are wretchedly complex and difficult to keep. While progress in environmental management appears to be the order of the day, recent history gives cause for concern.

Toronto, for example, made headlines around the world in 1990 by becoming the first city to commit to reducing its 1988 level of carbon dioxide emissions 20 percent by 2005. Included in its "call for action" was a goal of "significantly reducing the number of commuting autos" and a strategy to "promote significant reductions in the energy intensity of transportation in the city" by promoting public transit, bicycling, and walking (City of Toronto 1989). Yet *10 years earlier* Toronto City Council had passed an energy conservation bylaw designed, among other things, to encourage development and redevelopment that would contribute to energy-efficient urban form, reduce the need for transportation, discourage automobile use, and encourage public transit and bicycle transportation (Lang and Armour 1982). That the same environmental legislation was passed twice in 10 years is a strong indicator that the earlier measures were not implemented.

Another example of purported progress is the recent mushrooming of municipal and local government environmental departments, coordinators, task forces, staff committees, and citizen boards. At one level this certainly deserves applause. Yet a major survey of environmental management in nearly 3,000 North American local governments *in 1973* found that 20 percent had staff environment committees, 40 percent had designated environmental coordinators, and 24 percent had citizen environmental boards. Inadequate funding, uncertainty and delay in program administration, inadequate communication with senior levels of government, and inadequate technical assistance were all perceived in the mid-1970s as major impediments to adequate local responses to environmental problem solving (Magazine 1977). A quarter-century later, this list still sounds all too familiar.

No single person can raise the wind that might blow us into a sustainable future. But we can all help put up the sail so that when the wind comes, we can catch it. If we can create now the possibility of a sustainable future, we can genuinely breathe some hope into our communities for ourselves and for our children.

Our communities provide enormous, largely untapped opportunities for making our society more sustainable. This final chapter reviews some lessons for policy-making that emerge from the foregoing chapters, and explores the challenges ahead.

LESSONS FOR POLICY-MAKING

Communities are coming to recognize their responsibility to develop sustainably. Taken together, the initiatives described in this book begin to delineate a strategy for encouraging a globally conscious culture of sustainability in our communities. They also indicate some practical suggestions on how to design effective sustainable community development policies. The key features of any sustainable development policy framework should recognize the following:

Sustainable development requires sustainable communities: Global sustainable development requires local authority and capacity for sustainable community management and development. Despite the concentration of population in urban areas, many city and local governments do not have the regulatory and financial authority required to effectively contribute to sustainable urban development. Other levels of government must provide resources and support for the financing, management, and policy-making authority necessary for local governments to achieve sustainable development in their communities.

To make wise decisions about key aspects of their communities, particularly land use, local governments need more generous national funding for infrastructure, education, and social services. The experience of recent years has demonstrated that placing the burden of all these costs on property taxes can lead local governments to act irresponsibly — for example, allowing ecologically destructive development of valuable open space, or excluding low-taxpaying land uses such as affordable housing. Deteriorating municipal services, along with failing roads, bridges, and sewerage systems in major urban areas worldwide, also testify to the need for giving more financial resources to communities (Lowe 1991).

Rules can and must be changed: Many community policy-makers are stuck in the paralyzing belief that our market society and our bureaucratic nation-state system cannot be changed in any basic sense. To play by those rules means that both the environment and the less fortunate members of society always lose until eventually everything is lost.

Sustainability can mean "less" as well as "more:" So long as sustainable development is conceived merely as "environmental protection," it will be understood as an "added" cost to be "traded" against. Once sustainable development is conceived as *doing development differently*, such trade-offs become less critical: the new focus is instead on finding ways to *stop* much of what we are already doing, and use the resources thus freed for socially and ecologically sustainable activities.

Where the market works, use it: As one utility executive explained his sudden interest in energy conservation, "the rat has to smell the cheese." Create and promote incentives for ecologically sound practices. Well-designed ecological incentive programs are also cost-effective, since larger expenditures for clean-up and restoration are avoided.

Where the market fails, don't be afraid to mandate changes: The prevailing economic orthodoxy is that we must have a political and economic environment that welcomes foreign-owned companies and supports business through a reduction in regulations to become globally competitive, no matter what the consequences in our society and in our communities.

Yet the evidence may suggest otherwise. For example, in 1989 the Los Angeles area adopted a far-reaching mandatory environmental plan which, among other elements, phases out the use of petroleum-based transport fuels over a 20-year period. No less a source than *The Economist* (1991) attributes California's economic success in the $130-billion-a-year environmental services industry to strict environmental laws — the toughest in the world. This would not have been possible if Los Angeles had opted instead to impose a modest gasoline tax to encourage energy efficiency (Morris 1990).

Polluters should pay for the costs of remediation, but it is even more important to prevent pollution and the waste of resources in the first place: This principle is particularly significant in the debate over "green" taxes. Governments can reflect new priorities without increasing the total tax burden by shifting taxes away from income and toward environmentally damaging activities. If governments substituted taxes on pollution, waste and resource depletion for a large portion of current levies on employment and income, both the environment and the economy would benefit. The Worldwatch Institute estimates that a set of potential U.S. green taxes (particularly on carbon content of fuels and on generation of hazardous wastes) could substitute for *reducing income taxes* by nearly 30 percent (Postel 1991). Citizens, corporations, and the environment could all come out ahead.

Social equity is not only desirable but essential: Inequities undermine sustainable development, making it essential to consider the distributive effects of actions intended to advance sustainable development. Growth management ordinances in many western U.S. cities, for example, enacted to safeguard the environment and protect the quality of community life, have caused local housing supplies to tighten, driving up prices and causing serious affordability problems for low- and moderate-income households. As these households leap-frog across preserved open space to less expensive communities in the region, additional commuting, traffic congestion, and air pollution threaten the very quality of life at which the control measures were aimed in the first place (van Vliet 1990).

Public participation is itself a sustainable development strategy: To a considerable extent, the environmental crisis is a creativity crisis. By soliciting the bare mini-

"The enduring legacy of the environmental movement is that it has taught us the distinction between price and cost. Price is what the individual pays. Cost is what the community pays. The marketplace works efficiently only when guided by accurate price signals" (Morris 1990).

mum of public "input," rather than actively seeking community participation from agenda-setting through to implementation and evaluation, local and senior decision-makers have failed to tap the well of human ingenuity. They have failed to recognize that *only* from this well can the myriad challenges to redevelop our communities be met successfully. Effective and acceptable local solutions require local decisions, which in turn require the extensive knowledge and participation of the people most affected by those decisions, in their workplaces and in their communities.

THE CHALLENGES AHEAD

Sustainable communities will not come easily — they require significant change in our structures, attitudes, and values. Sustainable development implies a shift in the capacity of individuals, companies, and nations to use resources which they have the right to use — and are encouraged to use — under present legal and economic arrangements. Although even the most conventional analyses recognize the need for changing these arrangements, few openly acknowledge that moving toward a sustainable society requires more than minor adjustments to existing practices.

The key to a sustainable future lies not in making us more competitive, but rather in making us more perceptive, more able to realize what we have, what we need, and what are the long-term consequences of the short-term choices we are making (Wachtel 1989). Many North Americans intuitively understand that the reason why economic growth no longer brings a sense of greater well-being, why the pleasures of our new possessions swiftly melt away is that "what really matters is not one's material possessions but one's psychological economy, one's richness of human relations and freedom from the conflicts and constrictions that prevent us from enjoying what we have." Indeed, we have attempted "to use economics to solve what are really psychological problems" (Wachtel 1989).

Like others writing in the growing sociological literature on the "communitarian approach" (e.g., Bellah 1991; Lasch 1991), Wachtel (1989) argues that our societal focus on productivity and economic efficiency as defining values leads to greater emphasis on competition, the pursuit of self-interest, and the stimulation of demand:

> This in turn means still more decline in the security to be gained via shared ties and a stable, securely rooted place and way of life, still more need to compensate by organizing everything around what enables us to have "more," still more decline of traditional sources of security, and so forth. Thus, the more fully we have committed ourselves to increasing material abundance as our ultimate societal value, the more we have undermined older sources of security and made ourselves dependent on material goods for our sense of well-being to an unprecedented degree.

The challenge ahead is to explore the implications of a sustainable future and to find a new set of guiding images and metaphors suited for it. Sustainable communities are the next steps in suggesting an alternative vision of the future that is not just a bitter necessity (for example, the need to reduce materials and energy consumption), but promises a genuinely better life. Sustainable communities do not mean settling for less, but rather thinking of new opportunities along a different, and likely more satisfying, dimension.

With their relatively wealthy and well-educated populations, North American communities have a moral obligation to demonstrate leadership (and consequently benefit from) developing the knowledge, technologies, and processes the world requires for sustainability in the coming decades. Citizens and their governments have the ability to frame issues, assume leadership, champion initiatives, and demonstrate sustainable alternatives in their everyday practice. With creative leadership, we may yet be proud of the legacy left for our children.

Sustainable communities require unprecedented and simultaneous emphasis on the efficient use of urban space, on minimizing the consumption of essential natural capital, on multiplying social capital, and on mobilizing citizens and their governments toward these ends. This synergistic approach will enable our communities to be cleaner, healthier, and less expensive; to have greater accessibility and cohesion; and to be more self-reliant in energy, food, and economic security than they are now. Sustainable communities will not, therefore, merely "sustain" the quality of our lives — they will dramatically *improve* it.

REFERENCES

Bellah, R.N., et al. 1991. *The Good Society.* New York: Knopf.

City of Toronto. 1989. *The Changing Atmosphere: A Call To Action.* Toronto: City of Toronto.

Economist, The. 1991. "Going Green in Smog Valley." Reprinted in *Vancouver Sun,* 20 November, p. D9.

Lang, R., and A. Armour. 1982. *Planning Land to Conserve Energy: 40 Case Studies From Canada and the United States* . Ottawa: Lands Directorate, Environment Canada.

Lasch, C. 1991. *The True and Only Heaven: Progress and Its Critics.* New York: W.W. Norton.

Lowe, M.D. 1991. "Shaping Cities: The Environmental and Human Dimensions." *Worldwatch* 105. Washington, D.C.: Worldwatch Institute.

Magazine, A.H. 1977. *Environmental Management in Local Government: A Study of Local Response to Federal Mandate* . New York: Praeger Publishers.

Morris, D. 1990. *An Environmental Policy for the 1990s: Fashioning the Molecular Basis for a Green Economy.* Washington, D.C.: Institute for Local Self-Reliance.

Postel, S. 1991. "Accounting for Nature." *Worldwatch* 4(2) March/April: 28-33.

van Vliet, W. 1990. Human Settlements in the U.S.: Questions of Even and Sustainable Development. Prepared for the Colloquium on Human Settlements and Sustainable Development, Toronto, 21-23 June.

Wachtel, P. 1989. *The Poverty of Affluence: A Psychological Portrait of the American Way of Life.* Gabriola Island, B.C.: New Society Publishers.

SUSTAINABLE COMMUNITY RESOURCES

The following are useful sustainable community resources for citizens and their governments. These are generic resources of value to all aspects of sustainable community development. They are listed under Organizations and Journals. This listing is by no means exhaustive, but it provides some good places to start.

ORGANIZATIONS

Alliance for National Renewal brings together a network of people and organizations who want to better their communities. The web site is a comprehensive resource and includes a list of publications to order from the following address.

National Civic League
1445 Market Street, Suite 300
Denver Colorado
USA 80202-1717
E-mail: ncl@ncl.org
Web site: www.ncl.org/anr/index.htm

Center of Excellence for Sustainable Development is a demonstration project operated by the U.S. Department of Energy's Denver Office of Energy Efficiency and Renewable Energy. Regional support offices are also in Boston, Chicago, Philadelphia, Atlanta, and Seattle. They provide consultation on sustainable development for communities, and link them to relevant public and private programs.

U.S. Department of Energy
Office of Energy Efficiency and Renewable Energy
Denver Regional Support Office
1617 Cole Boulevard
Golden, Colorado
USA 80401
Tel: 303/275-4826
Toll-free: 800/357-7732
Fax: 303/275-4830

E-mail: sustainable.development@hq.doe.gov
Web site: www.sustainable.doe.gov

Center for Livable Communities is a national initiative of California's Local Government Commission (providing technical assistance to local governments) and a principal partner in the Environmental Protection Agency's Transportation Partners program. The Center helps local governments and community leaders be proactive in their land-use and transportation planning, and adopt programs and policies that lead to more livable and resource-efficient land-use patterns. The Center organizes workshops and conferences, distributes several publications and a monthly newsletter, maintains the Land Use Library, has a useful catalogue of slides and videos, and runs a toll-free hotline and referral number.

Local Government Commission
909 12th Street, Suite 205
Sacramento, California
USA 95814
Tel: 916/448-1198
Toll-free: 800/290-8202
Web site: www.lgc.org/clc/

Center for Neighborhood Technology promotes public policies and resources on sustainable, just, and vital urban communities.
2125 W. North Avenue
Chicago, Illinois
USA 60647
Tel: 773/278-4800
Web site: www.cnt.org/

Center for Renewable Energy and Sustainable Technology
1200 18th Street, N.W., Suite 900
Washington, D.C.
USA 20036
Tel: 202/530-2202
Fax: 202/887-0497
E-mail: www-content@solstice.crest.org
Web site: solstice.crest.org/

Coalition for Environmentally Responsible Economies (CERES)
711 Atlantic Avenue
Boston, Massachusetts
USA 02111
Tel: 617/482-2028
Fax: 617/482-2028.
E-mail: ceres@igc.apc.org
Web site: www.ncat.org/sustainable/redesign/cesdbeta3/business/ceres.htm

Environmental Protection Agency
401 M Street, S.W.
Washington, D.C.
USA 20460
Tel: 202/260-5922
Fax: 202/260-6257
E-mail: OW-General@epamail.epa.gov
Web site: www.epa.gov/glnpo/grnmakrs/ga-tool.htm

Institute for Local Self-Reliance is a nonprofit research and educational organization founded in 1974, providing technical assistance and information on environmentally sound economic development strategies.
National Office
2425 18th Street, N.W.
Washington, D.C.
USA 20009-2096
Tel: 202/232-4108
Fax: 202-332-0463
Web site: www.ilsr.org/

Institute for Sustainable Communities was founded in 1990 by former Vermont Governor Madeleine M. Kunin to promote sustainable development, environmental protection, and participatory democracy in Central and Eastern Europe. The Institute is interested in developing community-based approaches to solving and preventing environmental problems by emphasizing activities that reinforce and complement the region's move toward economic restructuring and democratic decision-making.
56 College Street
Montpelier, Vermont
USA 05602
Tel: 802/229-2900
Fax: 802/229-2919
E-mail: isc@iscvt.org
Web site: www.iscvt.org

Intergovernmental Committee on Urban and Regional Research is an information exchange service and research program on sustainable urban development in Canada.
150 Eglinton Avenue East, Suite 301
Toronto, Ontario
Canada M4P 1E8
Tel: 416/973-5629
Fax: 416/973-1375
Web site: www.icurr.org/icurr/

International City Management Association is the professional and educational association for appointed administrators and assistant administrators serving cities, villages, boroughs, townships, counties, and councils of governments. Membership also includes directors of state associations of governments, other local government employees, members of the academic community, and concerned citizens who share the goal of improving local government. For environmental management, the Association offers assistance in solid waste management, ground water protection, and wastewater treatment. *Cities International* is its quarterly newsletter on municipal development and management training programs in developing countries.

777 N. Capitol Street, N.E.
Washington, D.C.
USA 20002-4201
Tel: 202/289-4262

International Council for Local Environmental Initiatives (ICLEI) is an international association of local governments dedicated to the prevention and solution of local, regional, and global environmental problems. Members include more than 175 local governments of all sizes. ICLEI's *Local Agenda 21 Planning Guide: An Introduction to Sustainable Development Planning* helps local governments plan toward sustainability, offering planning elements, methods, and tools used by local governments worldwide.

New City Hall, East Tower, 8th Floor
Toronto, Ontario
Canada M5H 2N2
Tel: 416/392-1462
Fax: 416/392-1478
E-mail: 75361.3043@compuserve.com
Web site: www.iclei.org

U.S. Projects Office
15 Shattuck Square, Suite 215
Berkeley, California
USA 94704
Tel: 510/540-8843
Fax: 510/540-4787
Web site: www.iclei.org

International Institute for Sustainable Development
161 Portage Avenue E., 6th Floor
Winnipeg, Manitoba
Canada R3B 0Y4
Tel: 204/958-7715
Web site: http://iisd.ca

National Round Table on the Environment and the Economy is an independent agency of the Canadian government that seeks to provide objective views and information regarding the state of the debate on the relationship between the environment and the economy.

Canada Building
344 Slater Street, Suite 200
Ottawa, Ontario
Canada K1R 7Y3
Tel: 613/992-7189
Fax: 613/992-7385
Web site: www.nrtee-trnee.ca/

Planners Network is an association of professionals, activists, academics, and students involved in physical, social, economic, and environmental planning in urban and rural areas; they believe that planning should be used to assure adequate food, clothing, shelter, medical care, jobs, safe working conditions, and a healthful environment. A bi-monthly newsletter is published.

1601 Connecticut Ave., N.W.
Washington, D.C.
USA 20009
Tel: 202/234-9382
Fax: 202/387-7915

Pratt Institute Center for Community and Environmental Development

379 DeKalb Avenue, 2nd Floor
Brooklyn, New York
USA 11205
Tel: 718/636-3486
Fax: 718/636-3709
Web site: www.picced.org/

President's Council on Sustainable Development was created in 1993 to advise the President on sustainable development and to develop new approaches to integrate economic, environmental, and equity issues. The Council is a partnership of diverse leaders from business, government, community, environmental, labor, and civil rights organizations.

730 Jackson Place, N.W.
Washington, D.C.
USA 20503
Tel: 202/408-5296
Toll-free for reports: 800/363-3732
Fax: 202/408-6839
E-mail: infopcsd@aol.com
Web site: www.whitehouse.gov/PCSD

Public Technology, Inc. is the technical arm of the International City Management Association and the National League of Cities. As a nonprofit organization, it helps local governments throughout North America cut costs and improve services by practical use of technology and management systems. The U.S. Environmental Protection Agency funded the organization's Urban Consortium Environmental Task Force to conduct applied research on local environmental problems, develop innovations, and transfer results.

1301 Pennsylvania Avenue, N.W.
Washington, D.C.
USA 20004
Tel: 202/626-2400
Toll Free: 800/852-4934
Fax: 202/626-2498
E-mail: press@pti.nw.dc.us
Web site: pti.nw.dc.us/

Renew America is a nonprofit organization founded in 1989, coordinating a network of community and environmental groups, businesses, government leaders, and civic activists to exchange ideas and expertise for improving the environment.

1400 16th Street, N.W., Suite 710
Washington, D.C.
USA 20036
Tel: 202/232-2252
Fax: 202/232-2617
E-mail: renewamerica@igc.apc.org
Web site: www.crest.org/sustainable/renew_america/

Rocky Mountain Institute is a nonprofit research and educational foundation to foster the efficient and sustainable use of resources as a path to global security.

1739 Snowmass Creek Road
Snowmass, Colorado
USA 81654-9199
Tel: 970/927-3851
Fax: 970/927-3420
Web site: www.rmi.org/

Sustainable Communities Network is a comprehensive resource for citizens working to create healthy, vital, sustainable communities. The web site provides links and an extensive list of case studies.

CONCERN, Inc.
1794 Columbia Road, N.W.
Washington, D.C.
USA 20009
Tel: 202/328-8160
E-mail: concern@igc.apc.org
Web site: www.sustainable.org/index.html

JOURNALS

The following journals report regularly on sustainable community issues:

EcoCity Journal
Institute for Sustainable Cities
485 Leatherfern Place
Sanibel, Florida
USA 33957
Tel: 813/472-1450
Fax: 813/472-2625

*GreenClip*s is a bi-weekly summary of recent articles in the media on "green archi-tecture" and related government and business issues, published by Sustainable Design Resources in San Francisco. To request a free subscription, E-mail

GreenClips@aol.com.
Two Internet sites host GreenClips archives for reference and research:
http://solstice.crest.org/sustainable/greenclips/info.html
gopher://gopher.igc.apc.org/11/environment/pubs

Initiatives
ICLEI World Secretariat
City Hall, East Tower, 8th Floor
Toronto, Ontario
Canada M5H 2N2
Tel: 416/392-1462
Fax: 416/392-1478
E-mail: 75361.3043@compuserve.com
Web site: www.iclei.org

The Urban Ecologist
Urban Ecology
405 14th Street, Suite 701
Oakland, California
USA 94612
Tel: 510/251-6330
Fax: 510/251-2117
E-mail: urbanecology@igc.apc.org
Web site: www.best.com/%7Eschmitty/uejournl.htm

Planning and policy journals containing articles on sustainable community development:

LandLines
Lincoln Institute of Land Policy
113 Brattle Street
Cambridge, Massachusetts
USA 02138-3400
Tel: 617/661-3016

Plan Canada
Canadian Institute of Planners
116 Albert Street, Suite 801
Ottawa, Ontario
Canada K1P 5G3
Tel: 613/237-7526
Toll-free: 800/207-2138
Fax: 613/237-7045
E-mail: general@cip-icu.ca

Journal of the American Planning Association (JAPA) and Planning
American Planning Association
122 S. Michigan Avenue, Suite 1600
Chicago, Illinois
USA 60603-6107
Tel: 312/431-9100

Journals reporting on sustainable community issues as part of a broader social and/or environmental focus:

Alternatives: Environmental Thought, Policy and Action
Faculty of Environmental Studies
University of Waterloo
Waterloo, Ontario
Canada N2L 3G1
Tel: 519/888-4567 (ext. 6783)
Fax: 519/746-0292
E-mail: alternat@fes.uwaterloo.ca

Auto-Free Times
Fossil Fuels Policy Action Institute
P.O. Box 4347
Arcata, California
USA 95518
Tel: 707/826-7775

Coop America Quarterly
1612 K Street N.W., Suite 600
Washington, D.C.
USA 20006
Tel: 202/872-5307
Fax: 202/331-8166
E-mail: camember@envirolink.org

Earth Island Journal
300 Broadway, Suite 28
San Francisco, California
USA 94133
Tel: 415/788-3666
Fax: 415/788-7324
E-mail: earthisland@igc.apc.org

Earthword: The Journal of Environmental and Social Responsibility
The EOS Institute
580 Broadway, Suite 200
Laguna Beach, California
USA 92651
Tel: 714/497-1896

RAIN
P.O. Box 30097
Eugene, Oregon
USA 97403
Tel: 503/683-1504

Utne Reader
1624 Harmon Place
Minneapolis, Minnesota
USA 55403
Tel: 612/338-5040

World Watch
1776 Massachusetts Avenue, N.W.
Washington, D.C.
USA 20036
Tel: 202/452-1999
Fax: 202/296-7365
E-mail: Worldwatch@igc.apc.org

YES! (formerly *In Context*)
Positive Futures Network
P.O. Box 10818
Bainbridge Island, Washington
USA 98110

Tel: 206/842-0216
Fax: 206/842-5208
E-mail: yes@futurenet.org.

International journals:

The Ecologist
Corner House, Station Road
Sturminster Newton
Dorset, England
U.K. DT10 1BB
Tel: 0258-73476
Fax: 0258-73748
E-mail: gn:ecologist

Local Environment
Centre for Local Environmental Policies and Strategies
School of Urban Development and Policy
South Bank University
London, U.K. SW8 2JZ
Telephone orders (USA and Canada): 800/354-1420
E-mail: b.evans@sbu.ac.uk or julian.agyeman@sru.edu

Local Environment News
Environment Resource and Information Centre
University of Westminster
35 Marylebone Road
London, U.K. NW1 5LS
Tel: 0171-911-5000 (ext. 3135)
Fax: 0171-911-5171
E-mail: tuxworb@wmin.ac.uk

Public Innovation Abroad
International Academy of State and Local Governments
444 North Capitol Street, N.W., Suite 349
Washington, D.C.
USA 20001
Tel: 202/638-1445
Fax: 202/638-5109

INDEX — GENERAL

INDEX — NAMES

ABOUT THE AUTHOR

Mark Roseland is Director of the Community Economic Development Centre at Simon Fraser University (SFU) and is a professor in SFU's Department of Geography. In 1990, as Research Director for the City of Vancouver's "Clouds of Change" Task Force, he orchestrated a comprehensive municipal response to global atmospheric change and local air-quality problems. A former Editor of *RAIN* magazine, he is now North American Editor of the new international journal, *Local Environment.* He lectures internationally and advises communities and governments on sustainable policy and planning. He is also Editor of *Eco-City Dimensions: Healthy Communities, Healthy Planet* (New Society Publishers 1997).